A Comprehension on

Educational Technology
and
ICT for Education

"If the child is not learning the way you are teaching, then you must teach in the way the child learns."

- Rita Dunn

Vinod Kumar Kanvaria
University of Delhi
Delhi

Dedicated to

the Almighty,

my Godfather,

my Students

and

Teachers

Devotion to

the duty

is not a sacrifice

but,

it is a justification to one's

existence

in this

World.

PREFACE

This is the transition phase for learner and teacher fraternity. Every day we are struggling hard with the technology which has encrypted in the learning and teaching field. While talking about technology, it is pertinent question whether technology can replace teacher? Whether we should forget the teacher and teaching strategies? Whether we should forget about the classroom and classroom communication process?

The current book tries to deal with such several questions and takes a stand that teacher is a vital component for learning and teaching, but no doubt the role of the teacher has been transformed and become a much more demanding than the earlier.

The current book has a presumption that educational technology is nothing but pursuing each and every task in the field of education in a technological way which means with minimum possible resources, minimum possible energy and efforts and with optimum utilisation of available resources.

The book begins with conceptualizing educational technology. What does educational technology mean, what are its types, what are its ways, how did it evolved and developed. Then it talks about psychological bases of educational technology. Focus of it lies on the bases shared by Ausubel, Bruner, Vygotsky and Skinner. These have conceptualized learning in their way. The book briefly discusses about their views and theory. Communication in education focusses upon the classroom communication and communication in general. Various models, components and factors related to communication are dealt with in this section.

Now it comes about learning aids and media in educational technology. What are various types of learning aids and how these can be understood in various ways, which learning aids are suitable for various learners, keeping in mind their various characteristics? There are various ways of classification of learning aids. The book endeavours to have a close look over various media and learning aids. Light has been thrown on the use of computer in developing learning material and how to select an appropriate media for learner. Then it discusses various learning and instructional strategies for whole group, small group and individual.

System approach in education is a major field which tries to deal with problems arose in the field of education. It not only deals with the problems but also provides a scientific way to perform any task.

Recent development is the application of computer and technology in education . This book deals with online learning, social networking, computer system, application and authoring systems, technology for differently abled learners. And the most important is social and ethical issues in using computers and internet especially plagiarism and copyright issues.

Along with describing various aspects of computer technology in the field of education it also throws light on the most recent development in the education especially learning and teaching. These are ICT for education, web 2.0 tools in practices, open educational resources, opening up the new trend in education and OER for teaching-learning and professional development of teachers and teacher educators. These are especial features of this book which keeps in mind not only learners and their learning but also teachers and teacher educators.

In single line, this book is a good resource for learners, teachers, teacher educators and all the researchers in the field of education. This would also be like a handbook for all the practitioners and stakeholders in the field of education.

ACKNOWLEDGEMENT

Admiration is our polite recognition of another's resemblance to ourselves.

— **Ambrose Gwinnett Bierce**

First of all, all the authors, facilitators, developers, managers, and proprietors of the websites, published and unpublished material, whose works are cited or quoted with or without any changes in this entire document, including units, text and pictures, are highly and heartily acknowledged. Moreover, all of my students, along with all the past and present colleagues, during this life are acknowledged for fruitful interaction to bring the entire book to the current shape.

A book is never the whole sole contribution of the author, rather it is the result of many people's efforts and interests and paying thanks to their contribution is more a matter of realization and less that of expression. With the depth of my heart, I express my sincere thanks to all of them.

I am extremely grateful to my family members, without whose continuous cooperation, guidance and motivation, this study would not have been a reality.

I am deeply grateful to all of those, whose suggestions helped me, directly or indirectly, and so generously, in various aspects of this book. Their discussion and worthy suggestions gave me inspiration and confidence. Without their interaction and prescriptions, it would have been very difficult to give the present shape to the book.

I, today, pay my due regards to Prof. A. B. Saxena, Dr. R. P. Maurya, Prof. H. K. Senapaty, Prof. V. G. Jadhao, Dr. Kuldip Puri, Dr. Gakkhad, Prof. C. B. Sharma and exceptionally Dr. Kulwinder Singh for providing me insight before, during or after my formal studies, which helped me a lot in developing the current book, as well.

My uncle and aunt encouraged and supported me throughout the book. My Godfather helped me a lot when I was engaged in the selection of the units and preparation of the content. My Godmother's blessings and her words of concern have been extremely supportive for me.

Administrative as well as library staff of CIE (Faculty of Education, DU, Delhi), CPDHE-ILL (DU, Delhi), CRL (DU, Delhi), NCERT (New Delhi), NUEPA

(New Delhi), CASE (MSU, Baroda), IGNOU (Delhi), JNU (New Delhi), RIE (NCERT, Ajmer), RIE (NCERT, Bhubaneswar), RIE (NCERT, Bhopal), RIE (NCERT, Mysore), USOL (PU, Chandigarh) and PU (Chandigarh), too, were of great help to me in the completion of my book. I express my sincere thanks to all of them.

I am extremely thankful to the publisher for the proper printing and binding, and giving the current shape to this book.

Lastly, I, once again, express my sincere thanks to all my students and colleagues, since the beginning of my professional career; all my friends, since the beginning of my understanding of friendship; all my teachers, since the beginning of my academic career, and all my well-wishers, since the beginning of lighting the life-lamp in this body.

(VINOD KUMAR KANVARIA)

CONTENTS

SOME ABBREVIATIONS USED

AS	–	Application Software
AUP	–	Authorized Use Policy
BECTA	–	The British Educational Communications and Technology Agency
CAI	–	Computer Aided/Assisted Instruction
CASE, MSU	–	Centre of Advanced Study in Education, Maharaja Sayajirao University
CBE	–	Computer-Based Education
CBI	–	Computer-Based Instruction
CBSE	–	Central Board of Secondary Education, Delhi
CEI	–	Computer Enriched Instruction
CIE	–	Central Institute of Education
CMI	–	Computer Managed Instruction
CNL	–	Collaborative Networked Learning
COL	–	The Commonwealth of Learning
CRL	–	Central Reference Library
CSCL	–	Computer-supported Collaborative Learning
DU	–	University of Delhi
ERIC	–	Education Resources Information Center
GPL	–	General Public License
ICT	–	Information and Communication Technology or Technologies
IGNOU	–	Indira Gandhi National Open University
IOE	–	Instructional Objective Exchange

JNU	–	Jawaharlal Nehru University
LCD	–	Liquid Crystal Diode
LCMS	–	Learning and Course Management System
LMS	–	Learning Management System
MHRD	–	Ministry of Human Resource Development
NCERT	–	The National Council for Educational Research and Training
NCF	–	National Curriculum Framework
NCFTE	–	National Curriculum Framework for Teacher Educators
NCT	–	National Capital Territory
NCTE	–	The National Council for Teacher Education
NL	–	Networked Learning
OL	–	Online Learning
PL	–	Programmed Learning
PSI	–	Personalized System of Instruction
RIE	–	Regional Institute of Education (NCERT)
RTE	–	Right to Education
TPCK	–	Technology Pedagogy Content Knowledge
UN	–	The United Nations
UNESCO	–	The United Nations Educational, Scientific and Cultural Organization
USOL, PU	–	University School of Open Learning, Panjab University
VLE	–	Virtual Learning Environment

UNIT – 1

CONCEPTUALIZING

EDUCATIONAL TECHNOLOGY

This unit deals with concept, emergence, evolution, nature, types and scope of educational technology

'We need technology in every classroom and in every student and teacher's hand, because it is the pen and paper of our time, and it is the lens through which we experience much of our world.'

— David Warlick

Unit 1
Conceptualizing Educational Technology

1.1 CONCEPT OF EDUCATIONAL TECHNOLOGY

Educational technology (ET) consists of two terms: education + technology.

Education is derived from a Latin word 'educare' which means 'to train', 'to instruct', 'to nourish' or 'to draw out'.

Technology is a science of techniques and methods of doing or getting things done. Basically, it is the application of arts and science to needs of individuals and society.

According to Mitra (1968), 'ET is a science and art of techniques and methods by those educational goals of instruction and learning can be achieved'. According to Leith (1967), 'ET is the systematic application of scientific knowledge about instruction, learning and conditions of learning to improve efficiency of instruction and learning'.

Analysis shows that ET is

- ✦ Systematic study of the process of instruction.
- ✦ Objective knowledge of instruction.
- ✦ Breaking instruction into components.
- ✦ The goal is to improve the instruction-learning situation.

According to Richmond (1979) : ET is concerned with providing appropriately designed learning situations that, holding in idea the objectives of instruction or training bring to bear the best possible means of instruction.

Universities today are aware of how technology use by learners has evolved from the elite and hidden mainframe to the ubiquitous presence of desktop and hand-held technology, the user community now encompasses everyone on board. Its tools have evolved as indispensable utilities for our functioning (Cohen and Smith, 2005). The message that an enhanced use of technology brings change is being heard across the world. Several are joining to say that the traditional context of learning is experiencing a radical change (Nun Maker and Zhang, 2003), although the nature of that change is not well defined. Cohen and Smith (2005) suggested that change is often obstructed, but the advantages and outcomes are already being witnessed in the fresh and new tools and objects that are being created from this fresh and new community of facilitators and learners. Communication trends for teens have changed to reflect their multi-communicative culture. When the bell of the mother's mobile rings at home, children, aged 16 to 23, almost never answer it. They know it is not for them. They let it continue ringing (Maslow, 2005), though they are sitting in front of their computers, chatting electronically or holding a portable device allowing them to chat, explore the web and talk with friends on a mobile. When learners begin to use technology to multi-task as a normal part of their communication pattern, it fundamentally challenges our traditional patterns of communication in classrooms. We, therefore, must analyse how learners now communicate, and adapt our systems to accommodate their fresh and new ways of thinking and learning. We are living in electronic and cyber times. There is no longer a debate about the use of computers in school. The issue is how to use them in instruction and learning.

Some important definitions of ET

+ Association for Educational Communication and Technology— ET is the study and ethical practice of facilitating learning and improving performance by creativity, using and managing appropriate processes and resources.
+ Richmond—ET is the appropriate design of teaching and learning.
+ Leith: ET is a systematic application of scientific knowledge about instruction learning and condition of learning to improve the efficiency of instruction and training.
+ Mathis: ET refers to the development of set of systematic methods, practical knowledge for designing, operating and testing schools.
+ Derik Unwin: ET is concerned with the application of modern skills and techniques to the requirements of education and training.
+ Commission of Instructional Technology— ET is the application of psychology, sociology and scientific principles of knowledge to bring about effective instruction.
+ Kulkarni: ET is the application of laws as well as recent discoveries of science and technology to the process of education.'
+ Mitra: ET can be conceptualized as a science of techniques and methods by that educational goal could be realized.
+ Descryver—Technology means the systematic application of scientific and other organized knowledge to practical task. Hence, ET is based on theoretical knowledge from different disciplines as well as experimental knowledge from educational practice.

Meaning of ET

ET is the study and ethical practice of facilitating learning and improving performance by creating, using and managing appropriate technological processes and resources. ET encompasses software, hardware as well as internet applications and activities. ET is the media born of the communication revolution that can be used for instructional purposes.

The second meaning of ET is the mechanization of educational process.

The mechanization is being done in all the three phases of human knowledge very rapidly.

+ Preservation of knowledge: The first phase of human knowledge is to preserve it. Most of the knowledge used memorized orally and transmitted by facilitators to their learners. But now the knowledge is being preserved in books by the use of printing machines.
+ Transmission of knowledge: The second phase is to transmit the knowledge to the fresh and new generation. A limited number of learners can be benefited by the classroom instruction, but a large number of learners sitting in distant places can be taught with the help of radio and television. In this way ET has reversed the process of instruction.
+ Advancement of knowledge: The third phase of human knowledge is to advance the knowledge. The function of research process is to advance fresh and new knowledge. The education process is being mechanized and this aspect of ET refers to hardware approach.

According to Unwin, 'ET is concerned with the application of modern skills and techniques to the requirements of education and training'. According to Sattler, 'ET can be defined as a systemic way of designing, carrying out and evaluating the total process of instruction and learning.' According to Hubbard, 'ET is the complement of curriculum reform concerned with the method where curriculum reforms are concerned with the content.'

Given an acceptance to the concept of ET as the process of improving learning method, we are facing the problem of encouraging innovation in an educational system whose biggest strength is in decentralisation and autonomy.

1.2 EVOLUTION OF EDUCATIONAL TECHNOLOGY

The earliest recorded concept of educational technology (ET) was linked with the use of audio-visual aids like charts, models, maps, specimens, etc. With the development of physical science, and hence the electronic revolution, there came era of sophisticated hardware and software devices, that could be used for presenting instructional material. Then, with the mass media coming into picture, programmed learning and programmed instruction, a fresh and new dimension of ET evolved into the educational sphere.

ET is composed of two major concepts

- → **Technology in education**
- → **Technology of education**

And, these two give rise to a wider sphere termed Education and Technology.

Let us discuss about these two
A. Technology in Education

This is tool-technology that is also known as Hardware Approach or Physical Science Approach. This is responsible for an instructional media movement.

Tools of technology evolved under different phases. They are:

a) Oral dialogues: In the early period of human history, oral dialogue system was prevalent, and was used in Gurukulas.

b) Development of writing: The writing is the means and material of education. Writing systems on the whole, change more slowly than their spoken counterparts, and often preserve features and expressions that are no longer in fashion in the spoken language. The big benefit of writing system is the ability to maintain a consistent record of information that is expressed in a language and can be retrieved independent of the initial act of formulation. In all era, it has been customary to engrave on stone or metal, or other durable material, such as writing on leaves, tree trunk and engraving on the metals or rocks.

c) Audio-visual aids: This covers the use of charts, maps, models, pictures, specimens, blackboards, diagrams, slate-chalks, etc. This is good tool for making instruction fruitful and disseminating the knowledge. After the use of films and other visual aids during Second World War, audio-visual technology became more sophisticated. And, its use became more widespread in educational set-ups like schools, colleges, universities, museums and galleries. This method of technology is especially useful for learners who prefer to learn through visual learning style.

d) Electronic revolution: Physical sciences come under this category, that encompasses gadgets and mechanical devices for educational purposes i.e. hardware as well as software. Radio, television, tape recorder and films were used for presenting instructional media. Computers have become powerful enough for the creation of instruction machines that can manipulate the massive amount of information. Moreover, internet is now fast enough and widely distributed to change the instruction practices.

Technology used for understanding several subjects-

→ Optics : projected pictures.
→ Chemistry : paper, ink, photography.
→ Mechanical engineering : printing press, movies.
→ Electrical engineering : TV, films, audio recordings.

e) Massive communication revolution: This is characterised by the use of sophisticated apparatus and instruments for formal and informal education like teletext, and computer assisted instruments like video satellites, talking pen, etc. Advancement in telecommunications has led to the development of cable and satellite television and technologies to produce multiple copies of media products simultaneously and economically for different audiences. Development in social sciences made it possible to conduct sophisticated audience research and segmentation. This development resulted in one singular characteristic of contemporary media: increasing specialization in content and a fragmentation of audience. It is one medium that has the potential to contest the gatekeeping power of a typical mass medium.

The development of instruments, which brought out the massive communication revolution, is

i) *Development in Computer*

a) Pre-microcomputer era (1950 – late 1970s): University projects used mainframe and minicomputer systems to deliver instructions in schools; the computer literacy movement began.

b) Microcomputer era (late 1970s-1994) : Microcomputers entered schools and spawned the software publishing and integrated learning system movement.

c) Internet era (1994-present) – Mosaic, the first web browser made it possible to travel on the information superhighway.

ii) *Development in hardware/software*

a) Wireless connectivity

Global trends across computer systems and wireless connections are to simplify computer networks by reducing the number of cables required and to allow more freedom of movement. Instead of each computer having a cabled access point to the network, the wireless networks have one door, through that several computers can access the network. Some schools have 'hot spots' around the building, so that learners can use a portable computer. Facilitators, too, can connect to wireless networks and watch videos, lectures and other educational content from other educational ends. It also allows learners in one area to interact with those who are in other areas. Armed with such technology, facilitators and learners can better keep track of educational agenda. This is utilized in education by providing access to repositories of information.

b) Technology-merge

An increasing number of facilities available in a single device now combine so several communication capabilities, that were earlier limited to so several individual devices, e.g. – currently cellular phone allows not only voice communications, but can also create and share images and text messages.

c) Portable devices

Computers are becoming increasingly portable, that provide facilitators and learners with greater flexibility in learning environment. Laptop is becoming more popular along with handheld computers and tablets. Several schools are replacing their desktop computers with such portable devices so that learning activities need not be confined to classrooms or school premises.

d) High-speed communication (through cable modem, Wi-Fi, etc.) enhancement

Following the gradual spread of telephone access into all parts of the US during the early 1990's, high speed internet connections enhanced in the 2000's in other parts of the world. Faster connections due to digital subscriber lines, cable modems and Wi-Fi resulted into higher quality, more reliable voice and video communications, that are necessary to make distance learning environments as that of the face to face.

e) Visual immersion systems

These are computer generated environments that immerse learners in simulated applications and becoming increasingly available. Some applications encompass full immersion systems with head-mounted displays, augmented reality systems and 3-D models on computer screens. Though full immersion systems are still very expensive for most of the schools, experimental applications continue to appear. Virtual 3-D models on computer screens are becoming trendier.

f) Intelligent applications

Artificial intelligence has not the same level of impact on education as it had on activities such as chess playing, industrial training and problem solving. However, applications such as software that emulate human thought processes and responses to situations continue to appear in education as researchers explore more ways to utilize artificial intelligence capabilities to solve continuing problems in instruction and assessment.

Development	Instances	Applications
Wireless connectivity	-Mobile labs -School-hot spots (wireless connections to networks)	-Mobility makes it easier for facilitators to plan and implement better activities -Easier access to network makes it easier to get materials and update assessments
Merging of technologies for merging of general education and special education	-Handheld devices with built-in communication and digital imaging capabilities	-Combined capabilities mean fewer devices to keep and keep track of learning during instruction
Development in portable devices	-Laptops -Multiple-functionary handheld devices	-Portability makes it easier for each learner to have a computer, hence allowing

	-Tablet PC	individualized strategies -Learners can write and do research from any location -Facilitators can do continuous and comprehensive monitoring and assessment
Availability of high speed communications	-In homes: digital subscriber lines, cable modems and Wi-Fi -In schools: TI lines, DSL, and cable modems	-High-quality, reliable voice and visual communications make distance learning more like face-to-face classroom -Greater number of learners have access to virtual courses and degree programs
Visual immersion systems	-Head-mounted VR systems -Augmented reality systems -3-D imaging systems	-Learners with physical limitations can simulate movement in real situations -Simulated systems allow more realistic and authentic presentation of information
Intelligent applications Intelligent tutor	-Intelligent grading systems -Intelligent tutors	-Computer systems grade complex performances more quickly and reliably than facilitators -Computer tutors adapt more quickly to individual learners' learning needs.

B. Technology of education

It is educational application and implication of knowledge from the behavioural sciences. It encompasses psychological aspects.

Some psychological aspects are

+ Individual differences
+ Psychometrics
+ Learning theory
+ Task analysis
+ Instructional media research
+ Instruction machines

There are three phases of evolution under this area, described by Jonassen (1985)

+ Behaviourism movement: Emphasizes only upon observable change in behaviour, excluding study of mental process.
+ Neo-behaviourism approach: Acknowledges all behaviour that we can observe, but claims that the observed behaviour depends on mental process.
+ Constructive or cognitive science approach: It is psychological aspect that has replaced the mechanistic behaviourist model of human behaviour with the constructive model.

Technology of education versus technology in education

- Technology of education is also referred to as ET and is in reality the incorporation of technology into the realm of classroom. This is a constantly evolving field that depends upon technological advancements. The use of technology in education has several advantages just as technology has enriched the world in all walks of life. One can see and feel the change in air as classrooms are becoming modern and facilitators and learners are benefiting with gadgets such as smart boards and computers.

- The development of internet has made a sea of change in the way facilitators can demonstrate concepts and ideas to children and make learning almost fun. Information today has been encapsulated in internet that can be beautifully used to allow learning be fun rather than being drudgery that it used to be in earlier times.

- What this has meant is that education is no longer limited to the privileged few and even those who are downtrodden and poor can learn all the ideas and concepts that were like a dream for them in earlier times. Internet today has become very commonplace and its true potential can realized by disseminating knowledge through it to all, without any discrimination.

- Technology in education is not limited to making use of technology to make learning and imparting of education easier in all possible ways but is also a field of study in itself for those who are involved with developing technological tools for educational purposes. Keeping in mind the end user that are the learners and facilitators, technologists are busy inventing tools and gadgets for use in classrooms. These are the people who are behind this revolution and are working overtime in the field of ET to cover all the processes of learning and instruction.

- Technology in education refers to, but is not limited to the use of hardware and software, including internet and other related activities, for the purpose of increasing human capabilities. While the use of technology in education is always welcome as it enables both facilitators and learners to gain knowledge in a much better and faster rate, ultimately it is the facilitators, who make use of all the technology and hence they would remain as important as ever, and technology can never even think of replacing facilitators.

- Information technology has changed society in recent years. Just as the development of electronic media shaped society earlier, the capabilities of the internet are changing our current world. Concrete efforts have been made to ensure that schools are woven into the infrastructure of the web. Almost every school and virtually every classroom in the United States has been connected to the internet. Other efforts such as the one laptop per child initiative have been undertaken to extend the mesh of connections worldwide. Despite these investments, schools are not yet demonstrably more fruitful.

- The challenge of using technology effectively in schools is one that has been described as a wicked problem (Rittel and Webber, 1973) with incomplete, contradictory and changing needs characterized by complex interdependencies among a large number of contextually bound variables. The wicked problems of technology integration require all of us to develop innovative and creative ways of confronting this complexity. A critical aspect of thinking about technology integration is the diversity of disciplines. As Mishra and Koehler argued, realizing the potential of technology requires skills and knowledge not just of technology, pedagogy, and content in isolation but rather of all three taken together. Instruction successfully with technology requires continually creating, maintaining, and re-establishing a dynamic equilibrium among all three components.

↗ Facilitators constantly negotiate a balance between technology, pedagogy, and content in ways appropriate to the specific parameters of an ever-changing educational context. Facilitators construct curriculum through an organic process of iterative design and refinement, negotiating among existing constraints to create contingent conditions for learning. In particular the TPCK (Technology, Pedagogy and Content Knowledge) framework emphasizes the critical role of the facilitator as curriculum designer, the awareness that facilitators are active participants in any implementation or instructional reform we seek to achieve and, thus, require a certain degree of autonomy and power in making pedagogical decisions.

1.3 EMERGENCE AND SCOPE OF ET
(i) Emergence of ET

Technology of education deals with the active use of mass media and computer science for the individual learner's learning process under the facilitator's supervision. It begins with a discourse on the relationship between culture and ET. A key premise is that culture is an important influence in education. Similarly, the evolution of ET is very much intertwined with culture. ET was initially observed as technology in education, with the sole focus on it tools. Subsequently, a holistic perspective of the educational system was adopted and termed as the technology of education. In this larger idea, ET is informed by research from learning theories and other educational research.

Educational technology historian Sattler (1990) said that the earliest reference for ET seems to have been made by radio instructor Charters in 1948 and instructional technology was first used by audio-visual expert Finn in 1963. Charters brought revolution by radio instruction. There are two terms- Educational Technology and instructional technology. Both have more or less the same meaning. Sattler defined educational as well as instructional technology as the media born of the communication revolution that can be used for instructional purposes and the systemic way of designing, carrying out and evaluating the total process of learning and instruction. But today, ET has become equipment particularly, electronic equipment. In 1920, Cubans history placed emphasis on radio and television, with an afterthought. Now-a-days main focus is on the internet and in future it would become more intelligent computer-assisted instruction or virtual reality. In 1970, there was a commission that defined ET as one that encompasses both tools and processes belong to the future. Later on, Muffoletto (1994) said technology is not a collection of machines and devices, but a way of acting.

Four perspectives of ET

a) Media

This perspective came in 1930s as an audio-visual (AV) movement. Slides, films, etc. delivered information in more concrete and therefore more fruitful ways than lectures and books that had previously controlled the learning process. There are several more varieties of media and methods available for imparting instruction. No single method is suitable for all types of instructions.

b) Instructional systems

This idea originated after the Second World War It is based on the belief that both human (facilitator) and non-human (media) help in addressing any instructional need solutions to educational problems.

c) Vocational training

This idea came in 1980s. The important function of school learning is to prepare learners for the world of work in that they would use technology.
Exemplar: wood working\ metals and graphics\printing shops, computer assisted design (cad) and robotics systems.

d) Computer systems

This perspective was known as educational computing and encompassed both instructional and administrative support application.

By the 1990s, educators had begun to see computers as part of a combination of technical resources including media, instructional systems, and computer-based support systems. At that point educational computing came to be known as ET.

(ii) Scope of ET

Scope means the extent, range, boundaries, subject-matter or topics to be encompassed in any branch of knowledge. Scope of any subject depends on its definition. ET is concerned with bringing improvement in instruction-learning process. It is an applied or practical study that aims at maximizing educational effects by controlling such relevant factors as educational purposes, educational content and environment, instruction materials, conduct of learners, behaviour of facilitators and interrelationship between learners and facilitators. Thus its scope encompasses educational objectives, media and their characteristics for the selection of media and resources, management of resources as well as their evaluation.

The scope of ET

ET deals with all the variables, phases, levels and aspects of the instruction-learning process.
a. Analysis of the process of instruction and learning: ET discusses the concept of instruction, analysis of instruction process, variables of instruction, levels of instruction, the relevance of theories of instruction, principles and maxims of instruction, concepts of learning, the relationship between instruction and learning, etc. These all are for attaining optimum educational purposes.
b. Spelling out the educational goals and objectives: ET tries to discuss identification of educational needs and aspirations of the community and analyse of broad objectives in terms of the specific classroom objectives of instruction and learning etc.

c. Development of the curriculum: This aspect of ET is concerned with the designing of a suitable curriculum for the achievement of the stipulated objectives.

d. Development of instruction-learning material: This area is concerned with the production and development of the suitable instruction learning material in idea of designed curriculum, available resources and stipulated objectives. Here, more emphasis is on developing software and instructional material like programmed learning material, computer assisted learning material, mass media, preparation of lesson plans, etc.

e. Facilitator preparation or facilitator-training: ET encompasses topics like models of instruction, micro instruction, and simulated instruction, team instruction, and facilitator effectiveness, modification of facilitator behaviour, classroom interaction, and interacting analysis.

f. Development and selection of the instruction-learning strategies and tactics: It helps the facilitator to select suitable instruction strategies in terms of maximum learning and available instruction resources, for an instance if we have different types of models of instruction, devices and methods of instruction, then we would have to choose the one that gives a maximum output of learning with little effort.

g. Development, selection and use of the appropriate audio-visual aids

h. Fruitful utilization of the hardware and mass media

i. To work for the fruitful utilization of the subsystem of education

j. To provide essential feedback and control through evaluation

k. The art of instruction, the learners, the science of learning, educational planners the structure of planning

l. CCTVs in the class rooms: Radio broadcasting, television telecasting, computers (online education) etc. in education is the product of ET

It helps in understanding nature and structure of education.

Role of ET in improving theory and practice of education

+ Identification of educational objectives: ET helps in finding out the right objectives of education in terms of behavioural specifications. It analyses broad educational objectives in terms of specific classroom objectives of instruction and learning.

+ Improving instruction-learning process: ET helps in analysing and improving the instruction-learning process by making fruitful use of variables of instruction, levels of instruction, phases of instruction, theories of instruction, models of instruction, principles and maxims of instruction, and variables and theories of learning.

+ Development of suitable curriculum: ET helps in designing a suitable curriculum for the achievement of educational objectives.

+ Development and use of instruction-learning material: ET helps in the development of instruction-learning material in accordance with the desired objectives, curriculum and available resources. It consists of techniques of developing software and instructional materials like programmed learning material, computer-assisted learning material, mass media instruction material, individualized system of instruction and other instruction strategies.

+ Facilitator preparation: ET takes special care of the preparation of facilitators for performing their duties. For achieving this purpose, ET covers the topics like models of instruction, team instruction, simulated instruction, micro-instruction, facilitator effectiveness, modification of behaviour through classroom interaction and interaction analysis. Through ET, facilitators acquire necessary competencies that make them efficient facilitators academically, professionally and technologically.

→ Instruction-learning strategies: ET evolves different instruction-learning strategies and helps in selecting suitable strategies of instruction in terms of maximum learning and use of the available instruction resources.

→ Development of audio-visual aids: ET plays an important role in developing, selecting and using appropriate audio-visual aids, the software aids, the hardware aids, the computer and other such appliances, equipment etc. Computer assisted instruction helps the learner as well as the facilitator to achieve conveniently the goals of education.

→ Providing feedback and control through evaluation: ET develops suitable tools and devices for continuous and improved evaluation of the process and products of instruction-learning activities. Such an evaluation provides a proper feedback to the facilitators and learners for making improvement in their specific acts.

→ Improving the standard: The mass education has reduced the standard of education. The use of ET helps in maintaining and improving the standard by the use of instruction aids and programmed instruction. Bloom's taxonomy talks about programmed instruction and learning.

→ Providing life-long and continuing education: ET helps learners to keep themselves aware of the latest developments through television lessons, self-instructional programmed material.

Following functions have been made through INSAT-1b launched by India in 1983
   a) Rural TV transmission
   b) Expansion of transmission facilities
   c) Meteorological investigations
   d) Radio broadcasting
   e) Telecommunications

The programmes of education that are telecasted cater to the needs of formal and informal systems of education. The satellite instructional television experiment has revolutionized the education.

Characteristics of ET

→ Modern discipline: The question about whether or not ET is a fast developing modern discipline is not fresh and new. It might be encouraged in response to those who question or fail to appreciate what educational technologists do or might be encouraged by ET professionals (instructional designers, technology and media specialists, performance technologists, training developers, university professors, etc.) who are seeking to identify the central theories and principles that drive ET research and practice. An academic discipline can be defined in an operational way as simply any field of study or branch of knowledge that is typically taught and researched at the college or university level. Using this simple and straight forward definition, one would conclude that ET is a discipline, as there are relevant courses and programs at several colleges and universities in ET, instructional designs, instructional systems, instructional technology, learning design and technology, and so on.

+ Continuous and dynamic: Numerous sites and institutions all around the world are making efforts to specialise in designing and manufacturing learning resources to meet the needs of children of all ages. Technology is constantly changing. Therefore, planning to use only some particular technologies may be unwise. However, developing a robust framework for considering the use of technology in our future classroom would be useful irrespective of the context of our instruction. Several schools are adopting the latest technologies including mobile applications, web-based learning, and portable content, to help improve learning outcomes.

+ Based on application of scientific knowledge: ET is a science of techniques and methods. It involves adoption of scientific and technological innovations and inventions to educational situations. It gives way to adoption of scientific and technological methods of instructions. It enables facilitators to use multi-sensory instruction-learning aids leading to facilitator effectiveness and optimum learning.

+ Making instruction process objective, clear, interesting and scientific: With these technologies in the picture, all the sensory organs sense of sight, hearing, touch, smell and taste for the acquisition of the desired instruction-learning experiences has been made possible. It also suggests suitable instruction-learning methods, devices and strategies based on the psychology of instruction-learning. As a result, one can enjoy the serious task of instruction or learning him or her for the proper realization of his or her goals. A facilitator by using transparencies through overhead projectors, interacting with learners in their laboratories, and making them discover the facts by observing a video film and audio recording, or taking online tutorial help through e-mail or online-conferences may always help his learners relish the desired fruits of their efforts.

+ Providing technical guidance and solution to the problems of education: Technologically advanced classrooms, like virtual classrooms, provide flexibility to the learners in terms of time, space and distance; provide the joy and advantages of the real-time learning or doing away with the criticism, snubbing and ridiculing by other colleagues. Technology also helps in the collection, storage, retrieval, use, transmission, manipulation and dissemination of information as accurately and efficiently as possible for the purpose of enriching the knowledge. The use of information technology gives immense help and assistance to all connected with the task of education like learners, facilitators, and guidance and counselling personnel, education planners and research workers for performing their responsibilities as adequately as possible.

+ Improvising the educational system: ET locates the problems in the field of education, finds their remedy and ultimately aims at improving the educational system. It is bound to improve the facilitator, the learner and the instruction-learning process. It plays a fruitful role in the communication between facilitators and learner.

+ Based on research: ET makes use of research findings of psychology, sociology, social psychology, linguistics, communication, engineering and sciences and applies the same to the field of education.

- ✈ Practical discipline: ET is primarily a practical discipline and secondarily a theoretical one. It is a systematic application of technological knowledge to the field of education towards the attainment of practical goals.
- ✈ Attempt for modernization: ET attempts at the modernization of the education system by bringing into use varied electro- mechanical devices.
- ✈ A means: ET is a means to achieve an end, and not an end in itself.
- ✈ Wide scope: ET is not merely confined to the use of audio-visual aids, software material and hardware equipment nor be confined to the use of psychological principles and instructional theories for bringing improvement in the instruction- learning process. It encompasses the development, application and evaluation of systems, techniques and aids in the field of learning. As such its scope encompasses educational objectives, media and their characteristics, criteria for selection of media and resources, management of resources as well as their evaluation.

Objectives of ET

- ✈ To modernize the learning methods and instruction after systematizing them so that these may be turned fruitful according to the needs of changing era for the unknown future.
- ✈ To bring desirable modification in the behaviour of the facilitators and learners by improving the instruction, learning and evaluation conditions.
- ✈ To make the classroom instruction fruitful, easy, clear, interesting, understandable, scientific and objective.
- ✈ To help in increasing facilities by solving the most complicated problems of human life so that human life may carry on its progress continuously.

General objectives of ET

- ✈ To identify the educational needs of the community
- ✈ To determine the aims and objectives of education
- ✈ To prepare an appropriate curriculum
- ✈ To determine suitable strategies
- ✈ To identify human and non-human resources
- ✈ To identify problems standing in the way of development of personality of the learners
- ✈ To suggest remedies to solve the found problems
- ✈ To manage the entire educational system
- ✈ To improve the process and product of education

Specific objectives of ET (from the angle of specific classroom instruction)

- ✈ To identify the educational needs of the learners
- ✈ To determine the class-room objectives in behavioural terms
- ✈ To analyse and organize the content of instructions in logical or psychological sequence
- ✈ To plan the instruction methods and strategies of the presentation related to the content
- ✈ To make use of aid material, software and hardware, mass media and communication techniques

- To identify the human and non-human resources
- To evaluate class-room instruction in terms of performance of learners
- To provide continuous feedback to the learners and the facilitator for improving the instruction-learning process

Components of ET

- Defining educational goals
- Designing instructional strategies and learning sequences
- Evaluation of outcomes

ET relates to several activities in education

ET is the study and ethical practice of facilitating learning and improving performance by creating, using and managing appropriate technological processes and resources. The term ET is often associated with, and encompasses, instructional theory and learning theory. While instructional technology is 'the theory and practice of design, development, utilization, management, and evaluation of processes and resources for learning,' according to the Association for Educational Communications and Technology (AECT) definitions and terminology committee, ET encompasses other systems used in the process of developing human capability. ET encompasses, but is not limited to, software, hardware, as well as internet applications, such as wiki's and blogs, and activities. But there is still debate on what these terms mean.

ET is intended to improve education over what it would be without technology. Some of the advantages are listed below

- Easy-to-access course materials: Instructors can post the course material or important information on a course website, that means learners, can study at a time and location they prefer and can obtain the study material very quickly
- Learner motivation: Computer-based instructions can give instant feedback to learners and explain right answers. Moreover, a computer is patient and non-judgemental, that can give learner motivation to continue learning. According to Kulich, who studies the effectiveness of computers used for instruction, learners usually learn more in less time when receiving computer-based instruction and they like classes more and develop more positive attitudes toward computers in computer-based classes. The American educator, Whyte, researched and reported about the importance of locus of control and successful academic performance and later she wrote how important computer usage and information technology would become in the higher education experience of the future.
- Wide participation: Learning material can be used for long distance learning and are accessible to a wider audience.
- Improved learner writing: It is convenient for learners to edit their written work on word processors that can, in turn, improve the quality of their writing. According to some studies, the learners are better at critiquing and editing written work that is exchanged over a computer network with learners they know.
- Subjects made easier to learn: Several different types of educational software are designed and developed to help children or teenagers to

learn specific subjects. Exemplars encompass pre-school software, computer simulators, and graphics software

→ A structure that is more amenable to measurement and improvement of outcomes. With proper structuring it can become easier to monitor and maintain learner's work while also quickly gauging modifications of the instructions necessary to enhance learner's learning.

→ Differentiated instruction: ET provides the means to focus on active learner participation and to present differentiated questioning strategies. It broadens individualized instruction and enhances and supports the development of personalized learning plans. Learners are encouraged to use multimedia components and to incorporate the knowledge, they gained in creative ways.

With technology facilitators can instruct outside of the classroom. It is very beneficial for learners to learn quickly and easily. Learners would be more encouraged to learn. Using the internet would cut out the unwanted (extra) information provided in text books. Classrooms need to be updated. When the society changes, instruction-learning, also, needs to change. Using any kind of technology viz. cameras, computers, etc., learners can resort back to the saved images and to remember things that they can never look at again. For an instance, a class goes on a field trip to study rocks; learners take pictures of them so when they go back to the classrooms they can see exactly what each rock looks like instead of struggling to remember. Technology is beneficial to all of those who hands on children. Learners would be determined to learn as much as they can because it is a fun experience. Learners engaged would get their success. Education and training activities are increasingly employing the use of a variety of technologies to support pedagogy and learning. Several of the technologies used are computer-based. Word-processors, spread sheets, and databases are being utilized as tools in supporting instruction and learning. Graphics and desktop publishing software now allow facilitators to develop more instructional materials to their own specifications. Correspondingly, facilitators are utilizing testing and measurement software, CD-ROMs, DVD, hypertext, hypermedia, and multimedia tools to enhance classroom activities.

The internet and its resources (e.g. worldwide web, electronic mail, fresh and newsgroups, etc.) have provided access to information; resource personnel, facilitators and learners in other districts, counties, states, and even in other countries, enhancing classroom activities. Through internet, both facilitators and learners are exploring different countries and their cultures without leaving the classroom. The different ways in that facilitators respond to the need to integrate technology in classroom activities may be predicated on their pre-service training and additional encouragement provided in the different educational environments. The increasing application of technology to support instruction and learning provide a basis by that some facilitators reconsider the strategies they use in instructional activities. Different strategies are being employed in conjunction with the more familiar ones to accomplish the necessary learning objectives. The strategies adapted have resulted in learners playing a greater role in the instruction and learning process. This occurs, as learners become more involved in determining the sequence and strategies used in directing classroom activities. Under the facilitator's guidance learners are involved in collaborative learning activities. Together facilitators and learners use different technology to access information, communicate with others in different geographical locations, and explore fresh and new instructional media systems. Learners are playing a more significant role in classroom activities. Several learners are more familiar with some of the technologies employed in the educational environment, than others. By working cooperatively, learners help each other understand more about the technology and how to use it to accomplish set learning objectives, thereby increasing the level of interaction between and among them.

As efforts are made to get facilitator and learners to collaborate and cooperate in their classroom activities, more is heard about a constructivist approach to education. The constructivist perspective that evolved from some branches of thinking in cognitive learning theory is based on the concept that knowledge is produced by the individual learner rather than processed from information received from an external source. Despite the differences between the two perspectives on instruction and learning, they can both be employed to ensure a fruitful and efficient educational environment. Some uses of technology in instruction and learning are associated with directed instruction (e.g. Drill and practice, tutorials) but several other applications (e.g. Problem-solving, multimedia applications, telecommunications) can be used to enhance both the directed and the constructivist approaches, depending on how facilitators integrate them in classroom activities.

Recapitulation

The introduction of fresh and new information technology in instruction and learning has impacted the traditional classroom activities. The several technologies generate a greater level of interaction between and among facilitators and learners. They also help to enhance the educational environment while providing enrichment in the learning experience. However, technology used in the classroom should only be considered appropriate if it is used for specific purposes in the instruction and learning process. Its incorporation in this process should not just be as an appendage, but as an integral part of the instruction and learning objectives. Employing technology of any kind in the instructional process becomes valuable only when they are seen merely as elements in a well-constructed learning environment. The use of technology, therefore, should be driven by specific objectives related to instruction and learning with direct linkages to the curriculum.

1.4 APPROACHES OR TYPES OF ET
ET = Education + Science (Natural Science + Behavioural Science)

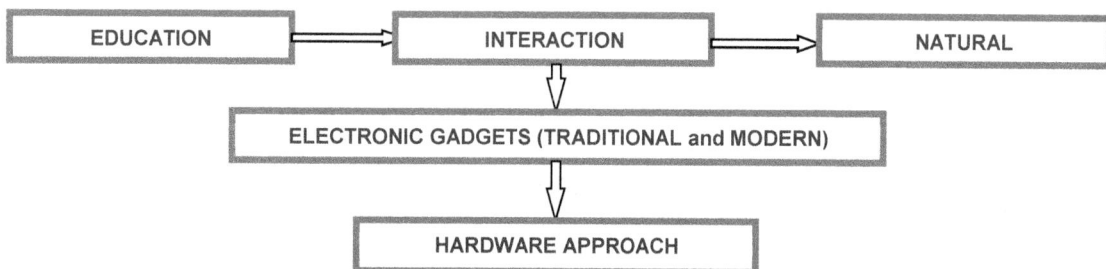

Lumsdaine (1964) gave three types of ET. They are
(1). ET 1 or hardware approach (audio-visual aids) natural science

It means application of technology to instrumentation or physical sciences useful to the process of instruction. Through this, instruction process is mechanized gradually so that maximum number of learners can be educated in minimum time at very low cost. It encompasses CCTV, projectors, motion pictures, radio, tape recorders, record player, epidiascope, computer, etc. Use of these machines makes instruction more fruitful and learning objectives can be easily achieved. Silverman (1968) termed this technology as 'relative technology' that refers to borrow and to apply technology, machines and devices in the process of instruction and learning.

(2). ET 2 or software approach (behavioural science)

In this, instead of engineering machines, psychological principles of instruction and learning are utilized so that desirable changes maybe brought

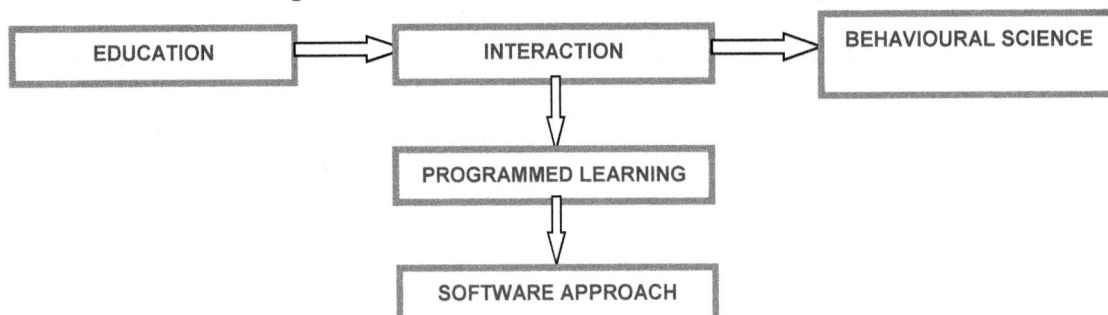

```
┌─────────────┐      ┌─────────────┐      ┌──────────────────────┐
│  EDUCATION  │ ───▶ │ INTERACTION │ ───▶ │ BEHAVIOURAL SCIENCE  │
└─────────────┘      └─────────────┘      └──────────────────────┘
                            │
                            ▼
                   ┌──────────────────────┐
                   │ PROGRAMMED LEARNING  │
                   └──────────────────────┘
                            │
                            ▼
                   ┌──────────────────────┐
                   │  SOFTWARE APPROACH   │
                   └──────────────────────┘
```

about in the behaviour of learners. If the machines are used it is only to make the subject matter fruitful. Its origin lies in the application of behavioural science to the problems of learning and motivation. This idea of ET is closely associated with the modern principles and theory of instruction, model of instruction, theory of instruction, and theory of facilitator-behaviour and principles of programmed learning. It is characterized by task analysis, writing objectives in behavioural terms, selection of appropriate instruction strategies, reinforcement for right responses and constant evaluation.

Silverman (1968) termed this ET as 'constructive technology'. In this, some constructive work is to be performed.

Distinction between hardware and software approach

Hardware approach	Software approach
Origin – in physical science	Origin – in behavioural science
It refers to the application of principles of physical sciences or engineering and technology in the development of electro-mechanical equipment used for instructional purposes.	It refers to application of instruction learning principles to the direct and deliberate shaping of behaviour.
Examples are chart, models, filmstrips, audio-cassettes, sophisticated equipment, gadgets like TV, film projectors, tape recorder, record player, computer etc.	The modern principles and theory of instruction, models of instruction, theory of instruction, theory of facilitator behaviour and principles of programmed learning.
It is concerned with production of audio-visual aids and utilization of	In this, we try to exploit the psychology of learning for the production and utilization

sophisticated instruments and mass media for helping facilitator and learner to achieve better results.	of instruction-learning strategies, tools of evaluation and other devices to soften the task of instruction and learning.
Hardware is useless without being accompanied by suitable software.	It is the software approach that makes hardware functional. While following this approach i.e. verbal manipulation of psychological principles of instruction we make use of aids and all that to make instruction fruitful i.e. we make use of hardware approach.
Hardware is prepared by assembling different gadgets. Same hardware can be used in different fields like industry, entertainment, education, corporate sector etc. Thus it is termed 'relative technology'.	It concentrates on the analysis, selection and construction of whatever is necessary to meet the educational needs. Thus it is termed 'constructive technology'.

(3). ET 3 or systems approach

This is the latest concept in technology of education. It is concerned with the systematic planning, designing, construction and evaluation of education system. System approach is applied to develop, implement and evaluate educational system, sub-system, and curriculum or even for designing an individual lesson. In this approach, one has to make continuous comparison of the different roles played my man, machine and media in a system of education and develops an appropriate instructional design and strategy in relation to the stipulated objectives. System technology helps the designer of instruction-learning system to proceed systematically, watching each component of system carefully and studying interaction of components with one another and with other outside systems.

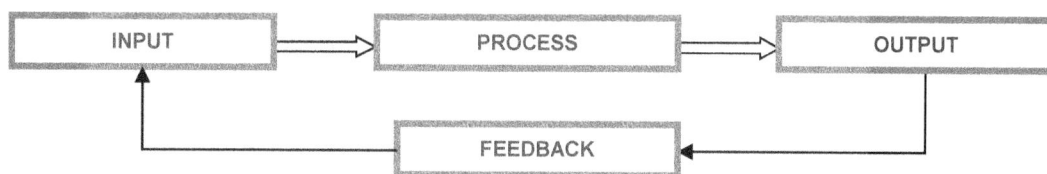

(4). ET 4 or management technology

Its focus is on management of instruction-learning process. It helps in managing educational resources including such activities as planning, programming, budgeting, management, decision making, and operational research system analysis. Management technology provides useful models, information systems and organisation theory for man-machine system.

(5). ET 5 or planning technology

Planning technology helps in reducing extra expenditure, time and energy and thus enhances the cost benefit of educational system. It is concerned with planning of instruction-learning process.

(6). Instructional technology

Instructional technology means a network of techniques or devices employed to accomplish certain defined set of learning objectives. It implies an application of psychological, sociological and scientific principles and knowledge to instructions for achieving the specific objectives of learning.

The origin of instruction technology is based upon psychological laboratory experiments the most important exemplar of instruction technology is programmed instruction. Programmed instruction and instructional technology can be used interchangeably.

According to McMinn, instructional technology is a systematic way of designing, carrying out and evaluating the total process of learning and instruction, in terms of specific objectives based on research, on human learning and communication and employing a combination of human and non-human resources to bring about more fruitful instruction.

Characteristics of instructional technology

- ✦ Cognitive objectives can be achieved effectively.
- ✦ The learner gets an opportunity to learn according to his own pace. Thus, the individual differences can be controlled through this technology.
- ✦ It incorporates the psychological learning theories and principles.
- ✦ The right responses of the learner are confirmed for providing the reinforcement continuously.
- ✦ It can be employed in storage of fruitful facilitator.
- ✦ It provides the deep insight to the content structure and sequence of its element.

In addition to the theory of instruction, principles of instruction, concept of operating conditioning, theory of learning, operant condition, model of instruction and schedules of reinforcement are also encompassed in instruction technology.

ET and instructional technology

They are not synonymous. ET deals with the whole instruction-learning process whereas the instructional technology deals with the instruction part of it only. ET is comprehensive and broad whereas instructional technology is a sub-system of the main system of ET. Moreover, it determines the media, methods and materials in a given instruction-learning situation for attaining instrumental objectives.

Similarities

- ✦ Both have certain goals and objectives.
- ✦ Both deal with the curriculum or subject-matter.
- ✦ Both try to analyse the characteristics of learners.
- ✦ Both measure academic performance of the learner.
- ✦ Feedback is an important activity in both. Feedback results in efficiency.

Dissimilarities

Criterion	ET	Instructional technology
Area and scope	It is a wider, more comprehensive and broad based concept.	It is one of the parts of ET and thus a narrow concept.

Skills and competencies	Efforts are made to discover the skills and competencies of learners all over the nation.	Efforts are made to discover skills and competencies of learners in specific and limited geographical area.
Behavioural outcomes	They are decided keeping in idea the ultimate needs of the nation.	They are decided in idea of the specific expectations from the learners.
Projects	It refers to projects that are large scale and involve long periods of time.	It is concerned with short term projects that are on a small scale.
Academic performance	Academic performance of the learner is measured at national or regional level.	Academic performance of the learner is measured in terms of specifically and rigidly laid down terminal behaviour at the end of each lesson.
Feedback	It is emphasized to improve instruction–learning at macro level.	It is emphasized to improve instruction – learning at micro level.

ET and engineering technology

Engineering technology is concerned with manufacturing devices-hardware for education like radio, television etc. While ET is concerned with planning, organizing, instruction and designing tests for learning outcomes. The use of hardware approach to instruction and training is termed ET. Engineering technology is supplementary to education.

ET and programmed learning

Programmed learning or programmed instruction is a learning methodology or technique first proposed by Skinner in 1958. According to Skinner, the purpose of programmed learning is to manage human learning, under controlled conditions. Programmed learning has three elements

- ✈ It delivers information in small bites,
- ✈ It is self-paced by the learner, and
- ✈ It provides immediate feedback, both positive and negative, to the learner.

It was popular in the late 1960s and through the 1970s, but pedagogical interest was lost in the early 1980s as it was difficult to implement and its limitations were not well understood by practitioners. It was revived in the 1990s in the computerized integrated learning system (ILS) approach, primarily in the business and managerial context. Programmed learning remains popular in self-instruction textbooks.

The methodology involves self-administered and self-paced learning, in that the learner is presented with information in small steps often referred to as 'frames'. Each frame contains a small segment of the information to be learned, and a question that the learner must answer. After each frame the learner uncovers, or is directed to, additional information based on a wrong answer, or positive feedback for a right answer.

Programmed learning is that part of ET that lays stress on instruction-learning strategy based on self-instructional texts or auto tutors. It is usually associated with those programmes that individualize instructions.

ET and audio-visual aids

Audio-visual aid is a part of ET. ET has a wider scope. It is not confined to the use of aids. It makes a functional analysis of instruction-learning process and locates the several components that operate from the stage of input to that of output. The development of instruction machines, radio, television, tape-recorder, computer and language laboratory gave a fresh and new dimension to the role of audio-visual aids.

1.5 DIGITAL VIDEO IN EDUCATION

There are, today, a number of educational video sites modelled on commercial or public web 2.0 technologies, viz. YouTube. These sites often archive video clips that educators are referring as employing technology as a conduit for the transmission of information. The impact of digital video technology on facilitators' beliefs encompassed shifts in reflections regarding children's thinking, planning and instruction informed by reflection, and notions of instruction expertise and requisite knowledge. There is undeniable value in capturing and sharing the world's most creative facilitators' discussions of their favourite subjects. However, we argue that limiting the use of digital video to the mere transmission of classroom lectures does not take full advantage of the capabilities of the medium.

In contrast, we believe that digital video technologies provide unique opportunities (through interactivity and user-generated content) to rethink the instructional paradigm particularly to match the needs of the subject to be taught. The technology now makes it possible to capture computer displays to create screen casts, combine images with learner narration for digital storytelling, and construct digital animations such as flash movies, among other possibilities. As a result of emergent technological advances and concomitant expansion of the affordances of the medium, the definition of digital video and digital movies is broader than in the past. As we shall see, the best uses of digital video can vary dramatically from one content area to another.

In sciences

Digital video can be used in several different ways for science education. One particularly important pedagogical role that can be played by digital video is in addressing common learner misconceptions. Learners at all levels have misconceptions about physical phenomena and often have difficulties conceptualizing scientific events. These conceptions occur due to a variety of reasons, and digital video can be an important tool in an educator's toolkit to help learners go beyond immediate perceptions toward more nuanced, complex and scientifically accurate understanding.

For an instance, consider the classic science demonstration where an egg is pushed into a milk bottle by the burning of a paper inside the bottle. There is a common misconception that the egg is forced into the bottle due to a drop in pressure caused by the depletion of oxygen as the paper burns. The actual story is little bit more complex. The heat of the flame causes the air inside the bottle to expand and, thus, initially enhances the air pressure inside the bottle. This enhanced pressure forces air out of the bottle, past the egg, that acts as a one-way valve. When the remaining air inside the bottle subsequently cools, a drop in the air pressure occurs, causing the egg to be pushed into the bottle by the external air pressure.

In social studies

In contrast, ready access to primary source documents provide social studies facilitators the possibility of different kinds of instructional approaches. Digital history centres and institutions, such as, the Smithsonian and The Library of Congress are increasingly making digital copies of historical documents such as photographs, artworks, and maps that are also available online. These digital resources afford learners the opportunity to create digital documentaries–short digital movies contain a montage of images, text, or video accompanied by a narration done in the learner's voice. Educators believe that learners who effectively use primary source documents can develop enhanced historical thinking skills. Development of digital documentaries incorporating primary source documents has been used to good impact in isolated classrooms. However, widespread classroom use faces significant barriers. Digital movies can be resource intensive and time consuming to develop. The digital movies we envision do not embody the turn the projector on and let the film instruct methods of 40 years ago. Instead, they provide a platform from that learners can dive into inquiry-to interact and engage with the content. Adequate facilitator preparation and support are crucial to fruitful use.

In languages and arts

Evidence exists that struggling readers, sometimes, have difficulty forming accurate images associated with the words that they are reading. The ability to combine images with words to create digital movies provides an avenue for reinforcing visual imagery — contextualizing the text in ways not previously possible. When the words are narrated in the learner's own voice, the process may also provide opportunities for auditory reinforcement. To instruct thinking and analysing skills, visual learning techniques are found to be quite fruitful. Visual diagrams stimulate creative thinking thus helping in processing, organizing and retaining fresh and new information.

Conclusion

Technology and emerging media are rapidly finding their ways into society and schools. Several schools now subscribe to video streaming services. Schools are rapidly acquiring interactive whiteboards and projectors for the classroom. Multimedia literacy is an equal and complimentary form of expression, alongside textbook education. Research is needed to guide the future use, but recommendations are also needed to guide the use of current and emerging technologies based on our best understanding of the needs of each discipline at this time. Facilitators cannot be expected to set these tools aside while waiting for perfect understanding of best use to develop. They need to incorporate the available technologies to their best knowledge and capabilities to explore the possibilities during the instruction-learning process.

EXEMPLARY QUESTIONS

1. What is Educational Technology? Describe its scope in several subsystems of education. How can Educational Technology improve the theory and practice of education? Elaborate by taking an exemplar.
2. In what way does the concept of Educational Technology get related to several process activities in education? Discuss with exemplars.
3. In what way can Educational Technology as a multidimensional approach strengthen the existing classroom practices? Discuss with the help of exemplars.

UNIT – 2

PSYCHOLOGICAL BASES OF EDUCATIONAL TECHNOLOGY

This unit deals with contribution of learning theories with special reference to Skinner, Bruner, Ausubel and Vygotsky.

'The object of psychology is to give us a totally different idea of the things we know best.'

— Paul Valery

Unit 2
Psychological Bases of Educational Technology

2.1 SUBSUMPTION THEORY OF AUSUBEL

David Paul Ausubel (1918–2008) was an American psychologist born in N. York. His most significant contribution to the fields of educational psychology, cognitive science, and science education learning, was the development and research on advance organizers. Ausubel's subsumption theory of learning, basically, deals with 'advance organizers'.

Advance organizers

These are the abstracts and outlines that help structure and organize the content to be taught. The advance organizers help the learners to learn a large body of fresh and new content more readily by relating it upfront to previously learned information within the learner's existing schema. Advance organizers not only structure the information but also provide initial contextual information already familiar to the learner (existing schema).

This helps learner take existing knowledge and relate it to fresh and new content to be learned. Hence, a great deal of emphasis is placed on prior knowledge providing an important foundation for the development of fresh and new concepts.

Chief learning concepts
Meaningful learning

It is the part and parcel of higher order thinking. Such thinking takes place when the learner grasps the interrelationship between two or more ideas, which may be old and/or fresh and new. First prerequisite for meaningful learning is that the learner should be able to relate to the material presented in some sensible fashion. The fresh and new information must be fitted into a larger pattern. Also, the learner must possess relevant ideas to which the fresh and new idea can be related or anchored. Finally, the learner must actually attempt to relate, in some sensible way, the fresh and new ideas to those which he presently possesses. If any of these conditions are missing, the end result will be 'rote learning' (that is, the learner merely memorizing the material)

Reception learning

Reception learning is not necessarily rote; likewise, discovery learning is not always meaningful. Rote is simply based on the memory, while meaningful is related to the understanding. Either one - reception learning or discovery learning - can be rote or meaningful. Everything depends upon how the knowledge is treated. If the learner merely memorizes the material (even if the conclusions have been arrived at by the discovery method), then, the learning outcomes must necessarily be rote and thus, meaningless. Reception learning or discovery learning may promote either rote or meaningful consequences. One does not inherently infer the other. Thus the whole question of rote learning versus meaningful learning depends upon whether or not the fresh and new information is integrated into the learner's cognitive structure.

Expository instruction

Expository instruction provides the educator the most direct route for laying a foundation for higher order thinking. Ausubel believes most facilitators favour this method of instruction. Expository instruction is an efficient and effective way of organizing classroom learning. Even laboratory sciences -which lend themselves to the discovery method - can be taught as well by using the expository method. Though expository instruction has been criticized as being authoritarian, such criticism is unjustified. There is nothing inherently authoritarian in presenting or explaining ideas to others as long as they are not obliged, either explicitly or implicitly, to accept them on faith. Facilitators have an obligation to share their understanding with their learners. According to Ausubel, to cast out the facilitator's understanding as it might impose some structure on the learners' thinking is not correct.

Mapping techniques in subsumption theory
Mind mapping

This involves a tree-like structure. Here, a topic is represented by a central image or a graph. The main themes of the topic radiate out from the central image as primary branches which further radiate into minor themes. All the branches are interconnected to form a series of links. Mind mapping helps break large projects or topics down into manageable chunks, so one can plan effectively without getting overwhelmed and without forgetting something important. A good 'mind map' shows the 'shape' of the subject, the relative importance of individual points, and the way in which facts relate to one another. Hence, mind maps are very quick to review, as one can often refresh information in his/her mind just by a glance.

Uses of mind maps

- Brainstorming - individually and as a group.
- Summarizing information and note taking.
- Consolidating information from different research sources.
- Thinking through complex problems.
- Presenting information in a format that shows the overall structure of the subject.
- Studying and memorizing information

Concept mapping

This involves, basically, a web structure. Concept maps are tools to organize and represent knowledge. They include concepts, usually enclosed in circles or boxes. The relationships between concepts are depicted by a connecting line between two concepts. Words on these lines can be used to specify the nature of the relationships between different concepts. An important characteristic of concept maps is the existence of cross-links which depict the relationships between concepts or ideas or information in different parts of the concept map. Hence, concept maps provide a visual representation of knowledge structures and arguments.

Uses of concept maps

- To generate ideas (e.g. Brain storming)

- ✤ To design a complex structure
- ✤ To communicate complex ideas
- ✤ To illustrate the relationships between different components or processes
- ✤ To aid learning by explicitly integrating fresh and new and old knowledge
- ✤ To assess an understanding
- ✤ Or diagnose a misunderstanding

Differentiating mind mapping and concept mapping

Mind mapping	Concept mapping
A mind map tends to have a single main concept or a central theme	A concept map may have several related and interconnecting ideas, themes or topics
It is basically a tree-like structure	It is basically a web structure

Knowledge mapping

Knowledge mapping is a less formal and vaguer concept than concept mapping and mind mapping. It is a collaborative technique where the learners brainstorm and create visual maps of their thoughts. A knowledge map is an association of items of information, mainly visual, where the association itself creates fresh and new, actionable information. The process of creating a knowledge map is known as 'knowledge mapping'.

This process consists of five steps

- ✤ Acquire data
- ✤ Manipulate data
- ✤ Store data
- ✤ Process data
- ✤ Visualise data

Uses of knowledge maps

- ✤ To compile internal and external resources
- ✤ To identify opportunities to reuse information
- ✤ To identify knowledge dependencies within cross-functional work groups
- ✤ To categorize value-added information
- ✤ To identify knowledge sharing opportunities
- ✤ To develop formal communities of practice
- ✤ To create a knowledge tool that helps users find what they need

Criticism

The most persuasively voiced criticism of advance organizers is that their definition and construction are vague and, therefore, that different researchers have varying concepts of what an organizer is and can only rely on intuition in constructing one, since nowhere, as claimed by the critics, is specified their criteria and their construction.

In a response to critics, Ausubel defends advance organizers by stating that there is no one specific exemplar in constructing advance organizers as they always depend on :

→ the nature of the learning material,

→ the age of the learner, and

→ his degree of prior familiarity with the learning passage.

Another criticism of Ausubel's advance organizers is that the critics often compare the idea of advance organizers with overviews. However, Ausubel has addressed that issue by saying that advance organizers differ from overviews 'in being relatable to presumed ideational content in the learner's current cognitive structure'.

Thirdly, critics also address the notion of advance organizers on whether they are intended to favour high ability or low ability learners. However, Ausubel shares that advance organizers are designed to favour meaningful learning.

Therefore, to question whether advance organizers are better suited for high or low ability learners is unrelated as Ausubel argues that advance organizers can be catered to any learner to aid them in bridging the gap between what they already know and what they are about to learn.

Applying Ausubel's learning theory to prepare instruction materials

While preparing instruction material, the facilitator's role is:

→ to focus on the lesson and its relevancy.

→ to activate any of the learner's prior knowledge and to motivate the learners to tap into their past education, experiences, and notions in order to use this as a base to build fresh and new information.

→ to introduce some form of text that the learners are familiar with to further connect the lesson to the learner's prior knowledge and build upon it.

→ to restate the focus of the lesson and revisit the advance organizers those were presented.

→ to engage the learners as much as possible in discussions.

→ to place fresh and new and old information together and using both simultaneously.

Application of Ausubel's theory in Economics

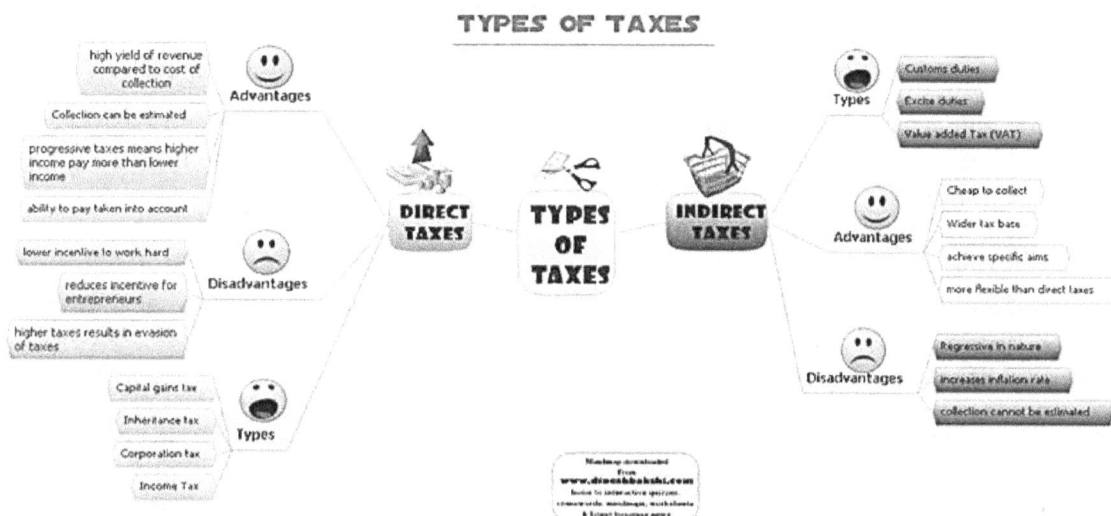

TYPES OF TAXES

Ausubel's Advance Organizer model

→ Phase one: Advance organizer to clarify the aim of the lesson; present the organizer; relate the organizer to learners' knowledge.

→ Phase two: Presentation of learning task or material to make the organization of the fresh and new material explicit; to make logical order of learning material explicit and to present material and engage learners in meaningful learning activities.

→ Phase three: Strengthening cognitive organization to relate fresh and new information to advance organizer in order to promote active reception learning.

Ausubel's expository instruction: Expository instruction is probably the most commonly used instruction method in the schools today. Ausubel is one of the strongest proponents of expository instruction. Expository instruction is where the facilitator is the major provider of information. The abstraction is stated by the facilitator before exemplars are given, and the exemplars are provided to help illustrate the abstraction.

There are some reasons that expository instruction is widely used

→ Facilitators are thought to be the persons who have all the knowledge and whose job is to pass this knowledge to learners.

→ Expository instruction is the easiest kind of instruction as giving lecture is easier than using other kinds of instruction.

→ It has the potential for being a very efficient means of instruction facts and abstraction.

→ It minimizes misconception.

→ It is very efficient in terms of time.

What facilitators should do in an expository lesson is

→ Set definite learning objective.

→ Plan what, when and how to teach.

→ Use structured and sequential learning material.

→ Begin lesson with an advance organizer.

→ Present fresh and new information in an organized way (step by step and deductively).

→ Define concept clearly and clarify terms.

→ Use both positive and negative exemplars when presenting fresh and new concept.

→ Encourage learners to think.

→ Encourage learner involvement and interaction in class.

→ Monitor and check learner progress toward the objectives and provide them with a corrective feedback.

→ Allow learners reflect at the conclusion of the lesson.

Advantages of expository instruction

→ Expository instruction is the easiest kind of instruction.

→ Misconception is minimized.

→ It is very efficient in terms of time.

+ It is useful for large number of learners.
+ Lesson summaries and closures are best accomplished.

Disadvantages of expository instruction

+ It is difficult to have the attention of all children.
+ It makes learners passive.
+ It is highly dependent on the skills of the facilitator.
+ It is not suitable for all age levels.
+ It reduces the ability to use the material and thinking processes outside the classroom.

Expository instruction and discovery instruction

Discovery instruction	Expository instruction
Learner centred	Facilitator centred
Facilitator's role is as a supporter	Facilitator gives information directly
Needs more time	Needs less time
Learners may have misconceptions	Misconceptions are minimized
More motivational for learner	Less motivational for learners

2.2 BRUNER'S THEORY

We know different learners, in a class, have different learning needs and the right method depends on the situation. As different learning needs call for different instruction methods, the effective technology integration depends on a well-planned match of needs with resources and instruction strategies, along with classroom conditions that support them. The goals of education keep on changing with changing times. Earlier the focus was on acquiring the knowledge of the 3 R's (Reading, wRiting and aRithmetic), now with technological advancements, the society has different challenges and hence different strategies are required to serve today's educational goals. In order to respond to modern challenges, these changes must reflect in the instruction-learning processes inside as well as outside the classrooms!

In an attempt to understand the intricate (instruction) learning process, different scholars gave different theories which can be crystallized into two different views on instruction and learning, viz., objectivism and constructivism.

Objectivism: knowledge has a separate, real existence of its own outside the human mind. Learning happens when this knowledge is transmitted to people and they store it in their minds.

Constructivism: humans construct all knowledge in their minds by participating in certain experiences. Learning occurs when one constructs both mechanisms for learning and his or her unique version of knowledge, colour by background, experiences, and aptitude.

Bruner postulated three stages of intellectual development

+ The first stage was termed 'enactive', when a person learns about the world through actions on physical objects and the outcomes of these actions.

- The second stage was called 'iconic', where learning can be obtained through using models and pictures.
- The final stage was 'symbolic', in which the learner develops the capacity to think in abstract terms.

Practical applications based upon this three-stage notion are:

Bruner's constructivist theory can be applied to instruction, by applying the following principles:

- Instruction must be concerned with the experiences and contexts that make the learner willing and able to learn (readiness).
- Instruction must be structured so that it can be easily grasped by the learner (spiral organization).
- Instruction should be designed to facilitate extrapolation and or fill in the gaps (going beyond the information given).

An exemplar: This exemplar belongs to Bruner (1973). The concept of prime numbers appears to be more readily grasped when the child, through construction, discovers that certain handful of beans cannot be laid out in completed rows and columns. Such quantities have either to be laid out in a single file or in an incomplete row-column design in which there is always one extra or too few to fill the pattern. These patterns, the child learns, happen to be called prime. It is easy for the child to go from this step to the recognition that a multiple table, so called, is a record sheet of quantities in completed multiple rows and columns. Here is factoring, multiplication and primes in a construction that can be visualized.

Exemplary activities

- Video-based scenarios
- Multimedia products
- Simulations and problem-solving software

Discovery learning theory by Bruner

The primary variable in his theory of learning is the coding system into which the learner organizes these categories. The act of categorizing is assumed to be involved in information processing and decision making. Hence, he suggested a coding system in which people have a hierarchical arrangement of related categories. Bruner's theory of cognitive learning emphasizes the formation of this coding system. He believed that the systems facilitate transfer, enhance retention and increase problem solving and motivation. He advocated the discovery oriented learning methods in schools which he believed helped learners discover the relationships between categories. A major theme in this theory is that 'learning is an active process in which learners construct fresh and new ideas or concepts based upon their current or past knowledge' (Kearsely).

Bruner contends that the instructor should try and encourage learners to construct hypotheses to makes decisions and discover principles by themselves.

Cognitive construct instructional theories

Bruner talks that we should teach the 'structure' of subjects. He advocated the introduction of the real process of a particular discipline to learners. For an instance, when learning history, learners should become involved in genuine historical enquiry. This might involve examining a bridge, a building, or even a head stone in a cemetery, then using the information acquired to trace records of various kinds in order to answer the questions generated about the origins, purposes, and history of that structure, or the life the person concerned.

Bruner's theory about instruction

Bruner was one of the founding fathers of constructivist theory. His was a theoretical framework based on the theme that learners construct fresh and new ideas or concepts based on existing knowledge. Learning is an active process. Bruner's theories emphasize the significance of categorization in learning. To perceive is to categorize, to conceptualize is to categorize, to learn is to form categories, to make decisions is to categorize. Interpreting information and experiences by similarities and differences is a key concept.

Four features of Bruner's theory of instruction
a. Predisposition to learn: This feature specifically refers to experiences which move the learner towards love for learning in general, or of learning something in particular. Part of the task of a facilitator is to maintain and direct a child's spontaneous explorations.
b. Structure of knowledge: Details are better retained when information or knowledge is placed within the context of an ordered and structured pattern. Understanding the fundamental structure of a subject makes it more comprehensive. To generate knowledge, which is transferable to other contexts, fundamental principles or patterns are best suited.
c. Effective sequencing- Sequencing in increasing difficulty will fit every learner than a unique sequencing for all. Sequencing, or lack of it, can make learning easier or more difficult.
d. Modes of representation: Visual, words, symbols.

a. Predisposition to learning

Bruner stated that experiences should be designed in a way that will help the learner be willing and able to learn. He believed that the desire to learn and undertake problem solving could be activated by devising problem activities in which learners would explore alternative solutions. The major condition for the exploration of alternatives was 'the presence of some optical level of uncertainty. This related directly to the learners curiosity to resolve uncertainty and ambiguity. According to this idea, the facilitator would design various activities that would arouse the learners' curiosity.

b. Structure of knowledge

Bruner expressed this component by proposing that the curriculum specialist and facilitator must specify the ways in which a body of knowledge should be structured so that it can be most readily grasped by the learner. Any idea or problem or body of knowledge can be presented in a form simple enough so that any particular learner can understand it in a resizable form. During the presentation of, the cognitive level needs to be taken consideration.

c. Sequencing

The most effective sequences of instruction should be specified. According to Bruner, instruction should lead the learner through the content in order to increase the learners' ability to 'grasp, transform and transfer', what is learned. In general sequencing should move from enactive (hands- on, concrete), to iconic (visual), to symbolic (description in words or mathematical symbols). However, this sequence will be dependent on the learner's symbolic system and learning.

d. Motivation (form and pacing of reinforcement)
The last aspect of Bruner's theory is that the nature and pacing of rewards and punishment should be specified. Bruner suggests that a movement form extrinsic reward, such as facilitator's praise, toward intrinsic reward inherent in solving problems or understanding the concepts is desirable. To Bruner, learning depends upon the knowledge of results when they can be used for correction. Feedback to the learner is critical to development of knowledge.

Discovery learning
Jerome Bruner was influential in defining discovery learning, which employs cognitive psychology as a base. Discovery learning is 'an approach to instruction through which learners interact with their environment- by exploring and manipulating objects, wrestling with questions and controversies, or performing experiments'. The idea is that learners are more likely to remember concepts that they discover on their own.

Advantages of discovery learning

+ Supports active engagement of the learner in the learning process.
+ Fosters curiosity.
+ Enables the development of lifelong learning skills.
+ Personalizes the learning experiences.
+ Highly motivating as it allows individuals the opportunity to experiment and discover something for themselves.
+ Builds on learner's prior knowledge and understanding.

Disadvantages of discovery learning

+ Potential to confuse the learner, if no initial framework is available.
+ It requires close monitoring on account of the fact that learners don't hesitate to make mistakes.
+ Learner have different pace of learning, thus, the pace of instruction will be affected accordingly.
+ Discovery learning may not be applicable to each and every topic.

Bruner's Theory and Implications
According to Bruner's theory, learners construct fresh and new ideas or concepts based upon existing knowledge and that learning is an active process. Bruner's theories emphasize the significance of categorization in learning. To perceive is to categorize, to conceptualize is to categorize, to learn is to form categories, to make decisions is to categorize. Interpreting information and experiences by similarities and differences is a key concept. Being an ardent constructivist, he also emphasized on the significance of a social setting to stimulate and enhance learning.

The immediate implications that arise from Bruner's theories are that:

a. Group learning skills should be fostered in the learners in order to provide 'social setting'.

Chemistry provides such opportunities for learners to learn with each other. This is achieves with the help of group projects/presentations, problem-solving that requires mutual help and experiments/practical performed in groups.

b. The content discussed in the classroom should be such that the learners are able to bring their daily life experiences into the classroom and apply the content back to their daily lives.

Science instruction is essentially about understanding the various phenomena in which the curriculum is designed in such a manner that learners are able to relate what they see around them to what is being discussed in the class.

c. Learners should be engaged to learn in a hands-on manner with real experiences of the things discussed in a class.

Chemistry provides immense opportunities for learners to engage in hands-on learning. With a plethora of scientific activities and experiments, learners can be made to familiarize themselves with the numerous apparatus involved and know how to use them.

2.3 VYGOTSKY AND HIS THEORY OF LEARNING

Lev Semenovich Vygotsky talks about constructivism. He elaborated the sociocultural theory/perspective of development. He wrote about language and thought, culture, cognitive development, psychology of art learning and development and educating learner with special needs. His work was banned in Russia for many years as he referred to western psychologists. But in the past twenty five years, with the rediscovery of this work, he provides an alternative to Piagetian theories. Yet the significance and usefulness of Vygotsky's work was not fully appreciated by western psychologists until his writings were translated into English (Vygotsky, 1962; 1978; 1981; 1987).

His significant contributions to cognitive development which are very profitable to us can be given as:

(1). The importance of social interaction for cognitive development:

It means we are socializing with others. In other words, we can say that we are guided by others. Vygotsky says that this is a cultural setting and cannot be understood apart from this setting. These social interactions are more than simple influence on cognitive development. In fact, Vygotsky conceptualized development as the transfer of socially shared activities into an internalized process.

(2). Psychological view of cognitive development:

Psychologists recognize that the child's culture shapes his cognitive development by determining what and how the child will learn about the world.

(3). Social sources:

(a) Individual thinking

(b) Individual learning

Vygotsky assumed that every function in a child's cultural development appears twice: first on the social level, (i.e. between the people), and later, on the individual level, (inside the child). In other words, higher mental process appears first between as they are co-constructed during shared activities.

So, for Vygotsky, social interaction was more than an influence, it was the origin of higher mental process such as problem solving. Co- constructed process is a social in which people interact and negotiate to create an understanding or to solve a problem. The final product is shaped by all participants.

He believed that cultural tools, including real (such as printing presses, abacus- today, we would add PDAs, computers, the internet) and symbolic tools (such as numbers and mathematical system, braille and sign language, maps, works of art, signs and codes, and language) play very important roles in cognitive development.

Vygotsky emphasized the tools that the culture provides to support thinking. He believed that all higher- order mental processes, such as reasoning and problem solving, are mediated by (accomplished through and with the help of) psychological tools, such as language, signs, and symbols. Adults teach these tools to children during day to day activities and the children internalize them. Then the psychological tools can help learners advance their own development. The process is something like this: as children engage in activities with adults or more capable peers, they exchange ideas and ways of thinking about or represent spaces concepts- drawing maps, for an instance, as a way to represent spaces and places. These co-created ideas are internalized by children.

In this exchange of signs and symbols and exchange of planation, children begin to develop a 'cultural tool kit' to make sense of their world. The kit is filled with physical tools such as pencils or paint brushes directed toward the external world and psychological tools such as problem- solving or memory strategies for acting mentally.

In Vygotsky theory, language is the most important symbol system in the tool kit and it is the one that helps to fill the other tools. Language is critical for cognitive development. It provides a means for expressing ideas and asking questions, the categories and concepts for thinking, and the links between the past and the future. When we consider a problem, we generally think in words and partial sentence. Vygotsky thought that human capacity for language enables children to provide for auxiliary tools in the solution of difficult task.

The role of learning and development
Vygotsky and Piaget views compared

Piaget defined development as the active construction of knowledge and learning as the passive formation of association. He was interested in knowledge construction and believed that cognitive development has to come before learning; the child had to be cognitively ready to learn. He said that learning is subordinated to development and not vice-versa. But Vygotsky believed that learning was an active process.

The role of adults and peers

Vygotsky believed that cognitive development occurs through the child conversations and interactions with more capable members of the culture- adults or more able peers. These people serve as guides and facilitators, providing the information and support necessary for the child development.

Implications of Vygotsky theory for facilitators

There are at least three ways through which cultural tools can be passed from one individual to another:

→ Imitative learning (where one person tries to imitate the other),
→ Instructed learning (where learner internalize the instructions of the facilitator and use these instructions to self-regulate), and
→ Collaborative learning (where a group of peers strives to understand each other, and learning occurs in the process).

Vygotsky was most concerned with instructed learning.

Assisted learning

It means providing strategic help in the initial stages of learning and gradually diminishing as learner gains independence.
Assisted learning requires scaffolding-giving information, prompts, reminders, and encouragement at the right time in the right amount.

Scaffolding learning

When adults and other skilled individuals assist children in performing difficult tasks, they often use a technique called scaffolding to support children in their efforts. Exemplar: while erecting a fresh and new building a builder sometimes construct an external structure – a scaffold- around the building. This scaffold provides support for the worker (a place where they can stand) until the building itself is strong enough to support them. As the building gains stability, the scaffold becomes less necessary and is gradually removed.

The zone of proximal development

This is an area where the child cannot solve a problem alone but can be successful under adult guidance or in collaboration with a more advanced peer. This is the area where instruction can succeed, as real learning is possible. This is an important concept that relates to the difference between what a child can achieve independently and what a child can achieve with guidance and encouragement from a skilled peer. For an instance: the child finds it difficult to solve the jigsaw puzzle by him / her and takes a long time to do so, but is able to solve it following interaction with father and has developed competence at this skill which will be applied in future while solving jigsaw puzzles.

Vygotsky sees the zone of proximal development (ZPD) as the area where the most sensitive instruction or guidance should be given, allowing the child to develop skills which they will use on their own, and developing higher mental functions. Vygotsky also views interaction with peers as an effective way of developing skills and strategies. He suggests that facilitators should use cooperative learning exercises where less competent children develop with help from more skilful peers, within ZPD.

Evidencing Vygotsky and ZPD

Freund (1990) conducted a study in which children had to decide which items of furniture should be placed in particular houses of a dolls house. Some children were allowed to play with their mother in a similar situation before they attempted it alone (ZPD) whilst others were allowed to work on this all by themselves (Piaget's discovery learning). Freund found that those who had previously worked with their mother showed greatest improvement compared with the first attempt at the task.

Conclusion: Guided learning, within ZPD, leads to greater understanding / performance than working alone i.e. discovery learning.

Applications of Vygotsky theory

→ Use ZPD – instruction should begin towards the zone's upper limit, where the learner is able to reach the goal only through close collaboration with the instructor. With adequate continued instruction and practice, the learner organizes and masters the behavioural sequences required performing the target skill. As the instruction continue the performance transfers from the facilitator to the learner. The facilitator gradually reduces the explanations, hints, and demonstrations until the learner is able to perform the skill alone. Once the goal is achieved, it can become the foundation for the development of a fresh and new ZPD.

→ Use scaffolding: look for opportunities to use scaffolding when learner need help with self-initiated learning activities. Also use scaffolding to help learner move to a higher level of skill and knowledge. Provide just enough assistance. You might ask, 'What can i do to help you?' Or simply observe the learner' intentions and attempts, smoothly providing support when needed. When the learner hesitates, provide encouragement. Encourage the learner to practice the skill. You may watch and appreciate the learner's practice or provide support when the learner forgets what to do.

→ Use more- skilled peers as facilitators: remember that it is not just adult that Vygotsky believed are important in helping learner learn important skills. Learner is also benefitted from the support and guidance from more-skilled person.

→ Encouraging collaborative learning and recognize that learning involves a community of learners: both children and adult engage in learning activities in a collaborative way. Peers, facilitators, parents and other adults work together in a community of learner rather than the child learning as in isolated individual.

→ Consider the cultural context of learning: an important function of education of education is to guide children in learning the learning the skills that culture in which they live.

→ Monitor and encourage children's use of private speech: be aware of the developmental change from externally talking to oneself when solving a problem during the preschool years to privately talking to oneself in the early elementary school years. In the elementary school years, encourage learner to internalize and self-regulate their talk to themselves

→ Assess ZPD, not IQ. Like Piaget, Vygotsky did not believe that formal, standardized test is the best way to assess children's learning or their readiness to learn. Rather, Vygotsky argued that assessment should focus on determining the learner ZPD. The skilled helper presents the child with tasks of varying difficulty to determine the best level at which to begin instruction. ZPD is a measure of learning potential. IQ, also a measure of learning potential, emphasizes that intelligence is a property of the child. By contrast, ZPD emphasized that learning is interpersonal. It is inappropriate to say that the child 'has' a ZPD in the same sense that the child might 'have' an IQ.

Suggestive reading: Educational Psychology by A. Woolfolk.

Role of social interaction in the cognitive development of learner

Vygotsky's theory stresses the fundamental role of social interaction in the development of cognition, as he believed strongly that community plays a central role in the process of 'making meaning.'

Vygotsky's theory highlights three main points. It :

+ places more emphasis on culture affecting/shaping cognitive development
+ places considerably more emphasis on social factors contributing to cognitive development
+ places more and different emphasis on the role of language in cognitive development.

Cultural tools and cognitive development:

According to Vygotsky, infants are born with the basic materials/abilities for intellectual development.
Vygotsky refers to elementary mental functions –

+ Attention
+ Sensation
+ Perception
+ Memory

Eventually, through interaction within the socio-cultural environment, these are developed into more sophisticated and effective mental processes/strategies which he refers to as higher mental functions, e.g. Memory. In young children this is limited by biological factors. However, culture determines the kind of memory strategy we develop. E.g., in our culture we learn note-taking to aid memory, but in pre-literate societies other strategies must be developed, such as tying knots in string to remember, or carrying pebbles, or repetition of the names of ancestors until large numbers can be repeated. Vygotsky also refers to tools of intellectual adaptation - these allow children to use the basic mental functions more effectively/adaptively, and these are culturally determined (e.g. memory mnemonics, mind maps).

Vygotsky therefore sees cognitive functions, even those carried out alone, as affected by the beliefs, values and tools of intellectual adaptation of the culture in which a person develops and therefore socio-culturally determined. The tools of intellectual adaptation therefore vary from culture to culture - as in the memory exemplar.

Social influence on cognitive development:

Vygotsky believes that young children are curious and actively involved in their own learning and the discovery and development of fresh and new understandings / schema. Hence, he places more emphasis on social contributions to the process of development.

According to Vygotsky, much important learning by the child occurs through social interaction with a skilful tutor. The tutor may model behaviours and/or provide verbal instructions for the child. This is referred as co-operative or collaborative dialogue. The child seeks to understand the actions or instructions provided by the tutor (often the parent or facilitator) then internalises the information, using it to guide or regulate their own performance.

For an instance, a young girl, who is given her first jigsaw; alone, she performs poorly in attempting to solve the puzzle. The father then sits with her and describes or demonstrates some basic strategies, such as finding all the corner/edge pieces and provides a couple of pieces for the child to put together herself and provides encouragement when she does so. As the child becomes more competent, the father allows the child to work more independently. According to Vygotsky, this kind of social interaction involving co-operative or collaborative dialogue promotes cognitive development.

Role of language and talk
According to Vygotsky, language plays two critical roles in cognitive development:
(1). It is the main means by which adults transmit info to children.
(2). Language itself becomes a very powerful tool of intellectual adaptation.

Vygotsky sees private speech or talk as a means for children to plan activities and strategies and therefore aid their development. Language is therefore an accelerator to thinking/understanding. Vygotsky believed that language develops from social interactions, for communication purposes. Later language ability becomes internalised as thought and 'inner speech'. Thought is the result of language.

Language is a critical aspect for cognitive development. It provides a means for expressing ideas and asking questions, the categories and concepts for thinking, and the links between the past and the future. When we consider a problem, we generally think in words and partial sentence. Vygotsky thought that human capacity for language enables children to provide for auxiliary tools in the solution of difficult task.

Reciprocal instruction
It used to improve learners' ability to learn from text. In this method, facilitator and learners collaborate in learning and practicing four key skills:
a. Summarizing
b. Questioning
c. Clarifying
d. Predicting.

The facilitator's role in the process is reduced over time with various kinds of learning like apprenticeship, where a facilitator or more advanced peer helps to structure or arrange a task so that all can work on it successfully, assisted learning and scaffolding learning.

2.4 SKINNER'S LEARNING THEORY
B. F. Skinner was considered as the most influential psychologist of the 20th century. Skinner (1904-1990) was born in Susquehanna, Pennsylvania. He received his master's degree in 1930 and his Ph.D. in 1931 from Harvard

University. He obtained his graduate degree from Hamilton College in N. York, where he majored in English.

While once at Hamilton, Skinner had lunch with the American poet Robert Frost, who encouraged him to send a sample of his writing. Frost favourably reviewed the three short stories that Skinner sent and Skinner decided to become a writer. This decision was a great disappointment to his father, who was a lawyer and wanted his son to become a lawyer. Skinner's early efforts for writing were so frustrating that he thought of seeing a psychiatrist. He gradually developed distaste for most literary pursuits. In his autobiography (1967), he said that he had failed as a writer as he had nothing important to say, but couldn't accept that explanation. It was literature which must be at fault. When he failed in describing human behaviour through literature, Skinner attempted to describe human behaviour through science. Clearly, he was much more successful at the latter pursuit.

Skinner's philosophy and theory: Skinner adopted and developed the theory of radical behaviourism. He stressed on the observable and measurable aspects of an organism's behaviour.

Operant behaviour: The behaviour, which is not elicited by a known stimulus, but is simply emitted by the organism, is called as operant behaviour. Instances include beginning to whistle, standing up and walking about, child abandoning a toy in favour of another. We can find exemplars of operant conditioning at work all around us. Consider the case of children completing homework to earn a reward from a parent or facilitator, or employees finishing projects to receive praise or promotions. Skinner doesn't say that operant behaviour occurs independently of stimulation. He says that stimulus causing such behaviour is unknown and that it is not important to know its cause. Operant behaviour is controlled by its consequence. It is also known as kind r conditioning.

Skinner's operant conditioning concepts build on the classical conditioning concepts of Pavlov but while Pavlov viewed learning as involuntary physical responses to outside stimuli e.g. Dog salivate at the sight of a dog food can. Skinner said that people have voluntary mental control over their responses and the consequences of their past actions can act as a stimulus to shape their future behaviour. He said that learning processes occur inside the mind and we can't see them directly, learning can only be inferred by observing behaviours. Behaviours are shaped by contingencies of reinforcement set up to shape desired responses. Positive reinforcement increases behaviour while punishment decreases the occurrences of the behaviours.

Operant conditioning principles

⤳ Any response that is followed by a reinforcing stimulus tends to be repeated.
⤳ Reinforcement is anything that increases the rate with which an operant response occurs.

These principles apply to a variety of situations. To modify behaviour, one merely has to find something that is reinforcing for the organism whose behaviour one wishes to modify, wait until the desired behaviour occurs and then immediately reinforce the organism. When this is done, the rate with which the desired response occurs goes up further. Any behaviour that the organism is capable of performing can be manipulated in this manner.

Skinner box

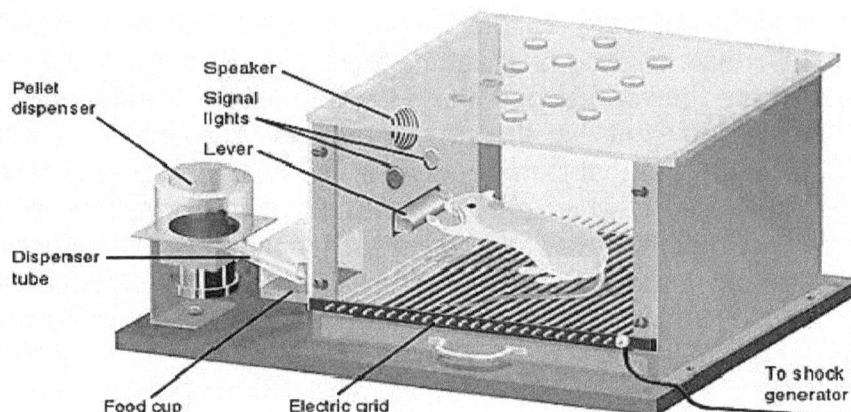

Skinner identified three kinds of responses or operant that can follow behaviour.

- ✦ Neutral operants: responses from the environment that neither increase nor decrease the probability of a behaviour being repeated.
- ✦ Reinforcers: responses from the environment that increase the probability of a behaviour being repeated. Reinforcers can be either positive or negative.
- ✦ Punishers: response from the environment that decrease the likelihood of a behaviour being repeated.

Punishment weakens behaviour while reinforcement strengthens behaviour.

Reinforcement (strengthens behaviour)
Positive reinforcement
Skinner showed how positive reinforcement worked by placing a hungry rat in his Skinner box. The box contained a lever on the side and as the rat moved about the box it would accidentally knock the lever. Immediately, a food pellet would drop into a container next to the lever. The rats quickly learned to go straight to the lever after a few times of being put in the box. The consequence of receiving food if they pressed the lever ensured that they would repeat the action again and again.
Positive reinforcement strengthens behaviour. By providing a consequence, an individual finds reward. For an instance, if your facilitator gives you Rs.50 each time you complete your homework (i.e. a reward) you are more likely to repeat this behaviour in the future, thus strengthening the behaviour of completing your homework.

Negative reinforcement
The removal of an unpleasant reinforcer can also strengthen behaviour. This is known as negative reinforcement as it is the removal of an adverse stimulus, which is rewarding to the animal. Negative reinforcement strengthens behaviour as it stops or removes an unpleasant experience. For an instance, if you speak Hindi, give your facilitator Rs. 25. You will speak English to avoid paying Rs. 25, thus strengthening the behaviour of speaking Hindi.

Skinner showed how negative reinforcement worked by placing a rat in his Skinner box and then subjecting it to an unpleasant electric current which caused it some discomfort.

a. As the rat moved about the box it would accidentally knock the lever. Immediately after it did so, the electric current would be switched off. The rats quickly learned to go straight to the lever after a few times of being put in the box. The consequence of escaping the electric current ensured that they would repeat the action again and again.

b. Skinner even taught the rats to avoid the electric current by turning on a light just before the electric current came on. The rats soon learned to press the lever when the light came on as they knew that this would stop the electric current being switched on.

These two learned responses are known as escape learning and avoidance learning.

Punishment (weakens behaviour)

Punishment is defined as the opposite of reinforcement since it is designed to weaken or eliminate a response rather than increase it. Like reinforcement, punishment can work either by directly applying an unpleasant stimulus like a shock after a response or by removing a potentially rewarding stimulus, for instance, deducting someone's pocket money to punish undesirable behaviour.

Skinner's observations can be divided into:

+ Independent variable: This can be manipulated by the experimenter.
+ Dependent variable: This cannot be manipulated by the experimenter and are affected by the independent variables.

Independent variables

Kinds of reinforcement

a. Primary reinforcement- These are the instinctive behaviours, which lead to satisfaction of basic survival needs such as food, water, sex, shelter. No learning takes place as the behaviours emerge spontaneously

b. Secondary reinforcement - The reinforcer is not reinforcing by itself, but becomes reinforcing when paired with a primary reinforcer, such as pairing a sound or a light with food.

c. Generalized reinforcement - Stimuli become reinforced through repeated pairing with primary or secondary reinforcers. Many are culturally reinforced. For an instance, in human behaviour, wealth, power, fame, strength, and intelligence are valued in many cultures. The external symbols of these attributes are generalized reinforcers. Money, rank, recognition, degrees and certificates, etc. are strongly reinforcing many individuals in the cultures that value the attributes they symbolize.

Schedule of reinforcement

+ Intermittent reinforcement - reinforcement is given only part of the times for the animal gives the desired response.
+ Ratio reinforcement - a pre-determined proportion of responses will be reinforced.

- Fixed ratio reinforcement - reinforcement is given on a regular ratio, such as every fifth time the desired behaviour is produced.
- Variable (random) fixed reinforcement- reinforcement is given for a predetermined proportion of responses, but randomly instead of on a fixed schedule.
- Interval reinforcement- reinforcement is given after a predetermined period of time.
- Fixed interval reinforcement - reinforcement is given on a regular schedule, such as every five minutes.
- Variable interval reinforcement - reinforcement is given after random amounts of time have passed.

In animal studies, Skinner found that continuous reinforcement in the early stages of training seems to increase the rate of learning. Later, intermittent reinforcement keeps the response going longer and slows extinction.

Dependent variables (measures of learning)

- Acquisition rate - it shows how rapidly an animal can be trained to a fresh and new operant behaviour through reinforcement. Skinner deprived the animals of food for 24, or more, hours before beginning a schedule of reinforcement. This tended to increase acquisition rate.
- Rate of response - this is a measure of learning that is very sensitive to different schedules of reinforcement. In most cases, animals were given intermittent schedules of reinforcement, to expect the desired response during other times as well. Rate of response is a measure of correct responses throughout a testing schedule including the times when reinforcement is not provided after a correct response. The animals build expectations when they are given rewards at predictable times (e.g.; animals which are fed at the same time each day become active as that time approaches, and a dog whose master comes home at the same time each day becomes more attentive around that time of day.).
- Extinction rate - the rate at which an operant response disappears following the withdrawal of reinforcement. Skinner found that continuous reinforcement schedules produced a faster rate of learning in the early stages of a training program, and also a more rapid extinction rate once the reinforcement was discontinued. A behaviour no longer followed by the reinforcing stimulus results in a decreased probability of that behaviour occurring in the future.

Skinner on education

- The information to be learned should be presented in small steps.
- The learners should be given rapid feedback concerning the accuracy of their learning.
- The learners are able to learn at their own pace.
- Course objectives be specified before instruction begins and be defined behaviourally e.g. Verbs like define, recall, draw, recite, list, name, write, recognize, classify, compare, select, predict, find, use, perform and so on should be encouraged. Verbs like know, understand, learn should be discouraged.

- ↷ Proceed from simple to complex.
- ↷ Extrinsic reinforcers are important as they can utilize in the classroom e.g. Verbal praise, positive facial expressions, golf stars and so on.
- ↷ Avoid the use of punishment.

Skinner's legacy

Skinner had proposed an alternative instruction technique called programmed learning (PL). Personalized system of instruction (PSI) is an off-shoot of PL.

Programmed learning

- ↷ Consists of a labour saving device.
- ↷ Can bring one programmer into contact with an indefinite number of learners.
- ↷ Involves mass production but the effect is of a private tutor.
- ↷ Induces sustained activity.
- ↷ Keeps the learner alert and busy.
- ↷ Makes sure that the learner moves on only when he has understood a frame properly.
- ↷ Helps the learner to come up with the right answer by hinting, prompting and suggesting and so on.
- ↷ Last but not the least, reinforces the learner for every correct response.

These are a number of variations possible in programmed learning e.g., some learners may skip information, if it is familiar. This procedure usually involves giving learners a pre-test on a certain section of the programme, and if they perform adequately, they are instructed to advance to the next section.

Another kind of programming allows the learners to 'branch' into different bodies of information depending on initial performance. After learners have been presented with a certain amount of information, they are given a multiple-choice question. If they answer correctly, they advance to the next body of information. If they answer incorrectly, the branching programs direct them to additional information, depending on the mistake that was made. For an instance, the program may say, 'if you picked a as your answer, go back and review the material on page 24; if you picked b as your answer, repeat section 3, if you chose c, you are correct; please proceed to the next section.'

Personalized systems of instruction

Like programmed learning, the psi method is individualized and involves quick, frequent feedback concerning learner performance. Providing an individualized course usually involves four steps, which can be summarized as follows:

- ↷ Determine the material to be covered in the course.
- ↷ Divide the material into self-contained segments.
- ↷ Create methods of evaluating the degree to which the learner has mastered the material in a given segment.
- ↷ Allow learner to move from segment to segment at own pace.

Developing instructional materials in Skinnerian framework

To develop instructional material in Skinnerian framework, we should adopt the behavioural approach that he had endorsed. Its offshoots are programmed learning; personalized system of instruction and online learning. We can begin by taking care of the basics involved which are as follows

- ✦ The information to be learned should be presented in small steps.
- ✦ The learners are given rapid feedback concerning the accuracy of their learning.
- ✦ The learners are able to learn at their own pace.
- ✦ Course objectives should be specified before the instruction begins and should be defined behaviourally e.g. Verbs like define, recall, draw, recite, list, name, write, recognize, classify, compare, select, predict, find, use, perform and so on should be encouraged. Verbs like know, understand, learn should be discouraged.
- ✦ Proceed from simple to complex.
- ✦ Extrinsic reinforcers are important as they can be utilized in the classroom e.g. Verbal praise, positive facial expressions, golf stars and so on.
- ✦ Avoid the use of punishment.

Under programmed learning the following things should be taken care of

- ✦ Keep the learner alert and busy.
- ✦ Make sure that the learner moves on only when he has understood a frame properly.
- ✦ Help the learner to come up with the right answer by hinting, prompting, suggesting and so on.
- ✦ Last but not the least; reinforce the learner for every correct response.

These are a number of variations possible in programmed learning e.g., some learners may skip information if it is familiar. This procedure usually involves giving learners a pre-test on a certain section of the programme, and if they perform adequately, they are instructed to advance to the next section.

Under personalized system of instruction, the following things should be taken care of

- ✦ Determine the material to be covered in the course.
- ✦ Divide the material into self-contained segments.
- ✦ Create methods of evaluating the degree to which the learner has mastered the material in a given segment.
- ✦ Allow the learners to move from segment to segment at their pace.

EXEMPLARY QUESTIONS
1. What measures will you keep in mind while applying Ausubel's learning theory to prepare instruction materials? Discuss with the help of a topic from your subject area.
2. Explain Bruner's theory and its implications with the help of-
   a) exemplars from your subject area
   b) experiences gained during school experience programme or instruction practice or internship.

3. Vygotsky emphasizes the role of social interaction in the cognitive development of learner. In this context what is the role of various aids provided by educational technology in the classroom. Support your answer with exemplar.
4. How should one develop instructional materials in Skinnerian framework?

UNIT – 3

COMMUNICATION IN EDUCATION

This unit deals with concept, component, process and factors influencing communication

'It is not about the technology; it's about sharing knowledge and information, communicating efficiently, building learning communities and creating a culture of professionalism in schools. These are the key responsibilities of all educational leaders.'

— Marion Ginapolis

Unit 3
Communication in Education

3.1 COMMUNICATION

Communication is a process in which we share our ideas, thoughts and emotions with others. The term communication is derived from a Latin word 'communis' which means 'to common' or 'to share mutually'. Thus communication refers to a common experience among people. Educationists have given various definitions for communication, e.g. according to Edgar Dale; communication is the sharing of ideas and feelings in a mood of mutuality.

One more view says: Communication is the sum total of directly or indirectly, consciously or unconsciously transmitted words, feelings, attitudes, gestures and tone. Even silence is also a form of communication. Simply defined, communication is the art of transmitting information, ideas and attitude from one person to another. It means a sharing of elements of behaviour or modes of life. Communication can take place between two persons or a group of persons, or between one person and a mass audience. Communication is also defined as the 'discriminatory response of an organism to a stimulus'. However, communication is not the response itself. Essentially it is the relationship established by the transmission of stimuli and evocation of responses. Effective communication is a two way process, including feedback.

People can communicate on many levels, for many reasons, with many people, in many ways. Ruesch and Bateson have prepared a hypothetical exemplar of the kinds of communication that a typical man, Mr A, might use in an average day: In the morning when Mr A enters his office he reads his incoming mail (written communication). In sorting his mail he encounters a number of pamphlets which are designed to describe the merits of various business machines (pictorial communication). Through the open window the faint noise of a radio is heard (spoken communication). When his secretary enters the room she gives him a cheerful 'good morning', which he acknowledges with a friendly nod of his head (gestural communication) while he continues with his conversation on the telephone (spoken communication). Later in the morning he dictates a number of letters to his secretary, and then he holds a committee meeting (group communication). In this meeting a number of fresh and new governmental regulations (mass communication) and their effect upon the policies of the firm are discussed.

After the committee adjourned, Mr A, engaged in thoughts concerning the unfinished business (communication with self), slowly crosses the street to his restaurant for lunch. On the way he sees his friend Mr B, who in a great hurry enters the same luncheon place (communication through action) and Mr A decides to sit by himself. While waiting, Mr A studies the menu (communication through printed words).

After lunch, he decides to buy a pair of gloves. He enters a store and with the tips of his fingers carefully examines the various qualities of leather (communication through touch). After concluding the purchase; he decides to take the afternoon off and take his son on visit to the zoo. On the way, John watches his father drive and asks why he always stops at a red light and not at a green light (communication by visual symbol). As they approach the zoo, an ambulance screams down the street and Mr A pulls over to the side of the road and stops (communication by sound).

After paying admission to the zoo (communication through action), they leisurely stroll over to see the animals. Later on in the afternoon Mr A yields to the pressure of his son, and they enter a movie house to see a cartoon (communication through pictures). After arriving home, Mr A dresses for attending a formal dinner and theatre performance (communication through the arts).

One of the perspectives adopted here is that communication is transactional- every element and every process influences every other element and process. Communication is an on-going, ever-changing process. It is never static, never at rest. Communication can only be fully understood as an event-in-motion.

We cannot 'not communicate'

Often we think of communication as being intentional, purposeful, and consciously motivated. In many instances, it is. But in other instances we are even though communicating, we might not think we are or might not even want to communicate, e.g. the learner sitting in the back of the room with an expressionless face, perhaps is staring at the front of the room, perhaps staring out of the window. Although the learner might say that he/she is not communicating with the facilitator or with the other learners, that learner is obviously communicating a great deal- perhaps disinterest, perhaps boredom, perhaps a concern for something else, perhaps a desire for the class to be over as soon as possible. In any event, the learner is communicating whether he/she wishes to or not. We cannot 'not communicate'.

Further, when we are in an interactive situation with this person, we must respond in some way. Even if we do not actively or overtly respond, that lack of response is itself a response and communicates. Like the learner's silence, our silence in response also communicates.

Nature

Communication is highly personal: Communication is influenced by large components of emotions, values and needs of individual who is communicating.

Communication is expectational. People perceive only what they expect to-depending upon their own needs, values, backgrounds, and the unexpected is ignored or misunderstood.

Communication makes demand: It is in terms of emotional selection, preferences or rejection on part of the receiver. It has been scientifically established that the words with pleasant association are retained easily and longer in a person's memory than otherwise.

Communication differs from information: Information presupposes communication as unless communication takes place, the information cannot be transferred.

Principles

Communication is a two-way process of giving and receiving information through any number of channels. Whether one is speaking informally to a colleague, addressing a conference or meeting, writing a newsletter, article or formal report, the following basic principles apply:

- ✈ Know the audience.
- ✈ Know the purpose.
- ✈ Know the topic.
- ✈ Anticipate objections.
- ✈ Present a rounded picture.
- ✈ Achieve credibility with the audience.
- ✈ Follow through on what one say.
- ✈ Communicate a little at a time.
- ✈ Present information in several ways.
- ✈ Develop a practical, useful way to get feedback.
- ✈ Use multiple communication techniques.

Communication is complex. When listening to or reading someone else's message, we often filter what's being said through a screen of our own opinions. One of the major barriers of communication is our own ideas and opinions.

Some suggestive readings
Communicology: An introduction to the study of communication by Joseph A. DeVito.
Educational technology by R. P. Pathak and Jagdish Chaudhary.
The process of communication by David K. Berlo.

3.2 COMMUNICATION IN INSTRUCTION-LEARNING
Communication plays an effective and essential role for running the show of any formal or informal instruction-learning process. Basically, instruction is communicating and in this sense good facilitators are always good communicators. It is equally true for the learners. The one who learns well is the one who participates well in the communication process. Good learners are always good receivers and responders. In this way, communication as a vehicle or tool for running the show of instruction-learning act must always be treated as a two-way process in which both the sources (facilitator) and the beneficiary (learner) interact for realization of the instruction- learning objectives. However for this proper interaction, facilitators and learners are required to acquire the art and technique of good communication.

Characteristics
Communication is dynamic as the process is constantly in a state of change. As the expectations, attitudes, feelings and emotions of the persons who are communicating change, the nature of their communication also changes.

Communication is continuous as it never stops, whether we are asleep or awake we are always processing ideas or thoughts. Our brain remains active.

Communication is irreversible as once we send a message we cannot take it back. Once we have made a slip of tongue, given a meaningful glance, or engaged in an emotional outburst, we cannot erase it. Our apologies or denials can make it light but cannot stamp out what was communicated.

Communication is interactive as we are constantly in contact with other people and with ourselves. Others react to our speech and actions, and we react to our own speech and actions, and then react to those reactions. Thus, cycle of action and reaction is the basis of communication.

Kinds of communication

Based on senses, there are mainly three kinds of communication, which are as follows:

a. Speaking-listening: In this kind of communication interaction is face to face, viz., conversation or listening to a lecture. In this case the listener shares the feelings and ideas of the source as in case of eye-to-eye contact. This kind of communication ranges from personal dialogue to distant broadcast.

b. Visualizing- observing: In this kind of communication the source and receiver are often physically separated but share the ideas and feelings as in viewing TV or films. Such communication also takes place effectively as in case of dramatization where gestures and postures add additional impact and support.

c. Writing-reading: In this kind of communication the sender and receiver never communicate directly. There is no conversation, no talk but one is able to analyse and appreciate the ideas and feelings of the other. For an instance: an author wrote a book and it is read by a reader.

Based on direction of flow of information, there are mainly two kinds of communication, which are as follows:

a. One-way communication: In this kind of communication sender is sending a message or information to the receiver but no feedback is sent by the receiver, e.g. some facilitators use lecture method in class room where the facilitator is giving information to the learners (receiver). Learners cannot send any feedback to the facilitator. Other exemplar is like watching TV, listening radio

b. Two ways communication: In this kind of communication sender sends a message or information to the receiver and receiver also sends his views/feedback to the sender. For an instance: in a classroom the facilitator is instruction and learners are asking questions from the facilitator. Other exemplar is news channels. In news channels, some programmes discuss major issues like corruption, poverty in their shows and also take the views of receiver by telephone calls.

Based on time, there are mainly two kinds of communication, which are as follows:

a. Synchronous : When sender & receiver are together talking to each other directly, it is called synchronous communication. At a time sender sends the message and receiver receives it and also gives feedback. For an instance: chatting live on TV shows or mobile

b. Asynchronous : When sender and receiver are not together. Sender sends message at a time but the receiver is not there and not responding. This is called asynchronous form of communication. Exemplar:-email, fax, voice mail, shows like daily soaps

Based on the level, there are mainly three kinds of communication, which are as follows

a. Intrapersonal communication: This involves communicating with oneself and comprises of activities such as thought process, personal decision making and focusing on self.

b. Interpersonal communication: It is the communication that takes place between two or more persons who establish a communicative relationship, e.g. two friends talking about an upcoming movie, or an event, or an interview situation between employee and employer.

c. Public communication: It is characterized by a speaker sending a message to an audience. It may be direct such as facilitator addressing a class or indirect such as message relayed over radio or television.

Basic functions

Education and instruction: This function of communication starts early in life, first at home, then in school and continues throughout life. Communication provides knowledge, expertise and skills for smooth functioning by the people in the society. It creates awareness and gives opportunity to people to actively participate in public life.

Information: Quality of our life would be poor without information. The more informed we are the more powerful we become. Communication provides information about our surroundings, information regarding wars, danger, crisis, famine, etc. is important for the safety and well-being of our life.

Entertainment: To break the routine life and divert our attention from the stressful life we lead today, entertainment is an essential part of everybody's life. Communication provides endless entertainment to people through films, television, radio, drama, music, literature, comedy, games, etc.

Discussion: Debates and discussions clarify different viewpoints on issues of interest to the people. Through communication we find out reasons for varying viewpoints and impart fresh and new ideas to others.

Persuasion: It helps in reaching for a decision on public policy so that it is helpful to govern the people, though it is possible that one can resort to persuasion for a bad motive. Thus, the receiver must be careful about the source of persuasion.

Cultural promotion: Communication provides an opportunity for the promotion and preservation of culture and traditions. It makes the people fulfil their creative urges.

Integration: It is through communication that a large number of people across countries come to know about each other's traditions and appreciate each other's ways of life. It develops integration, and tolerance towards each other.

The communication process

The process of communication can be

- ✛ Accidental (having no intent)
- ✛ Expressive (resulting from emotional state of the person)
- ✛ Rhetorical (resulting from the specific goal of the communicator)

3.3 COMPONENTS

Communication is process of transmitting and receiving messages (verbal and non-verbal).

Verbal communication: Verbal communication means when sender uses words to send and receive messages. We use words to share our messages, information, emotions, and directions. When we use verbal communication it is compulsory to know the language. It is compulsory for sender and receiver to know the same language when they communicate. For an instance: A man who knows only Telugu language cannot communicate to those who don't know the Telugu.

Non-verbal communication:It happens through touch, facial expressions, body language, body structure, silence. In this kind of communication, language is not important. Expressions, body language, body structure are given emphasis, e.g. maps, slides, charts, films stripes, written material given with visual communication.

Communication is a dialogue and not a monologue. So, a communication is said to be effective only if it brings the desired response from the receiver. Communication consists of six components or elements.

- → Context
- → Sender/encoder
- → Message
- → Medium
- → Receiver/decoder
- → Feedback

Context

Every message (oral or written), begins with context. Context is a very broad field that consists of different aspects. One aspect is country, culture and organization. Every organization, culture and country communicates information in their own way.

Another aspect of context is external stimulus. The sources of external stimulus include; meeting, letter, memo, telephone call, fax, note, email and even a casual conversation. This external stimulus motivates one to respond and this response may be oral or written.

Internal stimulus is another aspect of communication. Internal stimuli includes; the opinion, attitude, likes, dis-likes, emotions, experience, education and confidence. These all have multifaceted influence on the way one communicate the ideas.

A sender can communicate his ideas effectively by considering all aspects of context mentioned above.

Sender / Encoder

Encoder is the person who sends message. In oral communication the encoder is speaker, and in written communication writer is the encoder. An encoder uses combination of symbols, words, graphs and pictures understandable by the receiver, to best convey his message in order to achieve his desired response.

Message

Message is the information that is exchanged between sender and receiver. The first task is to decide what one want to communicate and what would be the content of the message; what are the main include. The central idea of the message must be clear. While writing the message, encoder should keep in mind all aspects of context and the receiver (how he would interpret the message). Messages can be intentional and unintentional.

Medium

Medium is the channel through which encoder would communicate his message. However, the message may be print, electronic, or sound. Medium may be a person as postman. The choice of medium totally depends on the nature of one message and contextual factors discussed above. Choice of medium is also influence by the relationship between the sender and receiver.

The oral medium, to convey the message, is effective when the message is urgent, personal or when immediate feedback is desired. While, when the message is ling, technical and needs to be documented, then written medium should be preferred that is formal in nature. These guidelines may change while communicating internationally or in complex situations.

Receiver/Decoder

The person to whom the message is being sent is called 'receiver'/ 'decoder'. Receiver may be a listener or a reader depending on the choice of medium by sender to transmit the message. Receiver is also influenced by the context, internal and external stimuli.

Receiver is the person who interprets the message, so higher the chances are of miscommunication as of receiver's perception, attitude and personality. There would be minor deviation in transmitting the exact idea only if the receiver is educated and have communication skills.

Feedback

Response or reaction of the receiver, to a message, is called 'feedback'. Feedback may be written or oral message, an action or simply, silence may also be a feedback to a message.

Feedback is the most important component of communication in business. Communication is said to be effective only when it receives some feedback. Feedback, actually, completes the loop of communication.

3.4 MODELS OF COMMUNICATION
a. Traditional model
According to the traditional model there are four aspects of the communication process

- ✈ Communicator [encoder]
- ✈ Message [words, pictures, signs, symbols]
- ✈ Channel [medium or means]
- ✈ Receiver [decoder]

An adept communicator knows what he wants to communicate as his message, understands the characteristics of the channels to be used as a media and the social and psychological background of person constituting audience or the receiver.

Anything which interferes with the transmission of message is called noise. It may be mechanical due to media disorder or semantic problem owing to meaning difficulty. The words are easily understood under particular context and not properly understood out of that context.

Each person has his own background, physical, social, psychological and emotional. He understands a message from his own background or past experiences. His physical and mental conditions like health, mood, and attitude and ego involvement influence his understanding or reception of the message. He helps the communicator by his reaction to the message which is called feedback. These bouncing effects or reactions occur along the communication process and are thus transmitted back to the communicator who modifies or revises his media and message according to the feedback effects.

b. **Shannon and weaver model of communication** [a mathematical model of communication or message centred model of communication, 1949]

Shannon was an American mathematician, electronic engineer and weaver was an American scientist both of them join together to write an article in 'bell system technical journal' called 'a mathematical theory of communication' and also called as 'Shannon-Weaver model of communication'.

This model is specially designed to develop the effective communication between sender and receiver. Also they find factors which affect the communication process called 'noise'. At first the model was developed to improve the technical communication. Later it's widely applied in the field of communication.

The model deals with various concepts like information source, transmitter, noise, channel, message, receiver, channel, information destination, encode and decode.

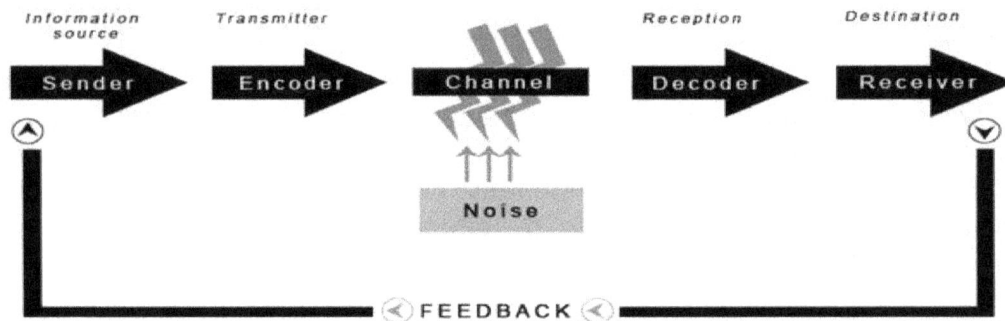

SHANNON-WEAVER'S MODEL OF COMMUNICATION

Sender: The originator of message or the information source selects desire message.

Encoder: The transmitter which converts the message into signals.

The sender's messages converted into signals like waves or binary data which is compactable to transmit the messages through cables or satellites. For an instance: in telephone the voice is converted into wave signals and it transmits through cables.

Decoder: The reception place of the signal which converts signals into message. A reverse process of encode.

The receiver converts those binary data or waves into message which is comfortable and understandable to receiver. Otherwise receiver can't receive the exact message and it would affect the effective communication between sender and receiver.

Receiver: the destination of the message from sender.

Based on the decoded message the receiver gives their feedback to sender. If the message is distracted by noise it would affect the communication flow between sender and receiver.

Noise: the messages are transferred from encoder to decoder through channel. During this process the messages may distracted or affected by physical noise like horn sounds, thunder and crowd noise or encoded signals may distract in the channel during the transmission process which affect the communication flow or the receiver may not receive the correct message.

The model clearly deals with external noises only which affect the messages or signals from external sources. For an instance: if any problem occurs in networks which directly affects the mobile phone communication or distract the messages.

Practical exemplar of Shannon-Weaver model of communication:

Thomson made call to his assistant, 'come here, I want to see one'. During his call, noise appeared (transmission error) and his assistant received, 'I want' only. Again assistant asked Thomson (feedback), 'what do one want Thomson?'

- ✈ Sender : Thomson
- ✈ Encoder : telephone (Thomson)
- ✈ Channel : cable
- ✈ Noise : distraction in voice
- ✈ Reception: telephone (assistant)
- ✈ Receiver: assistant.

Due to transmission error or noise, assistant could not be able to understand Thomson's messages.

Basic concepts of Shannon-Weaver model

The concepts of this model became staples in communication research:

(i) **Entropy** - The measure of uncertainty in a system. 'Uncertainty or entropy increases in exact proportion to the number of messages from which the source has to choose. In the simple matter of flipping a coin, entropy is low as the destination knows the probability of a coin's turning up either heads or tails. In the case of a two-headed coin, there can be neither any freedom of choice nor any reduction in uncertainty so long as the destination knows exactly what the outcome must be. In other words, the value of a specific bit of information depends on the probability that it would occur. In general, the informative value of an item in a message decreases in exact proportion to the likelihood of its occurrence.'
Entropy refers to messages which convey highly unpredictable information to the receiver.

(ii) **Redundancy** - The degree to which information is not unique in the system. Those items in a message that add no fresh and new information are redundant. Perfect redundancy is equal to total repetition and is found in pure form only in machines. In human beings, the very act of repetition changes, in some minute way, the meaning or the message and the larger social significance of the event. Zero redundancy creates sheer unpredictability, for there is no way of knowing what items in a sequence would come next. As a rule, no message can reach maximum efficiency unless it contains a balance between the unexpected and the predictable, between what the receiver must have underscored to acquire understanding and what can be deleted as extraneous.' Redundancy refers to the message which conveys highly predictable information to the receiver.

Redundancy and entropy with exemplars

Closely related to 'information' is the concept of redundancy. Redundancy is that which is predictable or conventional in a message. The opposite of redundancy is entropy. Redundancy is the result of high predictability and entropy of low predictability. So, a message with low predictability can be said to be entropic and of high information. Conversely, a message of high predictability is redundant and of low information. If i meet a friend in the street and say 'hi', I have a highly predictable and a highly redundant message. Redundancy is not merely useful in communication, but it is absolutely vital. Shannon and Weaver show that how redundancy helps the accuracy of decoding and provides a check which in turn enables us to identify errors. I can only identify a spelling mistake as of the redundancy in the language.

If I say, 'spring is...', then I am creating a context in which 'coming' is probable and thus more redundant than, say, a 'pane of glasses. It is of course possible that a poet or even an advertiser for fresh and new windows might write 'spring is a pane of glasses', but that would be a highly entropic use of language.

Redundancy also helps overcome the deficiencies of a noisy channel. We repeat ourselves on a bad telephone line when spelling words on radio or telephone. We say A for Apple, S for Sun, and so on. An advertiser whose message has to compete with many others for our attention would plan a simple repetitive predictable message. Increase in redundancy also helps overcome the problems of transmitting and entropic message. A message that is completely unexpected or which is opposite of which would be expected needs more information or increases redundancy.

(iii) **Noise** - The measure of information not related to the message. 'Any additional signal that interferes with the reception of information is noise. In electrical apparatus noise comes only from within the system, whereas in human activity it may occur quite apart from the act of transmission and reception. Interference may result, e.g. from background noise in the immediate surroundings, from noisy channels (a crackling microphone), from the organization and semantic aspects of the message (syntactical and semantic noise), or from psychological interference with encoding and decoding. Noise need not be considered a detriment unless it produces a significant interference with the reception of the message. Even when the disturbance is substantial, the strength of the signal or the rate of redundancy may be increased to restore efficiency.'

(iv) **Channel capacity** – It is the measure of the maximum amount of information a channel can carry. The battle against uncertainty depends upon the number of alternative possibilities the message eliminates. Suppose one want to know where a given Ghoda was located on a chessboard. If one start by asking if it is located in the first black square at the extreme left of the second row from the top and find the answer to be no, sixty-three possibilities still remain which is a high level of uncertainty. On the other hand, if one first asks whether it falls on any square at the top half of the board, the alternative would be reduced by half irrespective of the answer. By following the first strategy, it could be necessary to ask up to sixty-three questions; but by consistently halving the remaining possibilities, one would obtain the right answer in no more than six tries.

Criticism of Shannon-Weaver model

- One of the simplest model and its general applied in various communication theories.
- The model which attracts both academics of human communication and information theorist to leads their further research in communication.
- It is more effective in person-to-person communication than group or mass audience.
- The model based on 'sender and receiver'. Here sender plays the primary role and receiver plays the secondary role (receives the information or passive).
- Communication is not a one way process. If it's behaved like that, it would lose its strength, e.g. audience or receiver, who is listening a radio, reading the books or watching television is a one way communication due to absence of the feedback.
- Understanding noise helps to solve the various problems in communication.
- Chandler critiques this model by stating: It assumes communicators are isolated individuals, no allowance for differing interpretations and no allowance for situational contexts.

c. Lasswell's model of communication

Harold Dwight Lasswell, the American political scientist said that a convenient way to describe an act of communication is to answer the following questions

- Who
- Says what
- In which channel
- To whom
- With what effect?

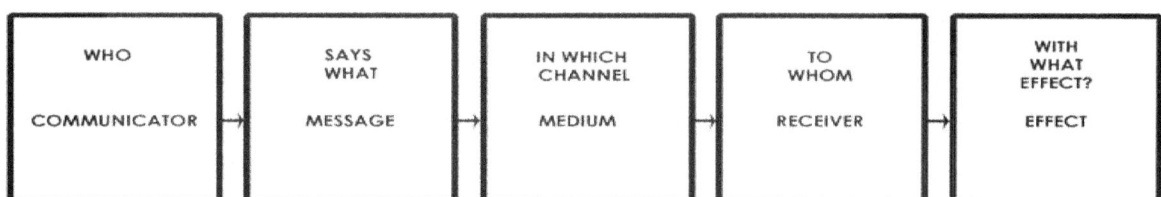

WHO COMMUNICATOR	SAYS WHAT MESSAGE	IN WHICH CHANNEL MEDIUM	TO WHOM RECEIVER	WITH WHAT EFFECT? EFFECT

This model is about process of communication. According to Lasswell there are three functions for communication:

- Surveillance of the environment
- Correlation of components of society
- Cultural transmission between generations

Lasswell model suggests the message flow in a multicultural society with multiple audiences. The flow of message is through various channels.

In this model, the communication component:
Who refers the research area called 'control analysis',
Says what refers to 'content analysis',

In which channel refers to 'media analysis',
To who refers to 'audience analysis',
With what effect refers to 'effect analysis'.

An exemplar
CNN News – a water leak from Japan's tsunami-crippled nuclear power station resulted in about 100 times the permitted level of radioactive material flowing into the sea, operator Tokyo electric power co said on Saturday.

Who – TEPC operator
What – radioactive material flowing into sea
Channel – CNN news (television medium)
Whom – public
Effect – alert the people of japan from the radiation.

Advantage of Lasswell model

+ Easy and simple
+ Suits for almost all kinds of communication
+ Supports the concept of effect

Disadvantage of Lasswell model

+ Feedback not mentioned
+ Noise not mentioned
+ Linear model

Communication process in instruction
Translating Lass well's model of communication into education situations:
Who: facilitator, textbook writer, TV, radio broadcaster etc.
Says what: content of the lesson, textbook, etc.
By what channel: face-to-face, audio- visual aids like power-point, projector, pictures, films, radio TV, etc.
To whom: learners/learners
With what effect: means to get reaction or feedback like doubts and questions the learners ask.

d. Berlo's SMCR model of communication
The Berlo's model follows the SMCR model. This model is not specific to any particular communication.

Berlos's SMCR Model of communication

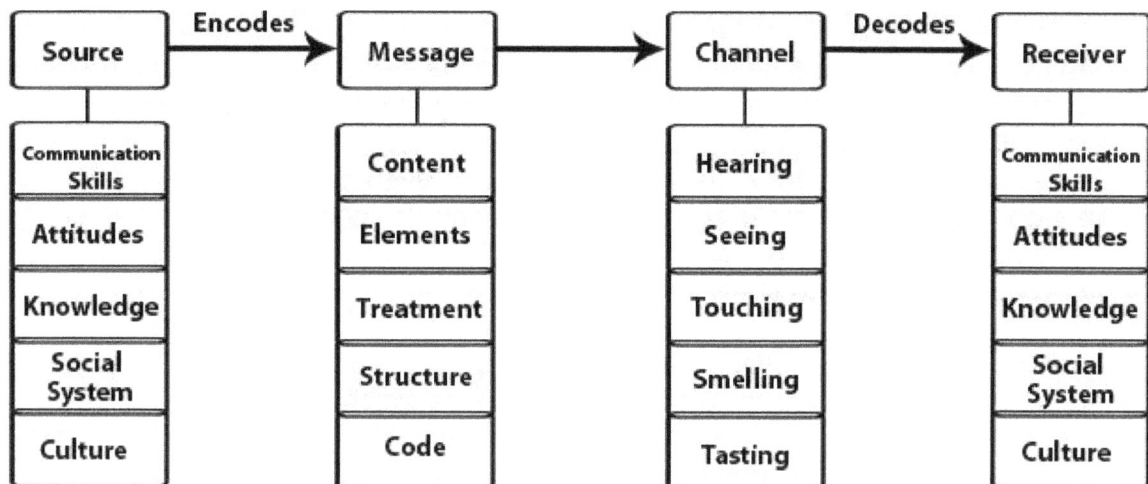

Source		Message		Channel		Receiver
	Encodes →		→		Decodes →	
Communication Skills		Content		Hearing		Communication Skills
Attitudes		Elements		Seeing		Attitudes
Knowledge		Treatment		Touching		Knowledge
Social System		Structure		Smelling		Social System
Culture		Code		Tasting		Culture

Berlo's model lives a number of factors under each of the elements:

S (Source): The source is where the message originates.
Communication skills – it is the individual's skill to communicate (ability to read, write, speak, listen etc.)
Attitudes – the attitude towards the audience, subject and towards one self, e.g. for the learner the attitude is to learn more and for facilitators wants to teach.
Knowledge- the knowledge about the subject one is going to communicate e.g. whatever the facilitator communicates in the class about the subject so having knowledge in what one is communicating. it is not talking about the general knowledge it is all about the knowledge of the subject, so it is the familiarity of what one are communicating.
Social system – the social system includes the various aspects in society like values, beliefs, culture, religion and general understanding of society. It is where the communication takes place. For an instance, class room differs from country to country like behaviours, how we communicate etc. We can communicate only to the extent that the social system allows, when we communicate take social system into account.
Culture: culture of the particular society also comes under social system.

All to this model, only if one has the above in the proper or adequate proportion, we can communicate.

Encoder: The sender of the message (message originates) is referred as encoder, so the source is encoding the message here.

M (Message): Content – the beginning to the end of a message comprises its content e.g. from beginning to end whatever the class facilitator speaks in the class is the content of the message.
Elements – it includes various things like language, gestures, body language etc., so these are all the elements of the particular message. Content is accompanied by some elements.

Treatment – it refers to the packing of the message. The way in which the message is conveyed or the way in which the message is passed on or deliver it. When it is too much treatment also the communication would not happen properly.

Structure- the structure of the message, how it is arranged, the way one structure the message into various parts.   Message is the same but if the structure is not properly arranged then the message would not get to the receiver.

Code- the code of the message means how it is sent in what form it could be e.g. Language, body language, gestures, music and even culture is a code. Through this one get/give the message or through which the communication takes place or being reached.   Only when the code is proper, the message would be clear, improper use may lead to misinterpretation.

C (Channel): It is nothing but the five senses. Through this only we do communication. The following are the five senses which we use:

- ✦ Hearing
- ✦ Seeing
- ✦ Touching
- ✦ Smelling
- ✦ Tasting

Whatever communication we do it is there either of these channels.

Hearing: the use of ears to get the message e.g. Oral messages, interpersonal etc.

Seeing: visual channels e.g. TV can be seen and the message is delivered.

Touching: the sense of touch can be used as a channel to communicate e.g. we touch and buy food, hugging etc.

Smelling: smell also can be a channel to communicate e.g. Perfumes, food, charred smell communicate something is burning, we can find out about which food is being cooked etc.

Tasting: the tongue also can be used to decipher e.g. Food can be tasted and communication can happen.

  Despite not mentioning a medium we need to assume that as communication is taking place channels can be any of the 5 senses or combinations.

R (Receiver): Decoder: who receives the message and decodes it is referred to as decoder. The receiver needs to have all the things like the source, communication skills, attitudes, knowledge, social system, culture.

        This model believes that for an effective communication to take place the source and the receiver needs to be in the same level, only if the source and receiver are on the same level communication would happen or take place properly. So source and receiver should be similar, e.g. Communication skills on source side are good then the receiver should equally have good listening skills.

        We cannot say the entire message passed doesn't reach the receiver as it is as the receiver may not good in listening, so only for the effective communication the source and the receiver to be in the same level.

  Self-image differs from person to person, for communicating the person should consider the receiver. Keep the receiver in mind, speak accordingly and give them what they need.

Criticism of Berlo's SMCR model of communication

- No feedback / don't know about the effect.
- Does not mention barriers to communication
- No room for noise
- Complex model
- It is a linear model of communication
- Needs people to be on same level for communication to occur but not true in real life
- Main drawback of the model is that the model omits the usage of sixth sense as a channel which is actually a gift to the human beings (thinking, understanding, analysing etc.).

3.4 COMMUNICATION SKILLS

We all use language to communicate, to express ourselves, to get our ideas across, and to connect with the person and to whom we are speaking. Chip Rose expressed that when a relationship is working, the act of communication seems to flow relatively effortlessly. When a relationship is deteriorating, the act of communication can be as frustrating as climbing a hill of sand.

Listening

The key to receiving messages effectively is listening. Listening is a combination of hearing what another person says and psychological involvement with the person who is talking. Listening requires more than hearing words. It requires a desire to understand another human being, an attitude of respect and acceptance, and a willingness to open one's mind to try and see things from another's point of view.

Listening requires a high level of concentration and energy. It demands that we set aside our own thoughts and agendas, put ourselves in another's shoes and try to see the world through that person's eyes. True listening requires that we suspend judgment, evaluation, and approval in an attempt to understand another is frame of reference, emotions, and attitudes. Listening to understand is, indeed, a difficult task.

Often, people worry that if they listen attentively and patiently to a person who is saying something they disagree with, they are inadvertently sending a message of agreement. When we listen effectively we gain information that is valuable to understanding the problem as the other person sees it. We gain a greater understanding of the other person's perception. After all, the truth is subjective and a matter of perception. When we have a deeper understanding of another's perception, whether we agree with it or not, we hold the key to understanding that person's motivation, attitude, and behaviour. We have a deeper understanding of the problem and the potential paths for reaching agreement.

Listening

- requires concentration and energy.
- involves a psychological connection with the speaker.
- includes a desire and willingness to try and see things from another's perspective.

✈ requires that we suspend judgment and evaluation.

John Powell says that listening in a dialogue is more focussed to meaning than to words. In formal listening, we reach behind the words; see through them, to find the person, who is being revealed. Listening is a sort of search to find the treasure of the true person as revealed verbally and nonverbally. There is the semantic problem, also. The words bear a different connotation for listener than they do for speaker. Consequently, one can never tell what speaker said, but only what listener heard. I would have to rephrase what speaker have said, and check it out with speaker to make sure that what left his/her mind and heart arrived in listener's mind and heart intact and without distortion.

Learning to be an effective listener is a difficult task for many people. However, the specific skills of effective listening behaviour can be learned. It is our ultimate goal to integrate these skills into a sensitive and unified way of listening.

Listening skills
Non-verbal

Giving full physical attention to the speaker; being aware of the speaker's nonverbal messages;
Verbal

Paying attention to the words and feelings that are being expressed; using reflective listening tools such as paraphrasing, reflecting, summarizing, and questioning to increase understanding of the message and help the speaker tell his story.

Giving full physical attention to the speaker attending is the art and skill of giving full, physical attention to another person. In his book, people skills, Robert Bolton refers to it as 'listening with the whole body'. Effective attending is a careful balance of alertness and relaxation that includes appropriate body movement, eye contact, and posture of involvement. Fully attending says to the speaker, 'what one is saying is very important. I am totally present and intent on understanding one'. We create a posture of involvement by: leaning gently towards the speaker; facing the other person squarely; maintaining an open posture with arms and legs uncrossed; maintaining an appropriate distance between us and the speaker; moving our bodies in response to the speaker, i.e. appropriate head nodding, facial expressions.

As psychiatrist Ernst, writes in his book, 'Who's listening?' that to listen is to move. To listen is to be moved by the talker - physically and psychologically. The non-moving, unblinking person can reliably be estimated to be a non-listener. When other visible moving has ceased and the eye blink rate has fallen to less than once in six seconds, listening, for practical purposes, has stopped. Being aware of the speaker's nonverbal messages, when we pay attention to a speaker's body language, we gain insight into how that person is feeling as well as the intensity of the feeling. Through careful attention to body language and para-verbal messages, we are able to develop hunches about what the speaker (or listener) is communicating. We can then, through our reflective listening skills, check the accuracy of those hunches by expressing in our own words, our impression of what is being communicated. Paying attention to the words and feelings in order to understand the total meaning of a message, we must be able to gain understanding about both the feeling and the content of the message. We are often more comfortable in dealing with the content rather than the feelings (i.e., the relationship), particularly when the feelings are intense. Our tendency is to try and ignore the emotional aspect of the message/conflict and move directly to the substance of the issues.

7 Cs of communication

(1). Clear

To be clear, try to minimize the number of ideas in each sentence, one should make sure that it's easy for the reader to understand the meaning. People shouldn't have to 'read between the lines' and make assumptions on their own to understand what speaker is trying to say.

(2). Concise

Speaker should be concise in communication, stick to the point and keep it brief as audience doesn't want to read six sentences when speaker could communicate the message in three.

(3). Concrete

When the message is concrete, then audience has a clear picture of what speaker is telling to them. There are details; facts and focus.

(4). Correct

When the communication is correct, it fits audience. Correct communication is also error-free communication.

(5). Coherent

When the communication is coherent, it's logical. All points are connected and relevant to the main topic and the tone and flow of the text is consistent.

(6). Complete

In a complete message, the audience have everything they need to be informed and, if applicable, they take action.

(7). Courteous

Courteous communication is friendly, open, and honest. There are no hidden insults or passive-aggressive tones. Speaker should keep reader's viewpoint in mind, and should be empathetic to their needs.

3.5 FACTORS AFFECTING COMMUNICATION PROCESS

There is more to communicating effectively than simply saying the right words at the right time. It's difficult to adequately convey the thoughts or feelings to another person efficiently and successfully. Many things affect effective communication, no matter what the situation, from work-related memos and text messages to presentations and casual conversation. Knowing the factors that can prohibit effective communication lets one achieve the meaning simply and articulately. Effective communication is about being understood. All that happens in a classroom is created and sustained through communication processes. e.g., Lesson plans, instruction methods, discipline strategies, explanations and the critique of learners work, all occur through communication only. Communication and its effectiveness depend very much on the difference in orientation and socio-cultural backgrounds of the components of communication process.

General factors

↬ Unclear or incomplete messages
↬ Jargon or words with multiple interpretation
↬ Disabilities and other impediments

- Age, gender or sexual orientation
- Relative status or respect for the sender
- Lack of empathy or concern
- Stereotyping or prejudice
- Conditions or distance
- Lack of time or other pressing priorities
- Poor spelling inaccurate sentence structure
- Personality traits and levels of EQ
- Ability of individual to send & receive messages
- Perceptions of sender & receiver
- Personal space/proxemics
- Territoriality
- Roles and relationships
- Time environment
- Attitudes
- Emotions and self-esteem

Barriers to effective communication

An effective communication barrier is one of the problems faced by many facilitators in the school. Many social psychologists opine that there is 50% to 70% loss of meaning while conveying the messages from a sender to a receiver. They estimate there are four basic places where communication could be interpreted wrongly.

A few barriers of effective communication in a classroom are given below.

- Language deficits
- Sensory deficits
- Cognitive impairments
- Structural/anatomical deficits
- Paralysis
- Anxiety
- Lack of Feedback
- Lack of non-verbal communication

A good facilitator is genuinely interested in learners' thoughts, feelings and opinions. Feedback is one way that a facilitator can tell how learners are absorbing and integrating the materials and lessons. This feedback calls upon the relationship facilitator have developed with the learner. If there are semantic barriers improper feedback may be given by learners to facilitator.

If a facilitator lacks non-verbal communication skill it may lead to ineffective communication. Good verbal skills combined with effective body language create interest, long-lasting impression on the minds of learners and off-course their involvement in the discussion. Also the voice modulation while instruction is essential.

Few exemplars of distortions during communication in classroom are

- Noise from the playground
- Learners talking in class

- Other facilitators/ learners coming in class to make some important announcements
- No expression on learner's face when a concept is explained to them. So facilitator does not get a feedback from learners
- When facilitator put up question in class learners do not answer. Interaction does not take place
- In extreme climatic situations learners and facilitators are unable to concentrate
- Language becomes barrier in classroom when learners from diverse background are present

Physical / External factors / environmental barriers

The environment can be a barrier to effective communication. It is important to learn how to improve the listening environment.
The most common external / environmental factors that affect communication are
Visual factors

- Lighting : poor lighting conditions can cause light should be on the talker's face
- Distractions : interfering objects 'visual noise'
- Talker's face: face/mouth should not be covered head movements should be well-lit no eating, chewing, smoking.
- Viewing angle : best to be seated in front of the talker
- Vision : use of corrective lenses if needed
- Auditory factors
- Noise: air conditioners, fans, TV, radio, other talkers, etc.
- Echo: too many hard surfaces
- Noise: Noise acts a distraction in the communication channel.
- Time: If proper time is not given, the communicator may not communicate effectively.
- Distance: The two communicators communicating should be audible to each other so distance should be appropriate.
- Defects in the medium: Medium can cause distraction during communication. Like distraction in telephone line.

Psychological barriers

- Emotions: same message can have different impact if the communicator is speaking in an angry or happy tone.
- Lack of trust: if communicator knows that receiver has negative attitude towards him, he may not be able to communicate and deliver the message effectively.
- Laziness: sometimes the communicator thinks that receiver knows about the message already and does not say or explain the message clearly again. This can cause misunderstanding. Like: if facilitator wants to teach media's role in democracy and she leaves explaining democracy thinking that it has already been done by learners in lower classes. That is laziness.
- Selective perception: receiver listens to only the messages which are of his/her concern and interest. This is a major barrier to communication.

Semantic barriers

→ Lack of common language: language should be understandable to both facilitator and learner. Inability to converse in a language that is known by both the facilitator and learner is the greatest barrier to effective communication. Being such a diversified class it becomes difficult for facilitator to decide which language to use for communication, e.g. even in the English medium schools, learners find it difficult to understand the English language and facilitator is expected to speak in bilingual medium. Thus, language constraint is a major distortion in effective communication.

→ Poor vocabulary: one should not fumble and stammer while communicating. To avoid this facilitator as well as learner should have a good vocabulary.

→ Poor knowledge of grammar and punctuation: grammar can be improved only when regular reading and writing practice is done. Poor grammar can change the meaning of a message. When a person uses inappropriate words while conversing or writing, it could lead to misunderstanding between the facilitator and a learner. It is not only the difference in language that causes a barrier to effective communication. People speaking the same language can sometimes find it difficult to comprehend what is being said.

→ Emotions- emotions could be a barrier to communication if a learner/ facilitator are engrossed in them for some reason. In such cases, one tends to have trouble listening to others or understanding the message conveyed to one. A few of the emotional interferences include hostility, anger, resentfulness and fear. People, who suffer from ailments such as anxiety and depression, tend to wrongly construct what is being said. Also, as they are battling something in their head, they may or may not be able to pay full attention to the speaker, which may make them appear disinterested and spaced-out. In the class we find cases where most of the learners seem to be only physically present in the class but mentally engrossed in some other work.

→ Lack of subject knowledge - if a facilitator who is instruction lacks subject knowledge then she may not be able to convey her message clearly. The learners could misunderstand her message and this could lead to a barrier to effective communication. This is visible in cases where facilitator may try to cover-up their ignorance with some unverified facts. In such cases facilitator should be prepared with good subject knowledge. Otherwise it may be misleading for learners.

→ Overdose of information - when too much of information is conveyed in a short span of time, there is possibility that the learners would not be able to comprehend the information fully. It creates confusion and ambiguity. Facilitators should design lesson plan keeping in mind the time allotted to them for the class. The ability of a facilitator to use silence is usually effective. Silence here means giving few more seconds to learners to respond to a query. Silence can help the learners as:

a) Length of learners' correctness of their response increase

b) The number of 'I don't know' decreases. The doubts can be cleared there and then.

c) More number of answers etc.
d) Better scoring by the learners.

Personal / Individual barriers

- → Fatigue, illness, stress: make concentration difficult
- → Inadequate ventilation : makes concentration difficult
- → Attitude : can affect success or failure
- → Preparation : can affect success or failure
- → Situation : some situations are easier than others
- → Personal attitude: if the facilitator/learner has lack of confidence to convey her message then communication cannot be effective. Like if facilitator has explained a concept and child does not ask doubts pertaining to the explained concepts due to lack of confidence then the feedback reaching the facilitator is not appropriate.
- → Message overload: when many messages are to be conveyed by the sender he may not be able to communicate messages effectively. Like a class facilitator has so many announcements to make in the class every day. She may forget some announcements and can even get confused. In such a case calmness and jotting down of points may help her to remember the points.
- → Improper listening by learners: one should listen and not hear. Hearing is a natural, physical and passive process, whereas listening is a physical mental and learned process. It requires activeness.
- → Inattentiveness: if a learner is not attentive in class he may not listen to what facilitator is communicating.
- → Inference: sometimes the receiver has some drawn past perceptions about the speaker, e.g. If a corrupt politician is reading out a manifesto related to social welfare, people may not listen to him.

Effective communication depends on:

- → Readiness
- → Appropriate use of language
- → Intonation
- → Precision
- → Lucidity

Verbal communication should have the following characteristics

- → Consciousness
- → Simplicity
- → Clarity
- → Relevance and timing
- → Adaptability
- → Credibility

Factors influencing interpersonal communication

Interpersonal communication is a process of sharing ideas and feelings between individuals. Interpersonal communication skills can be improved through appropriate knowledge, practice, feedback and reflection. Understanding interpersonal communication is essential in maintaining healthy relationships. It is important in our family life, too, as it affects nearly every aspect of our existence.

a. Cultural influence

Culture refers to the customs, language, arts, common dietary habits and attire of a particular region. It also includes the learned values, beliefs and behaviours common to a group of individuals. Culture and communication are inseparable. This means that culture can be a strong barrier to interpersonal communication between people of different cultures. Individuals from different cultural backgrounds often carry an attitude that their own culture is superior to that of others. This attitude hampers interpersonal communication between two individuals or groups from different cultural backgrounds. Individuals who are ethnocentric in nature often are under the impression that anyone who does not belong to their group is either strange or inferior. This perception also prevents healthy social and political communication between two groups.

b. Power

Power is the ability to influence others and have strong self-control under complex circumstances. All interpersonal communication or interactions reflect some form of power, which may be obvious or hidden. Obvious power refers to people who occupy a higher position in business or government and have to communicate with their employees or subjects. People in power positions may exert their power on individuals who are not equally competent, and this inequality could act as a barrier to effective communication.

c. Noise

Noise is one of the external factors that act as barriers to effective communication. Noise interferes with or disrupts communication by causing a divergence between the receiver and the communicator. Some exemplars of physical noise include running motors, horns, screeching brakes and children crying. In a classroom setting, if children create noise or murmur among themselves, this becomes a hindrance to communication, preventing the facilitator's message from being received the way she intended.

d. Technology

Electronic mail, most commonly referred to as email, is becoming the most popular medium for interpersonal communication. When exchanging emails, if a person makes grammatical errors or spelling mistakes, it can create a wrong impression on the receiver. People share messages or communicate via electronic media without visual or oral information. Lacking face-to-face contact with its sensory input, individuals start imagining other people based on their electronic communication style and pattern. This can become a technological hindrance that can hamper effective interpersonal communication.

Factors influencing group communication

Effective group communication is vital to a productive work environment. In fact, poor group communication is a primary reason for a failed career, according to the University of Northern Iowa. Effective group communication relies on understanding interpersonal communication basics and how they can improve or hinder messages. Interpersonal communication factors that influence effective communication include ability to listen, nonverbal communication, and culture and conflict resolution.

a. Ability to listen

Effective communication requires sharing ideas. This means not only sharing the ideas, but also listening to ideas from others. Using listening strategies, such as active and reflective listening, helps one to become a good listener. Active listening involves using nonverbal communication, such as eye contact and posture, to help one listen. Reflective listening requires rephrasing what the other person said to ensure that one understood the other person's idea correctly. For exemplar, if someone says 'scheduling more cashiers should help us keep lines down during the holiday season,' one could respond, 'yes, more cashiers should prevent long lines.'

b. Nonverbal communication

Group communication works best when members trust each other. Nonverbal communication, such as facial expressions and body language, can establish trust or raise suspicion. It builds trust when the nonverbal messages sent complement the verbal ones. On the other hand, nonverbal communication that contradicts verbal communication indicates trust issues, such as a person who says he just made a stressful decision but seems relaxed.

c. Culture

Biases and prejudices created by culture cause barriers to effective group communication. For instance, a man from a culture that views women as inferior to men might have trouble working as equals with women. Overcoming such barriers involves learning about different cultures and shattering stereotypes. Starting conversations about cultural diversity can increase knowledge and deflate stereotypes, according to Ohio State University. For the exemplar above, this would entail demonstrating to the man his female co-workers are equally capable and deserve respect.

d. Conflict resolution

With group-communication comes conflict. Conflict would more likely facilitate group communication if one confronts problems, in a respectful manner, as soon as possible. 'I' statements are one way to ensure one discuss issues respectfully without causing others to become defensive. 'I' statements put the focus on one rather than the other person, e.g. 'i feel we need to go into further detail about our marketing plan' would be better than 'one didn't give enough attention to our marketing plan.'

3.6 MAKING COMMUNICATION EFFECTIVE IN CLASSROOM

Instruction is generally considered 50% knowledge and 50% communication skills. One of the most neglected aspects of facilitator training is thorough preparation in the diverse communication skills that are needed by good facilitators in today's school.

Communication skills: communication skills are the most important when we talk about a good facilitator. The tone, volume, rhythm and emotions of the facilitator play a vital role while dealing with learners.

Positive motivation: good motivation usually produces learning outcomes. Some learners do not know why they should study a particular subject. We can show applications of that subject in the areas in which learners are interested. Thus they get motivated and take interest while studying that subject.

Empathy: facilitators' messages must convey empathy i.e. the ability to communicate care and concern along with an understanding of the child's problem that is, the ability to place oneself in a position to view the problem from the learner's perspective.

Effective body language: body language is the quiet, secret and a powerful tool to maintain healthy interpersonal skills. Good verbal skills combined with effective body language create interest, long-lasting impression on the minds of learners and off-course their involvement in the discussion.

Feedback: a good facilitator is genuinely interested in learners' thoughts, feelings and opinions. Feedback is one way that a facilitator can tell how one are absorbing and integrating the materials and lessons. This feedback calls upon the relationship one has developed with the learner.

Silence: the ability of a facilitator to use silence is usually effective. Silence here means giving few more seconds to learners to respond to a query.

Silence can help the learners as: Length of learners' correctness of their response increase, the number of 'i don't know' decreases. The doubts can be cleared then and there. More number of answers etc. betters the scoring by the learners.

Good sense of humour: a facilitator needs to have a keen sense of humour in order to keep learners learning & motivate. A facilitator who can't take a joke or give one, who can't lighten up, who is too serious would not survive.

Be reflective: we all filter and distort what we hear. This concept helps a facilitator to 'pay attention' and often helps the speaker stop and think about what is being said. It's also helpful sometimes to ask the listeners to paraphrase what they think one have said. This concept helps the facilitator to keep the attention of the learner and keep them participating in discussion.

Ask open-ended questions: make it a goal to find out what the learners think, not just what they know. Ask for information using open-ended questions that begin with how, what, when, where, and why. This strategy allows facilitators to help clarify a given question for both the child and itself.

Understand and then be understood: most learners don't like being told what to do. They often want a chance to have a say in what goes on in the classroom and a chance to prove it would work. In solving classroom problems, it is better to listen than to direct. Groups can be formed to figure out solutions to problems and facilitator can empower them to carry out the solutions. Learners who identify what should be done take on greater and greater responsibility for getting it done. Thus a facilitator seeks to understand the problem from the point of view of the problem solvers rather than force his own perspective on a solution to be understood. This helps to improve interpersonal skills among learners as well as between facilitator and learners.

Self-disclosure: often sharing a relevant story of the own experiences in similar situations can prove helpful in opening meaningful dialogue.

Use of technical skills: the latest method which is now a days used to improve interpersonal skills with learners is by using technical skills too i.e. Ability to work with latest instruction aids like computers, multimedia or other technical equipment. The uses of such technical skills bind the interest of learners in their lesson and also keep both the facilitator as well as learners up to date.

SMS, e-mail, scrap, chat, web spaces etc. can be used effectively for:

- Replying to the questions of the learners.
- Solving their doubts, queries etc.
- Giving some task for next class in advance.
- Having group discussions.

➔ Uploading lesson presentations on web spaces.
➔ Managing e- groups like wikispaces.

EXEMPLARY QUESTIONS
1. Explain Shannon-Weaver model of communication.
2. What are the various kinds of distortions possible during communication? Describe with the help of the experiences in the classroom.
3. How can facilitators make communication effective in classroom?

UNIT - 4

LEARNING AIDS AND MEDIA IN EDUCATIONAL TECHNOLOGY

This unit deals with various ways of classification of media with examples, use of computer in developing teaching-learning material and criteria for selection of appropriate media

'Excitement in education and student productivity, the ability to get a result that you want from students, go together and cannot be separated.'

— Major Owens

Unit 4
Learning Aids and Media in Educational Technology

4.1 EDGAR DALE'S CONE OF EXPERIENCE
Edgar Dale (April 27, 1900 – March 8, 1985)

According to Dale, the modern approach to learning places the facilitator in a fresh and new role-of a manager, an organizer, a motivator, and an evaluator of experiences. The facilitator makes choices from a rich variety of media and takes a larger role in the development of instructional materials. Confucius expressed that I see and I forget, I hear and I remember, I do and I understand. The Cone of experience is a visual aid meant to summarize Dale's classification system for the varied kinds of mediated learning experiences. It explains the interrelationships between various kinds of audio-visuals materials, as well as their individual positions in the learning process.

The original labels of Dale's ten categories in the cone of experience were
(1)   Direct purposeful experiences
(2)   Contrived experiences
(3)   Dramatic participation
(4)   Demonstrations
(5)   Field trips
(6)   Exhibits
(7)   Motion pictures
(8)   Radio, recordings, still pictures
(9)   Visual symbols and
(10)   Verbal symbols

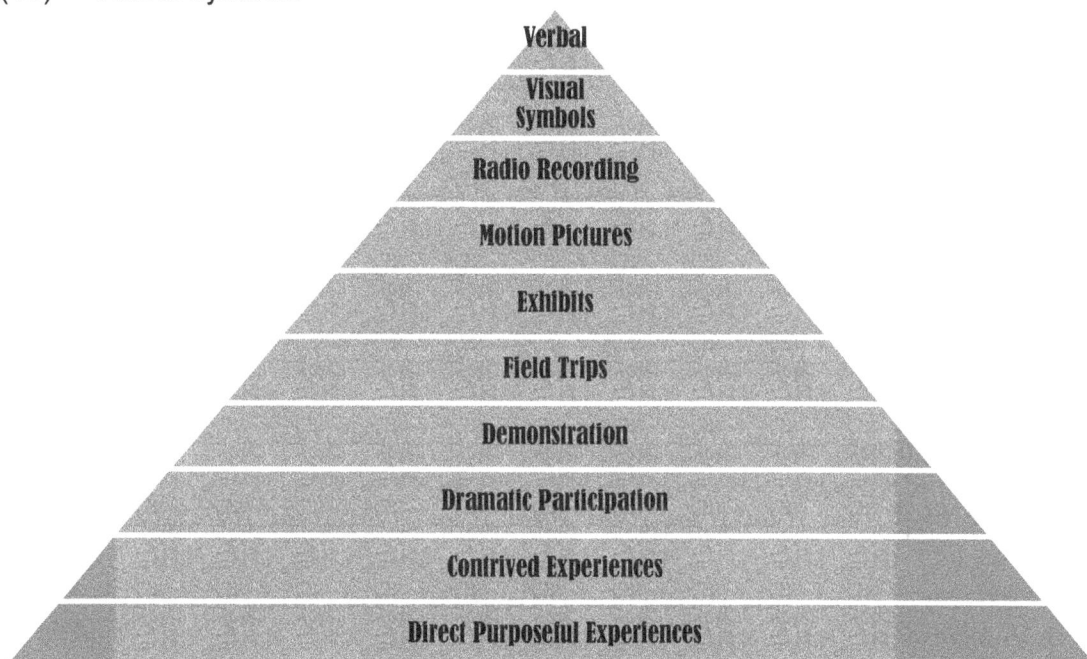

Dale's Cone of Experience

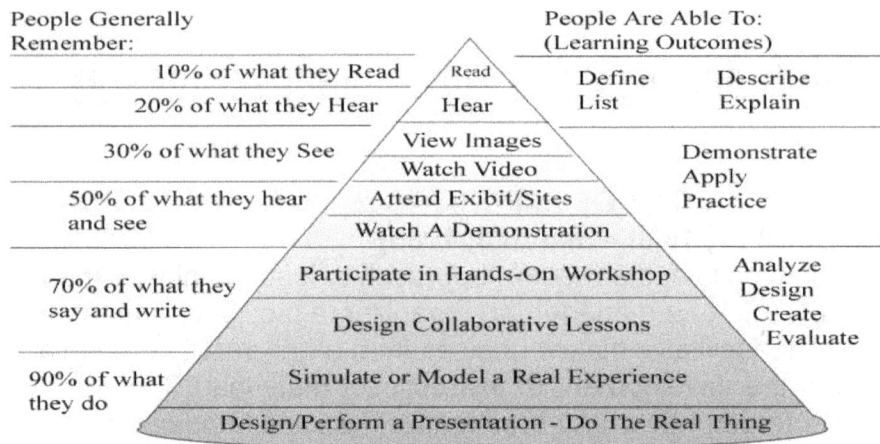

People Generally Remember:		People Are Able To: (Learning Outcomes)	
10% of what they Read	Read	Define	Describe
20% of what they Hear	Hear	List	Explain
30% of what they See	View Images / Watch Video	Demonstrate	
50% of what they hear and see	Attend Exibit/Sites / Watch A Demonstration	Apply Practice	
70% of what they say and write	Participate in Hands-On Workshop / Design Collaborative Lessons	Analyze Design Create Evaluate	
90% of what they do	Simulate or Model a Real Experience / Design/Perform a Presentation - Do The Real Thing		

Implications of Dale's Cone of Experience

The bottom level of the cone, 'direct purposeful experiences,' represents reality or the closest things to real, everyday life. If one travels upward from the base, one moves in order of decreasing directness/real life. Thus contrived experience is one step more direct than dramatized experience and so on. Similarly when one move downwards from the pinnacle of the cone, one move in the order of increasing directness: 'verbal symbols are more abstract than visual symbols; and visual symbols are more abstract than one-sense aids such as recordings, radio, and still pictures.

Cone as a flexible division a motion picture can be a silent or can combine sight and sound. One can view dramatization as a spectator or one may participate in it as an actor. Learners may merely watch a demonstration or they may watch it and then take part in it. The cone is a device, then, is a visual metaphor of learning experiences, in which the various kinds of audio-visual materials are arranged in the order of increasing abstractness as one proceeds from direct experiences.

Increasing abstractness versus increasing difficulty

Exhibits are nearer to pinnacle of the cone, not as they are more difficult than field trips, but, only, as they provide more abstract experience. Abstractness is not necessarily difficult. All words, whether used by children or by mature adults, are nothing, but a situation where we, as a facilitator, should understand that these are reading materials, without any pictures or other visuals, or a lecture, that is nothing, but words. Cone's utility in selecting instructional resources and activities is as practical today as was, when Dale created it.

Short explanation of various categories
  → Direct purposeful experiences- These are first hand experiences which serve as the foundation of our learning. These are derived from meaningful information and ideas through seeing, hearing, touching, tasting and smelling. Hence, it is considered as learning by doing.
  → Contrived experiences- These make use of representative models or mock ups of reality for practical reasons and make real-life experiences that are accessible to learner's perceptions and understanding.
  → Dramatized experiences- By dramatization, learners can participate in a constructed experience.

- Demonstrations – These are visualized explanation of an important fact, idea or process by the use of photographs, drawings, films, displays or guided motion. It is showing, how things are done.
- Study trips- These are excursions and visits conducted to observe event/events that are unavailable within the classroom.
- Exhibits – These are displays to be seen by spectators. They consist of working models arranged meaningfully or photographs with models, charts and posters. It is sometimes called 'for the eyes only'.
- Television and motion pictures- this are reconstruction of happenings of the past in an effective manner so that we are made to feel as if we were there. The value of the messages communicated by the films lie in the feeling of realism, emphasis on person's personality, their organized presentations and their ability to select, dramatize, highlight and clarify the situations.
- Still pictures, recordings and radio- these are visual and auditory devices used by an individual or a group. Still pictures lack the sound and motion of a sound film. The radio broadcast of an actual event may be like a televised broadcast minus its visual dimensions
- Visual symbols- they are no longer realistic reproduction of physical things for they are highly abstract representations. Exemplars are charts, graphs, maps and diagrams.
- Verbal symbols – they are not like the objects or ideas for which they stand. They usually do not contain visual clues to their meaning. Written words fall under this category. It may be a word for a concrete object (book), an idea (freedom of speech), scientific principle or a formula.

Pitfalls, facilitators should avoid, on the use of cone of experience
- Using one medium in isolation
- Moving to abstract without adequate foundation of concrete experience
- Getting stuck in the concrete without moving to the abstract hampers the development of learners as it prevents them from engaging in higher order thinking skills.

Classroom activity: Dale's cone of experience
Divide the whole class into small groups of 4-5 learners, using a fun strategy, such as playing cards, prepared ahead of time. Everyone is drawing the same suit forms a group, or everyone drawing an ace, two, three, etc. forms a group. Give each group a stack of sticky notes and ask them to brainstorm different ways of instruction say, mathematics in a classroom, listing only one idea per note. Then, ask them to post these notes on a sheet of paper, placing the instruction methods they believe are most effective in helping members learn at the bottom of the paper and progressing up the page in order, placing the least effective methods at the top of the page. Appoint a group leader in each group and ask from group leaders of each group to explain why they placed the instruction methods on the page in the order that they did.

Now, introducing Dale's cone of experience, explain to all groups that learners retain about:
- 20% of what we read or hear

- 30% of what we see
- 50% of what we hear and see
- 70% of what we say
- 90% of what we do

Ask the group leaders to think about the 'instruction of mathematics' methods posted on the sheet of paper and have each group reorganize the effectiveness of these methods.

Then, discuss the Dale's Cone: Dale, known as the father of modern media in education, arranged various audio visual aids in pictorial form, which is known as 'cone of experience'. According to Dale's cone of experience, more the sensory channels are involved in an interaction, better would be the learning. Thus, we can see that more the learners get chance to say or do a thing, better would be their chance of learning. The cone also shows that the base of the cone represents 'concrete' experiences and the top of the cone represents 'abstract' experiences.

Importance of Dale's cone of experience

Cone of experience helps to decide instruction strategy for maximum possible learning, e.g. if we want to teach about plants and animals, we should teach with the help of pictures and explain them or we can take the learners for a field trip. Dale's cone helps us to decide for field trip as it helps to get maximum possible learning. Learners taught through picture showing method would not be able to tell about the exact height of plants, how it looks like in natural habitat, in what kind of soil it grows etc. This method could be used for identifying the plant and explaining its characteristics. Moreover, learners would not be able to recall as much as they can do with the help of field-trip. So, Dale's cone of experience is helpful in deciding for instruction strategies available for maximum possible learning.

There are three ways of learning something:

- We can experience it directly- through experimenting or doing or imitating directly and immediately the performance of other person.
- We can observe the performance but postpone doing it ourselves.
- We can learn by reading or listening, about experiences that others have had.

The second and third steps are successively farther removed from actual doing. In truly organic instruction process, no such division is made. Direct experiencing in classroom is inseparable from reading and hearing verbal symbols. We normally tie our abstract verbal symbols to our direct experiencing. One may first see the motion picture' how it feels to travel by a metro-train in Delhi and then, as one really travel by a metro train in Delhi, experience at first-hand is what one experienced indirectly through the words of the commentary and the pictures if this film.

Advantages of direct experience over indirect experience

- It enables one to grasp many related details at once, not divisively but in a total act.
- They give us a foundation, a sound basis for our indirect experiences.
- Enables us to grasp a great deal of detail in a very short time.

We must have both direct and indirect experiences. But, all the experiences no matter how concrete or how abstract they are, and regardless of the instructional medium, must finally be tied firmly together, if they are to be both means and ends in an organic process of learning.

Now, let us discuss all the categories in detail:

(1) Direct purposeful experience

The base of the cone represents direct reality itself as we experience it at first hand. It is the rich full-bodied experience that is the bed rock of all education. It is the purposeful experience that is seen, handled, tasted, touched, felt, and smelled. Going to the store, preparing meal, making a piece of furniture, taking a trip or making a pot, and many other tasks involve direct participation. Life cannot, of course, be lived exclusively on this direct, concrete, sensory level. Whenever we remember something we have experienced, we begin to abstract. Even our earliest of experiences also do involve some degree of abstraction.

(2) Contrived experiences as an 'editing' of reality

A contrived experience differs from the original in size, in complexity, or in both. We simplify by means of a working model and the model makes the real life easier to understand. We usually use it when things we are interested in are obscured or confused or concealed.

(3) Models

A model is a three-dimensional representation of something not visible/abstract to the learner, such as a replica of the human ear, that may be smaller, larger, or the same size as the real thing. Hence, a model is three-dimensional recognizable imitation/representations of real things. It can be of the same size or larger or smaller than the thing it represents.

Principles of use (for facilitators) : models have a natural appeal which suggests some ideas regarding their effective use in instruction:

- ✈ Make certain that all learners can see the model.
- ✈ Use supplementary materials along with models.
- ✈ Make sure that correct concepts of size are given to the learners
- ✈ Arrange for the first –hand examination of three dimensional instruction materials. (Should be seen from different points)
- ✈ Show only such models and other three-dimensional materials as apply to work at hand.

Several characteristics of effective models for instruction purposes/significance or merits of using models as an aid:

- ✈ They are three-dimensional. They can be handled, operated, seen from different angles, and so it is generally more interesting and instructive than a picture or chart which is a two-dimensional representation.
- ✈ They reduce large objects or enlarge small objects to a size convenient for observation.
- ✈ They provide interior views of objects which are normally covered or otherwise invisible, e.g. replica of an ear.
- ✈ Non essentials are removed so that fundamentals can be more readily observed.
- ✈ Models accentuate important features and minimize less important features.

→ The most useful models can be taken apart and put together again. Models provide an environment for interactive learner engagement. Evidences from science education research shows that significant learning gains are achieved when learners participate in interactive engagement activities. Thus, the learning environment/activity created by a model provides an important interactive engagement experience.

→ Working with models can enhance systems thinking abilities.

→ Models and model development are useful for helping learners learn quantitative skills such as graphing, graphical analysis, and visualization; statistics; computational skills, mathematics.

→ Many models allow one to perform sensitivity studies to assess how changes in key system variables alter the system's dynamic behaviour. Such sensitivity studies can help one identify leverage points of a system to either help one affect a desirable change with a minimum effort or to help estimate the risks or advantages associated with proposed or accidental changes in a system.

→ Earth system models of intermediate complexity allow us to perform experiments related to the earth system without altering and potentially harming the actual earth. Many experiments, like understanding the future effects of atmospheric carbon dioxide increase, are taking place in the actual earth system today but the results of these would not be known for 50 to 100 years. An earth system model can run several such simulations using different assumptions in a matter of hours to days. The same is true for most models.

→ The knowledge gained while using models and the understanding of model development and implementation are transferable to other disciplines related to the earth system.

Application in a classroom situation

→ Models can be used in a variety of learning situations.

→ Many times it is impossible to show the learners the actual objects, they may be too big they may be too far, they may be dangerous. So, in these situations models according to requirement of the learners are brought and showed to the learners, e.g. learners have to be taught about a dam, it may not be possible to take them to the dam, for first-hand experience, and in that case a model is shown.

→ Where learners have to be taught about snakes, lion, which are dangerous animals, in that situation models can be used.

→ Certain things may be invisible, like the interior parts of eye, in such case a model is used to make learners understand it.

→ Certain real things may be too large or too small for study, exemplar earth and paramecium respectively.

→ Again, there are things which may be readily available and sufficiently large for study but from whose outward appearances we cannot understand anything.

→ Certain real things are things of past or things of future or things far away from us.

→ There are functions and processes in real-life that cannot be perceived directly.

+ Models can be used to introduce specific content. A model can introduce learners to important terms as well as provide an environment to explore relevant processes.
+ Models can be used to explore 'what-if' scenarios. 'What if atmospheric Nitrogen gets doubled?' is a common exemplar for a climate model.

Kinds of models

a. Scale models: large or small: in science classes, exact scale models are used-life size or larger-that can be handled and taken apart. Learners 'see' what the human brain is like as they work with various models of the parts that can be assembled and dissembled. Exactness of scale provides faithful reproduction that is often essential for learning.

b. Simplification models: for most study situations, precision models are not essential; indeed they are often less desirable than the clay figures and improvised models that the learners make as part of their learning experiences. A simplified model of farm animals may be sculptured in clay and painted or roughly drawn on cardboard and mounted on supporting woodblocks.

c. Cutaway or cross-sectional models: simplified models show the external form of the originals. We must look inside to see those parts or the processes hidden by covering, for which we use cutaway or cross-sectional models. Often these are life size or larger than life, and they are usually made to exact or approximate scale.

In any learning situation with a model the similarity and the differences from the real things should be emphasized. Learners should be given a clear idea of its actual size.

Some utilitarian criteria

+ Is the model necessary or can one make use of the original?
+ Could some other device portray the idea more effectively?
+ Is the idea appropriate for representation in the model? (Is it too elementary? Too complicated?)
+ Is each part of the model made to the same scale? (If human figures are included, are they of proportionate size?)
+ Are the important details of its construction correct?
+ Could wrong impressions of colour, shape and size result from using this model?
+ Does the model oversimplify the idea?
+ If it is workable, would it stand up under frequent use?
+ If it is to be made by learners, is the model to be worth the time, effort, and money involved?
+ If it is purchased, would the model be used often enough to justify it cost?
+ Would the model act as a stimulant to further learning?

Limitations

A model of the earth is named as a globe. Now the globe is not the same as earth. The globe would be labelled with a statement as to its scale, but a statement is not enough. There is a great difference between seeing the model of a house and seeing the full-sized house.

Every contrived experience, like every metaphor, would be true in certain respects and greatly different in others. We often speak the digestive system as a kind of machine that processes foods; we talk of the heart in terms of mechanics. Models of these organs have one serious deficiency: man is not a machine. He is like a machine in some ways, but in the most important respects he is very opposite. No machine repairs itself; no machine reproduces itself.

One should use models in combination with other required materials

It must not be assumed that we solve problems merely by making models available in the classroom. Direct instruction and demonstration relating to the model itself are essential. And when a model is used, its differences from reality must be made clear.

(4) Exhibits

It is an arrangement of realistic materials, primarily three dimensional, which are designed to inform the observer about a subject of educational significance. Large variety of exhibits can be used in instruction: school-made exhibits (school museum, classroom exhibits and others) and exhibits already available for instruction (loan exhibits and public museum). Every school made exhibit is planned either to communicate something to people outside the classroom or to teach subject matter to our own learners.

Classroom exhibit

Need for making and using displays with other learners

- ✈ The purpose is for approaching and motivating the fresh and new unit.
- ✈ For research and other work in the course of a unit.
- ✈ For summarizing and fixing in the learner's minds with the activities that have been completed and their meanings, some elaboration of these major purposes is worth undertaking.

Participation by the observer

Regardless of who produces the exhibit, one would aim for observer participation. For this one would make sure that the exhibit involves the viewer so that he feels somehow identified with its main idea that it is 'for him'.

Materials which can be used / methods of the production of exhibits:

An image of an old man held up before the class is not an exhibit, but a collage of pictures of same man at different stages of his life chosen to communicate a key idea and arranged in a skilful display constitutes an exhibit. Any material that can contribute in making the display better for learners to learn can be used. Three-dimensional arrangements may include objects, specimen, models, drawings, graphs, charts, duplicated pages, clippings, slides, photographs, or any other item that has a useful function in the total display.

Place, where an exhibit can be displayed or used:

One can set up the exhibit on the floor, on a table, on the shelves, on several layers of boxes. One can use a pin-up exhibit against a wall, using the bulletin board. One can use a felt board; adapt a chalk-board. More elaborate exhibit may use a glassed-in case or a 'shadow-box' made from an old picture frame. The possibilities are literally without limit-all one need is an imagination and awareness of how much can be accomplished without extensive labour or expense.

Remember that in the classroom the exhibit would be seen from close range. As East points out, effectiveness would be increased if learners can touch or pick up or examine things.

Planning exhibits so as to assure fair chance of achieving their purpose
+ Put only one, central idea in the exhibit.
+ Place the exhibit where it is certain to be seen.
+ An exhibit is seen, not read.
+ Make the labels short and simple.
+ Labels should be uniform and legible.
+ Motion attracts attention.
+ Be sure the exhibit is well lighted.
+ Colours may add interest and attractiveness.
+ Sound and various mechanisms add attractiveness.
+ One would look at this exhibit even if one had not produced it.

Exhibits already available for instruction (loan exhibits and public museum)
Loan exhibits are used with other instruction materials in the classroom. There are three main sources of loan exhibit
+ The public museum.
+ Organisations devoted to some civic or educational purpose.
+ Commercial firms.

Out of these the first one is likely to remain of primary importance to learners. To use museums for classroom subject matter, facilitator should do extensive planning before the visit. He should familiarize himself with the resources of the museum as well as its facilities for handling visiting groups of learners. And he should prepare his class in the general basic way in which he prepares them for a field trip. Sometimes the visit would be made at the beginning of the unit. But often the learners would be benefitted more of it if occurring in the second half. They would be able to interpret in a better way, what they see and would be able to ask more intelligent questions. Modern museums provide guides or instructors who are familiar with learner's needs. If they have had actual classroom experience, these guides are likely to prove invaluable to the facilitator.

(5) Field trips
Here, we watch and note the meanings of their actions. As spectators we are not responsible for what happens-we may be on the side-lines, without authority or ability to alter the event. We merely watch it getting unfold.

A) Trip selection
+ Start with identifying the aim, objectives and plan of evaluation for the field trip.
+ Select the site to be visited.
+ Contact the coordinator of the site and fix the date and time

✦ Collect as much information as one can about the site beforehand (e.g. Addresses, directions, contact persons, phone numbers, maps, email addresses and so on)

Pre-visit can be done for familiarizing with the key features of the field trip. Buy postcards and posters. Take photographs to share with the learners prior to the visit. Explore as much as one can (visit exhibitions etc.), so that one get a sound idea about pre-field trip activities.

B) Logistics planning

Administrative approval, bus transportation reservation, food, developing schedule, arrangement of camera, torch etc., collecting money, composing parent permission, collect the money and deposit it, create the list of phone numbers of all the learners and so on.

✦ Prepare learners before the trip- talk with the learners about the aim of the field trip and how it is related to the current unit of study.

✦ Encourage learners to observe things. Encourage them to give detailed description of day to day seen things, like a tomato sauce bottle, fan, classroom, or playground to their fellow classmates.

✦ Tell them about particular terms which would be used by the tour guide during the trip.

✦ Arouse interest in the trip (by displaying images or posters of the field trip site or related to exhibits).

✦ Assign learners 'particular' portion of the topic that they are supposed to study during the field trip. Learners could be grouped in different subject areas related to the field trip topic to research (e.g. history, art, religion, science, environment, etc.).

✦ Explore the website of the place one would be going.

✦ Discuss with the class and set a standard of conduct and rules to be followed for the trip and discuss about how much money should be spend, food plans, kind of clothes to wear for the trip and other requirements.

✦ Discuss with learners about what are good questions and what are open ended and close ended questions, how to ask open ended questions related to their observation so that they could get maximum information from the visit. Write the questions.

✦ Overview the field trip schedule.

C) Final planning

Check all permission slips the day before the field trip.

D) Conducting the trip

On the day of the trip

✦ Pass out name tags

✦ Divide class into small groups and assign chaperones to the groups

✦ Assign each learner a partner

✦ Place a class list and learner emergency forms in a folder

✦ Secure a cell phone if possible

✦ Take along an emergency kit

✦ Take inventory of food, specific equipment, and other supplies pertinent to the particular field trip

E) Activities that would occur during the field trip

→ Plan activities that engage learners in various activities, which allow learners to work in groups, in pair, as well as alone.

→ Provide time for learners to observe, ask questions, and record key words, ideas and phrases as journal entries in their field book after viewing each exhibit.

→ Ask follow-up questions as learners make observations and listen to presentations.

    a) What clues does one get by seeing this picture?
    b) How these two objects are related to each other?
    c) If one could change one thing in this exhibit, what would it be?
    d) Pretend one is an archaeologist in the future who has come to observe this object. What inferences would one draw about the culture of the past?
    e) Expand the title or name of this object into a detailed caption (sentence or paragraph) in the field book.
    f) Describe the place where one might have found this object.
    g) Out of all these objects, which one would be of greatest importance in next hundred years? Why?
    h) List the objects in the exhibit in the order of the story they tell or usefulness, or their origin.
    i) Which object did one observe for the most of the time and why?
    j) Which object took the most time and effort to produce?
    k) Pretend one area character in this exhibit. Tell us as much as one can about the life.
    l) What does this object tell us about the person's attitude toward?
    m) Can the object displayed be used in modern scenario?
    n) If one were to suggest the friend this particular location, what adjectives would one use to describe it?

→ Schedule a particular segment of the field trip for a scavenger hunt where learners look for particular objects and record them in their field book or on an observation sheet.

→ Provide time for learners to work in their field book writing questions, describing favourite displays or making sketches of artefacts, structures, scenery, etc. If they cannot complete their sketches, encourage them to label them for future completion as to colour, detail, etc.

→ Provide time for learners to use tape recorder, camcorder and digital camera for recording important resources viewed/heard.

→ Polling activity: After careful observation of an exhibit, ask learners to discuss an exhibit and vote on an artefact, artwork that they consider to be the most valuable part of the exhibit they viewed. Then ask learners to record one sentence in their field book describing why they felt the object was of key importance.

F) Post field trip activities

A good pre-planning is a necessity for the success of a field trip. However, planning for suitable follow-up activities is also an important phase in the process of learning as it would boost learner learning and increase the value of hands-on experiences outside the classroom. The following activities provide a general guide when planning for post-field trip classroom experiences—

- Allot some time for learners to discuss their observations and reactions to the field trip experiences
- Inform and discuss specific assignments that the learners completed while on the field trip.
- Create a classroom bulletin board displaying materials developed or collected while on the field trip.
- Develop a classroom museum that replicates and extends displays that learners observed on the field trip, e.g. if the field trip involved an art museum, develop a classroom art museum containing learner artwork.
- Link field trip activities to other curricular areas. (Learners can make a list of words of the objects that they observed while they were on field trip; record field trip observations in a classroom journal; why few learners were not able to accompany them to the trip, what all problems did they face when it started raining; etc.
- Share and evaluate learner assignments/activities from the field book.
- Ask the class to compose and send thank-one letters to the field trip site host, organisers, school administrators and other persons that helped them to organize the field trip. Include best objects or fresh and new information learned during the field trip.
- Create a short news report about what happened on the field trip. Publicize the trip via an article in the local newspaper, school bulletin board, trip presentation for parent's night, or class web page.

G) Evaluating the trip

Complete a 'facilitator journal' regarding the field trip. This would provide a good reference for future field trips.

- What was the main objective of this field trip? How much educational value did it have?
- Did the learners meet the objectives/expectations?
- Was time-management done appropriately?
- Were the route and the means of transportation satisfactory?
- Was there adequate staff and adult supervision?
- What else could be done to make this an even better experience in the future?
- What points should be emphasized next time?
- What special problems came up and how can they be addressed in the future?
- What could improve a visit to this site in the future?
- Share the evaluation with the learners, volunteers, hosts from the field trip site, and school administrators.

In evaluating the growth of the learners as a result of the trip, a facilitator would ask herself some obvious questions and others that are rather searching

- Did the class see what they wanted to see?
- What things did they like best?
- What things did they like least?
- Were any of the learners disappointed-if so why?

- Were attention and interest consistently maintained?
- Were the guide's services adequate or inadequate?
- Were there discipline problems that need to be considered?
- Have the learners developed fresh and new appreciations and attitudes?

Advantages for learners
- Response: It gives a richer experience in comparison to printed words. Learners get a chance to hear or read.
- Planning for insights: As facilitators, we must plan for insights. A learner's past experience would influence the meanings he obtains from the field trip. And these meanings can be in the form of questions to be answered, purposes to be achieved, and things to be discovered. We all tend to see what we are looking for.
- Planning for selectivity: The number of facts which could be learned from the field trip is endless. As there is so much to see, the facilitator and learners must work out ahead of time the key ideas that they wish to explore. There would be individual differences in what is learned. Learners with intellectually alert, active and curious minds would try to get much more meaning from the experience.
- Attitude change: It can produce realizations and appreciations on a non-intellectual level that are often essential for thorough understanding of a situation or a problem or a concept.
- Previewing and summarizing.
- Values in motivating and group planning

(6) Exhibits, Boards and charts

a. White boards: white board is easy to write and erase. There are three kinds of white boards which are
- Non-magnetic board: Non-magnetic board is sturdy; surface is smooth and ideal for regular use. One can easily write with white board marker.
- Magnetic board (resin coated) : this has a glossy metal surface coated with resin, which ensures smooth writing and easy erasing. It also doesn't leave ink stains during regular use.
- Magnetic board (ceramic/porcelain coated) : this board has matt finish metal surface that can be used as screen for projection apart from writing. It can also be used as a pinup board and is suitable to post papers and charts by using magnetic buttons.

b. Chalk writing boards

Advantages of using a chalkboard in the learning process
- Chalkboard can become an integral and valuable part of learner facilitator planning.
- The chalkboard can be a means of motivation. It can be used for recording the progress and status of learner-facilitator planning.
- The chalkboard is useful in recording progress by documenting trial-error approaches to subject matter responsibilities.
- The chalkboard permits quick change and rearrangement, both valuable in documenting developmental thinking.

↣ The chalkboard may become the medium through which group projects are worked out. Group projects in the social studies, arts, arithmetic, nature study, history, and in other subjects can be planned, illustrated, summarized by means of chalkboard techniques.

Chalk writing boards are usually used in educational institutions, schools, etc. for smooth writing with chalks. There are three kinds of chalk writing boards.

↣ Laminate surface: using special kind laminate surface for easy writing and erasing. These are available in green and black colours.
↣ Magnetic (resin coated) metal surface. This is more economical and ideal for occasional use.
↣ Magnetic board (ceramic coated) : this has metal surface and resistant to scratches. It is suitable for regular use and long lasting. It is available in sizes up to 4' x 16' without joint.

Charts
It is a visual symbol for summarizing or comparing or contrasting or performing other helpful services in explaining subject matter.

a) Charts should be sufficiently large to be seen easily.
b) It can tell a story but it should not contain too many words.
c) They should be attractive to look at.
d) They should be strong enough to stand rough use.
e) It should not contain any picture that is not related at all to their experience.

How to use charts effectively
↣ Facilitator-made charts should be preferred.
↣ Learners should be involved in the preparation of the charts.
↣ Charts should be so large that every detail depicted should be visible to every learner in the class wherever he is sitting.
↣ Charts should display information only about one specific area in a subject.
↣ A chart should not contain too much written material
↣ Too many details should not be included.
↣ A chart should give a neat appearance.
↣ When a chart is to be used in the classroom, the facilitator should make sure that there is the provision for hanging the chart at the vantage point.
↣ The facilitator should have a specific pointer to point out specific factors in the chart.
↣ Straight pins, staples, pegboard clips, gummed hangers, paperclips, folded making tapes may all be used for fastening charts without damaging them.
↣ Charts should be carefully stored and preserved for future use.

There are various kinds of charts
↣ Time chart
↣ Tree or stream charts
↣ Flow or organisation chart
↣ Comparison and contrast charts.

Time chart: it presents data in ordinary sequence, e.g. a list of the prime ministers of India, with dates of term on the left and other information in tabular form. One can obviously, add as many columns as one wish, depending upon how much are to be presented and how the chart would be used.

Tree or stream charts: tree or stem charts depicts development, growth and change by beginning with a single source which then spreads out into many branches; or by beginning with many tributaries which then converge into a single channel (stream).

Flow or organisation charts: it represents rectangles, lines, and sometimes arrows and circles - the functional relationship within the organisation.

Comparison and contrast charts: tell a summarized story by the simple device of showing two or more sets of data in the columnar form. When the comparison is essentially mathematical, a graph is used instead; but we are often less interested in numerical than in other differences.

(7) Motion pictures, mass media and multimedia

Media which has a very large audience is known as mass media. The term mass media was first coined back in the 1920s in the advent of radio networks, mass circulation of newspapers and magazines; although mass media was present since many centuries before the term became common. Before the invention of television, the mass media, commonly referring to newspapers and radios, was mainly a platform of news and information to the public. Today, however, mass media has become much more than that, it has become a necessity in our daily lives. We are very much dependent on mass media not only as a source of news and information, but also as a source of entertainment and leisure. With the help of mass media, the adult masses without the knowledge of reading and writing, not only understand what is happening in the outside world but, what is more important, they learn things which help them improve the conditions of health and hygiene, develop agriculture and industries, and attain higher social standard.

Significance and merits of using television as an aid
  + Availability of direct stimuli.
  + Consistency in instruction learning
  + Economically viable
  + Services of super facilitator
  + Education of a great number
  + Multiplication and magnification

Efficient use of educational television

Efficient, inspirational and practical educational television is cooperation among progressive administration, a dedicated and sincere faculty and an educationally aware and technically knowledgeable staff (group work and dedicated staff). The instructors appearing on television must be capable of accepting and assimilating criticism which they would not ordinarily receive in the classroom.

Relationship between the instructor and the production expert determines the quality of presentations. The producer of the instructional programme must be a versatile artist. There should be an expert in programme system analysis whose responsibility would be to analyse the educational needs of the educational institutions and to recommend the most efficient use of the medium.

An educational psychologist should be an important member of the group for testing and evaluating the result of the instructional methods as well as for advising on the method to be employed. A great deal of research is necessary to theorize ETV's impact on learning processes.

Multimedia

Multimedia is more than one concurrent presentation medium (e.g. on CD-ROMs or a web site). Although still images are a different medium than text, multimedia is typically used to mean the combination of text, sound, and/or motion video. Some people might say that the addition of animated images (e.g. animated gif on the web) produces multimedia, but it has typically meant one of the following

+ Text and sound
+ Text, sound, and still or animated graphic images
+ Text, sound, and video images
+ Video and sound
+ Multiple display areas, images, or presentations presented concurrently
+ In live situations, the use of a speaker or actors and
+ 'Props' together with sound, images, and motion video.

Multimedia can be defined generically as any combination of two or more media such as sound, images, text, animation, and video. For educational technology purposes, multimedia refers to computer-based systems that use associative linkages to allow users to navigate and retrieve information stored in a combination of text, sounds, graphics, video, and other media.

Effectiveness of multimedia packages as instructional aids

The technology that combines video, animation, sound and computers (multimedia technology) can help motivate learners in the learning process. The development of multimedia as the basis for a virtual reality environment is based on hypertext systems. Introduced by Vannevar Bush and extended by Theodore Nelson and others, hypertext systems were developed as valuable interactive approaches for presenting text and graphical information in which users can jump from a given topic to other related information. The hypertext systems comprises of links within generally text-based documents. Hypermedia incorporates hypertext with other media like video, illustrations, diagrams, animations and computer graphics, and sound. Hypermedia systems play major role in education through the ability of learners to access information in a wide range of media.

Advantages of multimedia

The role of hypermedia in developing virtual environments has several possible functions

+ Save time by allowing learners to browse information.
+ Provide nonlinear access to information to the learners

- ✦ It enhance and supports group activity, and allow learners working on partial information to be linked together and present the same information in multimedia formats
- ✦ Increased motivation.
- ✦ It provides more flexible learning modes /environment.(performed when and where the learner desires
- ✦ Development of creative and critical thinking skills.
- ✦ Improved writing and critical thinking skills.
- ✦ Combining hypermedia with artificial intelligence created intelligent hypermedia systems. This combination gives designers more freedom for communication and learners more ways to access information and instruction materials.
- ✦ It enables learners to communicate rapidly, easily and cheaply across time and space, and to more selectively control access and participate in communication network.
- ✦ Various data glove devices are available which allow complex and subtle motions of the human hands and fingers to be fed into a computer. When emerged in virtually real world, a data glove allows a learner to grasp and accurately manipulate objects in 3 D space. Sounds also play an important role in input devices and techniques.
- ✦ Multimedia-based learning provides a novel, and non- threatening way to learn that differs from traditional school learning.
- ✦ It does not require a human instructor to be actively instruction.
- ✦ Learning process is made possible on demand and is specific to immediate staff.
- ✦ Multimedia applications facilitate communication that plays a crucial role in any form of distance learning.
- ✦ It provides a way of working and learning that allows social and task specific activities to come together across time and space.
- ✦ It can track and graphically represent to the user her or his path through the interactive media space.
- ✦ Media rich distance learning systems.
- ✦ It can provide situations that can mimic reality, where one can experience situations that may be impossible in real life.
- ✦ Emphasis on visuals

Limitations
- ✦ To use multimedia-based learning in planning, one needs to provide both on-going support for learners and support for the technology. For a fruitful impact of multimedia, a highly dedicated group of administrators and staff, who have a high sense of responsibility for the technology, is required.
- ✦ It allows learners to manipulate the reality in the scope of micro world.

(8) Still pictures, recordings and radio
These are nothing but visual and auditory apparatus and devices used by an individual or a group. Still pictures lack the sound and motion of a sound film. The radio broadcast of an actual event may be like a televised broadcast minus its visual dimensions. These have sounds but not moving effects as that of the television and motion pictures. These may be recording of a song, lecture, dialogue, discourse, etc.

(9) Visual symbols

Non-verbal symbols are signs or gestures that are not spoken, but still try to convey meaning. These include the chalk board method, drawings and sketches, cartoon strips, diagrams, charts, graphs, and flat maps. These generally represent abstractions.

(10) Verbal symbols

The verbal symbol may be a word for a conception (cow), an idea (goodness), a scientific principle (the law of reflection), a formula (NH_3), a philosophic aphorism (Truth is god.) or any other representation of the experience that has been classified in some verbal symbolism. Thus, verbal symbols are used with every other material on the cone of experience, though they themselves are abstractions.

A young child learns through direct and purposeful experience. We show him a 'train' and tell him that this thing is called a train. Then, he learns the verbal symbol of the thing. When the train is no longer present physically, then also he can understand what does the word 'train' stands for. As he grows up, he can think in abstract and expands his schema, e.g. when we say life is a train too, he can understand the structure and journey of life is like a train.

In other experiences, like contrived experiences, drama, demonstration, field-trips, exhibitions, TV, still pictures, radio and recordings, the learner tries to understand the verbal symbols and makes sense of the experience, e.g. the word 'cow' does not look like an actual cow. But he can understand that we are referring to the animal cow.

4.2 NON-PROJECTED AIDS AND PROJECTED AIDS
Non-projected aids

Non-projected aids are those that do not require the use of audio-visual equipment such as a projector and screen. Basically aids which do not use electricity. Charts, graphs, maps, illustrations, photographs, brochures, and hand-outs fall under this category.

Chart : A chart is a combination of pictorial, graphic, numerical or vertical material which presents a clear visual summary.

Dale defines charts as, 'a visual symbol summarizing or comparing or contrasting or performing other helpful services in explaining subject-matter'. The main function of the chart is always to show relationships such as comparisons, relative amounts, developments, processes, classification and organization.
Educational motivation:

↣ Shows continuity in the process
↣ Shows relationships by means of facts, figures and statistics
↣ Presents matter symbolically
↣ Presents abstract ideas in visual form
↣ Summarizes information
↣ For effective impact, proper colour combination, spacing and margins should be kept in mind to avoid confusion.

Poster : The poster can be defined as a graphic representation of some strong emotional appeal that is carried through a combination of graphic aids like pictures, cartoons lettering and other visual arts on a placard. It aims for conveying the specific message, instruction a particular thing, giving a general idea etc. Posters exert a great influence on the observer.

Flash-cards : Flash cards are used for the presentation of an idea in the form of posters, pictures, words and sentences and for quick comprehension and retention.

Graph : Graph is defined as a visual representation of numerical data. It is an effective tool for comparisons and contrast or for presenting complicated facts.

Maps – Maps are encyclopaedia of man's existence. The map as a record of spatial concept tells a story that nothing else can. A map is an accurate representation of plane surface in the form of a diagram drawn to scale, the details of boundaries of whole of earth's surface, continents, countries etc. Geographical details like location of mountains, rivers, altitude of a place, contours of the earth surface and important locations can also be represented, taught and learnt accurately. Maps depict the climatic conditions, natural conditions, location etc. of certain countries and continents. Maps are graphic representations of the surface of the earth. They are used to simplify many of the disciplines- history, geography, economics, etc. Maps are usually drawn to scale. Other form of representation of map is in the form of a globe.

Photographs: Photographs may be passed from hand to hand or posted on a board in front of an audience.

Brochures and hand-outs: Brochures are small pamphlets composed of illustrations and printed material, but they are generally much briefer than hand-outs. When given to learners or an audience, these materials should help the people understand the presentation. Hand-outs are normally retained by the audience for purposes of reference and later review. Long after the presentation, they can review important points of the presentation.

Projected aids

It includes filmstrips, slides, overhead transparency projectors, stereographic projection, tachistoscope, micro projection, microfilms and screens.

- Overhead transparency projectors: The main advantage of these is that a class of hundred learners can see clearly as compared to a small group of learners if chalk-board method was used.
- Stereographic projection: 3-d (stereographic) slides can be shown by a twin-lens projector for viewing by whole class.
- Tachistoscope: It is produced by the addition of a phragm-kind shutter. This shutter allows the facilitator to produce time exposers of figures, words, sentences, and paragraphs on a screen at exposures varying from 1 - 1/100 seconds. But it has limited use.
- Micro projection: These projections are either attachments for a microscope or separate projectors with built-in microscope lenses. They are used much as slide-projectors, but the adjustment is more complex and the image is not bright.

- ✈ Microfilm: Refinement of photographic technique in recent years has made possible the reproduction of large pages of printed matter on 35-mm or 16-mm film. The use of microfilms is in infancy, but we can house vast quantities of information in a relatively small space.
- ✈ Screens: the screen partly determines the quality of the projected image. It must be chosen by taking into account the size of the image needed for the size of audience and their seating arrangement. It must also be chosen in terms of image brightness and the reflective qualities needed according to specific situations.

Projected medium

All media intended for projection (motion picture, video recording, filmstrip, slide, or transparency) are included in it. In this kind of record category, the material specifically designed for overhead projection, as well as archival projected items, is also included, where the distinguishing features of the format or medium are very much emphasized. Projected materials enable educators to convey information to large number of people at the same time. In all cases, they require three things: the material, screen and a projector.

Inadequacies in any one of these items can render the material, no matter how well the content is. In fact, the distractions of poorly projected materials, or the delays of having to set up screens or projectors, can make these expensive preparations less useful than a well-prepared talk or live demonstration. These problems are compounded when there is no available electricity.

4.3 EDUCATIONAL MEDIA AND AUDIO-VISUAL AIDS
Understanding educational media

At first, one thing must be understood that the subtopics under this heading would revolve around educational media and not mass media. Therefore, the portions covered here would not discuss the means of communication or channels of communication such as newspaper, television, radio and advertising. By saying, this we are not negating the educational purpose of media; we are just clarifying that while mass media does not have only one purpose (of learning-instruction purpose) but many other purposes like entertaining, informing, marketing and influencing; educational media, too, is a means by which instruction-learning process takes place.

Reasons to use educational media

Media provides different ways to communicate. Since instruction-learning is also one of the forms of communication, media acts as a strong tool for instruction-learning process. Educational media helps the learner to get more awareness about his 'environment' through varied 'experiences' (that a learner may not get through traditional means {namely use of language symbols}). It has now been widely accepted that facilitators should have a sound idea of learners learning capabilities and competence level. Thus, educational media can contribute a lot in accelerating learning process in comparison to traditional means.

Importance of audio-visual aids

Audio-visual aids impact the quality of instruction and learning process. They help to capture the attention and interest of the learner. Selection of appropriate media is a complex task considering the wide array of media available and differences between the learners and objectives pursued.

Importance of audio- visual media/aids
- ✦ They supply a concrete basis for conceptual thinking and hence reduce meaningless word responses of learners.
- ✦ They have a high degree of interest for the learners.
- ✦ They make learning more permanent
- ✦ They provide a reality of experience which stimulates self-activity on the part of pupils.
- ✦ They develop a continuity of thought; this is especially true for motion pictures.
- ✦ They combine to growth of meaning and hence lead to vocabulary development.
- ✦ They provide experiences not easily obtained through other materials and contribute to the efficiency, depth and variety of learning.

Considerations to be kept in mind while selecting an audio-visual aid :
Audio-visual materials should be selected or rejected in terms of how well they perform their intended function. The criteria for selection of appropriate audio-visual material include several things.

Suppose, we have to select an overhead projector (OHP) over all the other projected aids i.e. chalkboard, transparencies, film strips etc. Then the following considerations must be kept in mind:
- ✦ Position of aid in Dale's cone of experience: The aids situated in the bottom of the cone of experience prove to be more effective in imparting experience. Thus an OHP would be quite effective.
- ✦ According to objectives and goals: Instruction aids should fulfil the objective of the instruction. Since, through an OHP learners can visualize things; it would be helpful in the development of knowledge. Extent to which the audio-visual material/combination of materials helps the learners to reach their goals is very important aspect.
- ✦ Suitability according to age, grade and cognitive level of the learner: An OHP can be used for al level of learners and would suit the cultural and social environment of all the learners also. AV material/s should match the level of learners in terms of vocabulary, pace, and general understand ability.
- ✦ Hold the interest of the learners: Any audio-visual aid loses its effectiveness, if it is not able to hold the attention of the learners. But, since, OHP can show both stable picture and motion picture, it can successfully bind the interest of the learners.
- ✦ Accessibility: Audio-visual aid should be easily accessible.
- ✦ Flexibility: Audio-visual aid should not act as a hindrance. Instead, there should be scope of diversity in case the need arises. Since an OHP can be stopped in between thus it provides scope of in between discussion.
- ✦ User friendly and interactive: Audio visual aid should be such that the facilitator is well equipped with the skill of handling it.
- ✦ Accuracy and authenticity: The information given by the AV material/s is accurate and authentic.

+ Sense: AV material/s should have excellent audio-video sense (of sound, vocabulary, colour and other 'see and hear' factors).

4.4 SIMULATIONS AND EDUCATIONAL GAMES IN EDUCATION
Simulations
It is a computerized model of a real or imagined system that is designed to teach how the system works.

Kinds of simulations: According to Alessi and Trollip (2001), simulations are of two kinds, simulations that teach

+ About something.
+ How to do something

Simulations that teach about something
These are again of two kinds:

Physical: These simulations allow user to manipulate things or processes represented on screen. E.g. combining various chemicals to see the results

Iterative: These simulations, as the name suggests, can be repeated again and again by the learner. These simulations speed up the slow processes, or slow down the quick process, e.g. to allow user to understand the effect of changes in demographic variables on population growth or the effects of environment on ecosystem. These simulations are commonly popular in genetics, where learners can see the resulting offspring of their chosen pair.

Simulations that teach how to do something
These simulations are also of two kinds

Procedural: These simulations teach the appropriate sequence of steps to perform certain procedures, e.g. flight simulators, where learners simulate piloting an airplane.

Situational: These simulations give the hypothetical problems and situations to the learners and ask them to react, e.g. Learners play the stock market and operate business.

Criteria for selecting simulation software
System fidelity and accuracy

+ Simulations vary in purpose, so a uniform criterion is not possible. For some, a realistic and accurate system is necessary, but for others, the representation of screen elements is important.
+ Good documentation to explain system characteristics and uses. Since, the same set sequence of steps is not necessary for all the simulations, they need good accompanying documentation.
+ A set of clear directions helps the facilitator learn how to use the programme and show the learners how to use it popularly and easily.

Advantages of using simulations

+ Reduces time: Simulations speeds up the process that normally takes long time. E.g. Movement of glaciers.
+ Appropriate rate of process : Simulations speed up the slow processes and slow down the quick processes so that the learners can learn effectively.

- Involvement of learner: Simulations capture the interest and attention of learners and they can discover whole lot of possibilities themselves.
- Safe experimentation: Learners learn in simulated environments and thus can avoid physical injuries.
- Make impossible, possible: Learners can experience what would it be like to walk on moon, or can see cells mutating.
- Save money and other resources: Dissections can be shown, instead of doing actually, which is found to be equally productive in terms of learning.
- Observations of complex processes : When many things happen at once, simulations make it easier to focus on individual components.

Limitations of using simulations
- Accuracy: learners may get inaccurate perspective of the complexity of the process. Therefore, simulations must be followed by real-life experiences.
- Misuse: some simulations provide little information. Learners focus on 'trial-and-error' guessing, rather than the systematic analysis of available information

Games
These are the software designed to increase motivation by adding games rules, competition and fun for enhanced learning. The games should be in entertaining format which increase motivational level rather than induce frustration in the learners. Also, learners should not be exposed to violence. However, they should be used sparingly to avoid misuse; and they should emphasize the content area skills.

Criteria for selecting games
- Appealing formats and activities: most popular games include elements of adventure and uncertainty and level of complexity matched to learner's abilities.
- Instructional value: they should be valuable as instructional and valuable tools.
- Physical dexterity should be reasonable: learners should be motivated rather than frustrated.
- Minimum violence/aggression: careful screening should be done as these games often tend to point females as likely targets of violence.

Advantages
According to Randal et al. (1992), the games are more interesting. Traditional instruction is both a basis for using them as well as a consistent finding.
The games provide opportunity to the learners to focus and learn the topic most effectively.

Exemplars
- Arthur's math games - to practice math skills.
- Alice in Vivaldi's four seasons - to practice music skills.

Limitations

- The instructional purpose of the learning of the topic may get lost in pursuit of winning the game.
- Learners may get confused, which part of the activity is game and which part is skill.
- Some games may not have required educational value as desired.

Applications
- In place of worksheets and exercises.
- To teach cooperative group working skills.

Suggestive reading: Audio-visual materials: Their nature and use by Witch and Schuler.

EXEMPLARY QUESTIONS
1. Dale's cone of experience places visual and verbal symbols at the top of the cone. As a facilitator in the middle school, how would this information be useful to you? Support the answer with exemplars.
2. Discuss the effectiveness of multimedia packages as instructional aids.
3. What principles would you keep in mind while selecting and using audio-visual aid? Explain with the help of an exemplar of projected aids?
4. What are non-projected and projected aids?
5. Discuss the significance of 'educational games' and 'simulations' as facilitators in learning.
6. What criteria will help one in choosing an appropriate media for the class? Cite appropriate exemplars from the subject area to illustrate the answer.

UNIT - 5

LEARNING AND INSTRUCTIONAL STRATEGIES

This unit deals with whole group learning, collaborative learning, individualized learning and computer assisted instructions

'We cannot teach our students in the same manner in which we were taught. Change is necessary to engage students not in the curriculum we are responsible for teaching, but in school.'

— April Chamberlain

Unit 5
Learning and Instructional Strategies

5.1 COLLABORATIVE LEARNING

'Collaborative learning,' 'cooperative learning', and 'group learning' are the terms that are often used synonymously. While some people carefully try to differentiate between the three terms, we use them to refer to an instructional approach in which learners work together in small groups to achieve a common learning goal. Collaboration can be as simple as a two-minute, in-class exercise involving pairs of learners, but term-length projects in or outside of class are the most common.

Collaborative learning involves the grouping and pairing of learners with the target of achieving learning goals. Collaborative learning is a method of instruction and learning, in which learners group-up together, to explore a significant question or create a meaningful project. In this method learner can produce or collect the individual parts of a larger assignment individually and then 'assemble' the final work together, as a group. A group of learners discussing a lecture or learners from different schools working together over the internet on a shared assignment are both exemplars of collaborative learning. The learners are responsible for each-other's learning as well as their own. Thus the success of one learner helps other learners to become successful. Proponents of collaborative learning claim that the active exchange of ideas within small groups not only increases interest among the participants but also enhances and supports critical thinking. There is persuasive evidence that cooperative groups achieve higher levels of thought and retain information longer than learners who work quietly as individuals. In collaborative learning setting, learners have the opportunity to converse with peers, present and defend ideas, exchange diverse beliefs, question other conceptual frameworks, and they are actively engaged.

The elements of collaborative learning are

A. Positive interdependence
    a) Learners must fully participate and put forth their effort within their group
    b) Each group member has a task/role/responsibility therefore they must believe that they are responsible for their learning and that of their group
B. Face-to-face promoted interaction
    a) Members enhance and support each other's success
    b) Learners explain to one another what they have learned or are learning and assist one another with understanding and completion of assignments
C. Individual accountability
    a) Each learner must demonstrate master of the content being studied
    b) Each learner is accountable for their learning and work, therefore eliminating social loafing.
D. Social skills
    a) Social skills that must be taught in order to make cooperative learning successful.
    b) Skills include effective communication, interpersonal and group skill.
E. Group processing:

Every group must assess their effectiveness and decide how it can be improved. In order to make achievement of learners improving considerably, two characteristics must be present

a) Learners are working towards a group goal or recognition end

b) Success is reliant on each individual's learning.

While designing cooperative learning tasks and reward structures, individual responsibility and accountability must be identified. Individuals must know exactly what their responsibilities are and that they are accountable to the group in order to reach their goal.

Two major theoretical perspectives in collaborative learning are socio-cultural perspective and socio-cognitive perspective. Research in the socio-cultural perspective, represented by Vygotsky, tends to focus on asymmetrical pairs where guidance and tutoring mechanisms are central. The socio-cognitive perspective, represented by Piaget, tends to emphasize equivalent intellectual abilities where cognitive conflict is central.

Assumptions about learning supported by collaborative learning—

Smith & Macgregor identifies some of the underlying assumptions, and the goals, where these assumptions are manifested, that ties the different approaches in the area of collaborative learning together. These assumptions are:

- ✦ Learning is an active, constructive process: to learn fresh and new information, ideas or skills, learners have to work actively with them in targeted ways.
- ✦ Learning depends on rich contexts: Research suggests that learning is fundamentally influenced by the context activity in which it is situated.
- ✦ Learners are diverse: Learners have diverse backgrounds, learning styles, experiences and aspirations, they introduce multiple perspectives.
- ✦ Learning is inherently social: In collaborative learning; there is an intellectual synergy of many minds coming to bear on a problem, and the social stimulation of mutual engagement in a common endeavour.
- ✦ Learning has affective and subjective dimensions: Listening to and acknowledging diverse perspectives, working in a cooperative spirit, becoming a peer facilitator or a peer learner. All these activities are socially involving, as well as emotionally demanding.

Goals for education supported by collaborative learning

- ✦ Involvement: Involvement in the learning, involvement with other learners, and involvement with faculty are factors that make an overwhelming difference in learner retention and success in college. By its very nature, collaborative learning is socially and intellectually involving.
- ✦ Cooperation and group-work: In collaborative endeavours, learners inevitably encounter difference and must grapple with recognizing and working with it. Collaborative learning represents a value system that regards group work, cooperation, and community as just as important as academic achievement.
- ✦ Civic responsibility: Collaborative learning encourages learners to acquire an active voice in shaping their ideas and values and a sensitive ear in listening others. Dialogue, deliberation, and consensus-building out of

differences are strong treads in the fabric of collaborative learning and in civic life as well.

Strategies of collaborative learning

Unlike individualized learning, people engaged in collaborative learning depend on one another's resources and skills (asking one another for information, evaluating one another's ideas, monitoring one another's work, etc. More specifically, collaborative learning is based on the model that knowledge can be created within a population where members actively interact by sharing experiences and take on asymmetry roles. Put differently, collaborative learning refers to methodologies and environment in which learners engage in a common task where each individual depends on and is accountable to each other. These include both face-to-face conversation and computer discussions (online forums, chat rooms, etc.). Methods for examining collaborative learning processes include conversation analysis and statistical discourse analysis.

Collaborative learning is heavily rooted in Vygotsky's views that there exists an inherent social nature of learning which is shown through his theory of zone of proximal development. Often, collaborative learning is used as an umbrella term for a variety of approaches in education that involve joint intellectual effort by learners or learners and facilitators. Thus, collaborative learning is commonly illustrated when groups of learners work together to search for understanding, meaning, or solutions or to create an artefact or product of their learning. Further, collaborative learning redefines traditional learner-facilitator relationship in the classroom which results in controversy over whether this paradigm is more beneficial than harmful. Collaborative learning activities can include collaborative writing, group projects, joint problem solving, debates, study groups, and other activities. This approach is closely related to cooperative learning.

Some activities or assignments well suited for collaborative learning include:

- ✦ Case studies
- ✦ Discussions
- ✦ Learner moderated discussions
- ✦ Debates
- ✦ Collaborative writing ,collaborative presentation
- ✦ Games
- ✦ Demonstrations

Six exemplary collaborative learning strategies are
a) Think-pair-share

(1) The instructor poses a question, preferably one demanding analysis, evaluation, or synthesis, and gives learners a minute to think through appropriate responses. This 'think-time' can be spent on writing also. (2) Learners then turn to their partners and share their responses. (3) During the third step, learners' responses can be shared within a four-persons learning group, within a larger group, or within an entire class during a follow up discussion. The calibre of discussion is enhanced by this technique, and all learners get an opportunity to learn by reflection and verbalization.
b) Three-step interview

It is common as an ice breaker or a group building exercise. This structure can also be used to share information such as hypotheses or reactions to a film or article. (1) One learner interviews the other. (2) Learners switch roles. (3) One learner interviewer links with a second interviewer. This four-member learning group then discusses the information or insights gained from the initial paired interviews.

c) Simple jigsaw

The faculty member divides an assignment or topic into four parts with all learners from each learning group volunteering to become 'experts' on one of the parts. Expert groups then work together to master their part of the assignment and also to discover the best way to help others learn it. All experts then assemble in their home learning groups where they teach the other group members.

d) Numbered heads together

Members of learning groups usually composed of four individuals, count off: 1, 2, 3, or 4.The instructor then poses a question, usually factual in nature, but requiring some higher order thinking skills. Learners discuss the question, make sure that every group member knows the agreed upon answer. The instructor calls a specific number and the group members originally designated that number during the count off respond as group spokespersons. Because no one knows which number the facilitator will call, all group members have a vested interest in understanding the appropriate response. Again, learners get benefitted from the verbalization, and the peer coaching helps both the high and the low achievers. Class time is usually better spent because less time is wasted on inappropriate responses and because all learners become actively involved with the material.

e) A social science facilitator can use this strategy while instructing about continents, how to use atlas in class 6th and 7th. This can be used to enable the learners to understand that the atlas is a useful source of information, and to improve their skills in gathering information. This activity is based on prior knowledge of learner. The facilitator can divide learners in groups of 3-4. Each group needs an atlas and set of cards. The names of continent, their features and location are written on these cards.

- On few cards it will be written- 'Africa', 'north America, 'south America', 'Asia', etc.
- On others the locations like- 'This continent is to the north of equator', 'this continent is to the south of equator', etc.
- On some it can be written- 'It is the biggest continent', 'it is the smallest continent', etc.
- Few can have the name of the countries of the continent - 'This continent includes countries like India, japan, Pakistan, china.', 'and this continent includes countries like Brazil, Chile and Argentina', etc.
- On the rest of the cards there will be other features of the continents like name of the famous river in that continent, or the name of the famous mountain range, the ocean near that continent, etc.
- Then, learners have to group the cards with the help of atlas.

In each group different learners can have different roles like one can be a card reader, second child can be the atlas holder and another can be the card placer.

They first have to find the continent names and then place them in a row. Then they have to place all the cards in appropriate row/ column, checking their facts in the atlas. If they are stuck they can visit another group and, as a last resort. They can ask a facilitator. Different groups can later write/ speak on different continents and these can be discussed on the world map with the whole class. This is a very good exemplar of an activity which enhances and supports collaborative learning.

f) An elementary class maths facilitator can use this strategy to develop in learners the skill of working in a collaborative manner. Facilitator can begin the lesson by asking the learners all the different ways of writing 3 as a sum (for an instance, 1 + 1 + 1, 2 + 1, 3 + 0). She can write those responses on the board and note the number of possibilities. She will then ask the learners to work in pairs to identify all the ways to make sums of 4. The learners will feel encouraged to confer and pool solutions to determine whether they had found all possible solutions. Then she can ask small groups of learners to consider the number. Before the groups start, she will ask them to predict how many solutions there would be. It is expected that the groups will compete to find the greatest number of solutions, and much task-related conversation is likely to happen. The facilitator will then lead a follow-up discussion, asking each group to describe the system it had used to generate possible solutions. The class will then decide which system they thought was best. She will end by encouraging learners to think more about this problem. In this way the learners in group will work collaboratively, they will help each other and they know their own responsibilities as well.

Exemplars of collaborative learning

✦ Collaborative networked learning is a form of collaborative learning for the self-directed adult learner. According to Findlay (1987), collaborative networked learning (CNL) is that learning which takes place via electronic dialogue between self-directed co-learners, and learners and experts. Learners share a common target, depend upon each other and are accountable to each other for their success. CNL takes place in interactive groups in which participants actively communicate and negotiate with one another within a contextual framework which may be facilitated by an online coach, mentor or group leader.'

✦ In the late 1980s Findley headed the collaborative networked learning project at Digital Equipment Corporation on the east coast of the United States. Findley's project conducted trend analysis and developed prototypes of collaborative learning environments, which became the basis for their further research and development of what they called collaborative networked learning (CNL). Youth directed collaboration, another form of self-directed organizing and learning relies on a novel, more radical concept of youth voice.

✦ Computer-supported collaborative learning (CSCL) is a relatively fresh and new educational paradigm within collaborative learning, which uses technology in a learning environment to help mediate and support group interactions in a collaborative learning context. CSCL systems use technology to control and monitor interactions, to regulate tasks, rules, and roles, and to mediate the acquisition of fresh and new knowledge. Most recently, one study showed that using robots in the classroom to enhance and support collaborative learning led to increase effectiveness in learning and also increase in the learner's motivation. Researchers and practitioners in several areas, including cognitive sciences, sociology, computer engineering have begun to investigate CSCL, thus, it constitutes a fresh and new trans-disciplinary area.

+ Learning management system is a context that gives collaborative learning particular meaning. In this context, collaborative learning refers to a collection of tools which learners can use to assist, or be assisted by others. Such tools include virtual classrooms (i.e. geographically distributed classrooms linked by audio-visual network connections), chat, discussion threads, application sharing (e.g. A colleague projects spread sheet on another colleague's screen across a network link for the target of collaboration), among many others.

+ Collaborative learning development enables developers of learning systems to work as a network. Specifically relevant to e-learning where developers can share and build knowledge into courses in a collaborative environment. Knowledge of a single subject can be pulled together from remote locations using software systems. An exemplar of this could be content point from Atlantic link.

+ Collaborative learning in virtual worlds by their nature provides an excellent opportunity for collaborative learning. At first learning in virtual worlds was restricted to classroom meetings and lectures, similar to their counterparts in real life. Now collaborative learning is evolving as companies have started to take advantage of the unique features provided by virtual world spaces - such as ability to record and map the flow of ideas, use 3-D models and virtual worlds mind mapping tools.

+ Collaborative learning in thesis circles in higher education is another exemplar of people learning together. In a thesis circle, a number of learners work together with at least one professor or lecturer, to collaboratively coach and supervise individual work on final (e.g. Undergraduate or MSc) projects. Learners switch frequently between their role as co-supervisor of other learners and their own thesis work (incl. Receiving feedback from other learners).

Advantages of collaborative learning

+ Develops higher level thinking skills.
+ Enhances and supports learner-faculty interaction and familiarity.
+ Increases learner retention.
+ Builds self-esteem in learners.
+ Enhances learner satisfaction with the learning experience.
+ Enhances and supports a positive attitude toward the subject matter.
+ Develops oral communication skills.
+ Develops social interaction skills.
+ Enhances and supports positive race relations.
+ Creates an environment of active, involved, exploratory learning.
+ Uses a group approach to solve a problem while maintaining individual accountability.
+ Encourages diversity understanding.
+ Encourages learner responsibility for learning.
+ Involves learners in developing curriculum and class procedures.

- Learners explore alternate problem solutions in a safe environment.
- Stimulates critical thinking and helps learners clarify ideas through discussion and debate.
- Enhances self-management skills.
- Fits-in well with the constructivist approach.
- Establishes an atmosphere of cooperation and helping school wide.
- Learners develop responsibility for each other.
- Builds more positive heterogeneous relationships.
- Encourages alternate learner assessment techniques.
- Fosters and develops interpersonal relationships.
- Modelling problem solving techniques by learners' peers.
- Learners are taught how to criticize ideas, not people.
- Sets high expectations for learners and facilitators.
- Enhances and supports higher achievement and class attendance.
- Learners stay on task more and are less disruptive.
- Greater ability of learners to view situations from others' perspectives (development of empathy).
- Creates a stronger social support system.
- Creates a more positive attitude toward facilitators, principals and other school personnel by learners and creates a more positive attitude by facilitators toward their learners.
- Addresses learning style differences among learners.
- Enhances and supports innovation in instruction and classroom techniques.
- Classroom anxiety is significantly reduced.
- Test anxiety is significantly reduced.
- Classroom resembles real life social and employment situations.
- Learners practice modelling societal and work related roles.

Limitations of collaborative learning techniques

- Different learners work at different speeds.
- A learner may try to take over/dominate over the group
- Quiet learners may not feel comfortable
- Sometimes some learners in a group may not get along
- Sometimes a lot of time is wasted on discussing irrelevant topics, learners might deviate from the main topic of discussion

Conceptual components of collaboration

- Objectives: help participants (i.e. learners and facilitators) to work together to engage in efficient collaboration processes to reach specific objectives.
- Activities: identify the activities, and possible constraints, for completing the activities. Activities can include summarizing, questioning, giving an argument, stating a claim, etc.
- Sequencing: explain the expectations of the participants by specifying which activities should be performed and in what order.
- Distribute roles: clarify the roles individuals will assume throughout the activity to encourage participants to adopt and consider multiple perspectives.

✦ Kind of representation: textual, graphical, or oral representations of explicit instructions are presented to the participants

5.2 COOPERATIVE LEARNING

Cooperation is working together to achieve shared goals. Within cooperative situations, individuals seek outcomes that are beneficial to them as well as all other group members. Cooperative learning is the instructional use of small groups such that learners work together to maximize own and each other's learning (Johnson, Johnson & Holdback, 1998).

The terms group learning and cooperative learning are often used as the same thing. In fact, group work means several learners working together and working together doesn't necessarily involve cooperation. Cooperative learning is a sort of arrangement of learners where they work in mixed ability groups and are rewarded on the basis of the success of the group (Woolfolk, 2001).

Kinds of cooperative learning

✦ Formal cooperative learning is structured, facilitated, and monitored by the educator over time and used to achieve group goals in task work (e.g. completing a unit). Any course material or assignment can be adapted to this kind of learning, and groups can vary from 2-6 people with discussions lasting from a few minutes up to a period. Kinds of formal cooperative learning strategies include jigsaw, assignments that involve group problem solving and decision making, laboratory or experimental assignments, and peer review work (e.g. editing ,writing assignments). If one has experience and develops skill with this kind of learning, it often facilitates informal and base learning.

✦ Informal cooperative learning incorporates group learning with passive instruction by drawing attention to material through small groups throughout the lesson or by discussion at the end of a lesson, and typically involves groups of two (e.g. Turn-to-the-partner discussions). These groups are often temporary and can be changed from lesson to lesson (very much unlike formal learning where 2 learners may be lab partners throughout the entire semester contributing to one another's knowledge of science). Discussions typically have four components that include formulating a response to questions asked by the educator, sharing responses to the questions asked with a partner, listening to a partner's response to the same question, and creating a fresh and new well-developed answer. This kind of learning enables the learner to process, consolidate, and retain more information learned.

✦ Group-based cooperative learning helps peer groups gather together over the long term (e.g. Over the course of a year, or several years such as in high school or post-secondary studies) to develop and contribute to one another's knowledge mastery on a topic by regularly discussing material, encouraging one another, and supporting the academic and personal success of group members. Base group learning is effective for learning complex subject matter over the course or semester and establishes caring, supportive peer relationships, which in turn motivates and strengthens the learner's commitment to the group's education while increasing self-esteem and self-worth. Base group approaches also make the learners accountable to educating their peer group in the event that a member was absent for a lesson. This is effective both for individualized learning, as well as social support.

Brown & Parker (2009) discusses about the five basic and essential elements to cooperative learning.

Basic elements of cooperative learning
(a). Clearly perceived positive interdependence

In collaborative learning the success of one person is bound up with the success of others. This is referred to as positive interdependence. There are many ways to ensure positive interdependence. Goal sharing is one way. This might include shared subject matter, a particular assessment, and solving problem jointly or creating and discovering something of worth. Another way is role sharing. This takes place when each group member is given a specific role that also gives a person specific responsibilities. The role describes what group activities that person might take and the contribution to the overall task.

For an instance, one person has responsibility for checking the accuracy of information, another for making links between theory and practice, whilst another has responsibility for summarising information for the group. Resource information contributes to positive interdependence and exists when each group member has only part of the information, cases, material or other resources necessary for the group to achieve its task.

Finally, task interdependence is structured by creating a division of labour so that the actions of one group member have to be completed before the next member can complete the entire task.

Learners perceive that they need each other in order to complete the group's task (sink or swim together). Facilitators may structure positive interdependence by establishing mutual goals (learn and make sure all other group members learn), joint rewards (if all group members achieve above the criteria, each will receive bonus points), shared resources (one paper for each group or each member receives part of the required information), and assigned roles (summarizer, encourager of participation, elaborator).

(b). Face-to-face promotive interaction

Individual learners are encouraged to assist others in the group to complete tasks in order to reach the group's goal. In other words there is an expectation that learners will help each other so that common goals can be achieved. Help may be in the form of resources, advice, provision of feedback and challenging situations. Learners enhance and support each other's learning by helping, sharing, and encouraging efforts to learn. Learners explain, discuss, and teach whatever they know to their classmates. Facilitators structure the groups in such a way so that learners sit knee-to-knee and talk through each aspect of the assignment.

(c). Individual accountability and personal responsibility

Everyone is expected to do their fair share of work and it is important for all group members to know that they cannot 'free ride'. Fair sharing of work can be achieved by:

+ Keep the group small: the smaller the group, the greater individual accountability.
+ Testing every learner.
+ Observing the group and recording the frequency of each member contributing to the group work.
+ Ask one member to check the work of others through use of reasoning.
+ Ask learners to teach others whatever they have learned.

Each learner's performance is frequently assessed and the results are given to the group and the individual. Facilitators may structure individual accountability by giving an individual test to each learner or randomly selecting one group member to give the answer.

(d). Interpersonal and small group skills

Groups cannot function effectively if learners do not have and use the needed social skills. Facilitators teach these skills as target fully and precisely as academic skills. Collaborative skills include leadership, decision-making, trust-building, communication, and conflict-management skills.

Interpersonal skills are important. In order to achieve these goals learners must

+ Get to know and trust each other
+ Communicate clearly
+ Provide and accept support
+ Resolve conflict constructively

(e). Group processing

Groups need specific time to discuss and reflect how well they are achieving their goals and maintaining effective working relationships among members. Reflection may focus on such things as relationship between people, facilitation of collaborative skills, rewarding of positive behaviour and the celebration of success. Facilitators structure group processing by assigning such tasks as (a) list at least three member actions that helped the group be successful and (b) list one action that could be added to make the group even more successful tomorrow. Facilitators also monitor the groups and give feedback on how well the groups are working together to the groups and the class as a whole.

When designing cooperative learning tasks and reward structures, individual responsibility and accountability must be identified. Individuals must know exactly what their responsibilities are and that they are accountable to the group in order to reach their goal. Positive interdependence among learners in the task: All group members must be involved in order for the group to complete the task. In order for this to occur each member must have a task that they are responsible for and which cannot be completed by any other group member.

Researches support cooperative learning

Research on cooperative learning demonstrated 'overwhelmingly positive' results and confirmed that cooperative modes are cross-curricular. Cooperative learning requires learners to engage in group activities that increase learning and adds other important dimensions. The positive outcomes include: academic gains, improved race relations and increased personal and social development.

Brady & Tsay (2010) report that learners who fully participated in group activities, exhibited collaborative behaviours, provided constructive feedback and cooperated with their group had a higher likelihood of receiving higher test scores and course grades at the end of the semester. Results from Brady & Tsay's (2010) study support the notion that cooperative learning is an active pedagogy that fosters higher academic achievement.

Slavin states the following regarding research on cooperative learning which corresponds with Brady & Tsay's (2010) findings

- Learners demonstrate academic achievement
- Cooperative learning methods are usually equally effective for all ability levels.
- Cooperative learning is affective for all ethnic groups
- Learner perceptions of one another are enhanced when given the opportunity to work with one another
- Cooperative learning increases self-esteem and self-concept
- Ethnic and physically/mentally handicapped barriers are broken down allowing for positive interactions and friendships to occur

Limitations

Cooperative learning has many limitations that could cause the process to be more complicated than first perceived. Sharan (2010) discusses the issue regarding the constant evolution of cooperative learning as a threat. Due to the fact that cooperative learning is constantly changing, there is the possibility that facilitators may become confused and do not understand the method. Facilitators who implement cooperative learning may also be challenged with resistance and hostility from the learners who believe that they are being held back by their slower group mates or by the learners who are less confident and feel that they are being ignored or demeaned by their group.

Most collaborative/cooperative group models adhere to the following principles

- Group projects are selected and designed for group work.
- Learners usually work and learn in groups of three to six.
- Positive interdependence and cooperation is a necessary component.
- Interpersonal/cooperative skill building is addressed in class.
- The facilitator is viewed as a coach or facilitator.
- Learners are individually accountable for the work they do in the group.
- Learners are individually accountable for meeting the objectives of the unit of study.

Advantages of learning, if learners work in a group

- Collaborative learning groups can overcome learner resistance to class participation, even if one member of the group reports to the class as a whole.
- Promoting and modelling group cooperative behaviour in class can have positive effects on learners' interactions with one another outside the class, also.
- Cooperative working relationships are required for many jobs.

➤ Learner collaboration in learning enhances and supports active engagement with materials, critical thinking and communication skills, rather than passive forms of learning.

Strategies for incorporating group work in a classroom

Effective group work requires careful planning and structuring. The process must be planned in detail before it is communicated to learners. Group work should be based on objectives developed in the learning design of the course.

➤ Break projects into specific and sequential tasks the groups will perform.
➤ Small groups should present their findings to the class as a whole.
➤ Specify roles for group members and tasks for the group.
➤ Consider how one will provide learners with incentives to work as a group and hold learners individually accountable for contributing to the group's work and for mastering the content.
➤ Consider electronic communication (e-mail, discussion groups) as means for learners to work together.
➤ Half of each learner's grade will be an individual assessment of the sample cooperative learning activity.

Evaluating group learning

Some possibilities are as follow

➤ A portion of each learner's grade will be the average of grades earned by all members of the group for the group learning activities;
➤ A portion of the project grade will reflect each learner's participation and contributions as assessed by other group members.

Some common difficulties faced by learners while working in a group

➤ The difficulty of learners in getting together outside the class.
➤ Fairly evaluating the individual work, as some learners feel they do most of the work while others do not try to give their best.

Some suggestions for supporting effective group work

Provide groups with adequate descriptions of assignments, processes, evaluations, and objectives. Get the learners in their groups early in the course and let them remain together for the duration of the project. Allow groups to have a say in group assignments. Set group size by pedagogical objectives. Look for ways to train learners in skills that will help them to work in groups. Give sufficient instructions on outcomes and process. Identify and encourage the following defined roles: group facilitator, record keeper/folder monitor, timekeeper, or reader, reporter, checker, and encourager.

5.3 INDIVIDUALIZED LEARNING

Individualized learning is a training that is individualized to take into consideration the differences between learners. It is the most appropriately used in a one-to-one situation, such as training the successors or group members in the workplace. Unlike facilitated learning where the trainer takes a more passive role, with individualized learning the trainer needs to consider and cater to the needs of individual participants for an instance

- ✈ Rate of learning and learning style
- ✈ Attitude
- ✈ Maturity
- ✈ Interests which effect the level of learning
- ✈ Motivation
- ✈ Learning environment

It doesn't necessarily mean learners are at home — they can be in a classroom and still work through things at their own pace.
The main kinds of individualized learning are

- ✈ Distance learning
- ✈ Resource-based learning
- ✈ Computer-based training
- ✈ Directed private study

The advantages are

- ✈ Many learner differences can be taken into account.
- ✈ Learners can work at their own pace at the time which is the most convenient to them.
- ✈ Different learning styles can be accommodated.
- ✈ It is cost-effective for large number of learners.
- ✈ It is in the control of learners what they learn and how they learn.
- ✈ It is an active, not a passive learning.

Basic instructional principles for individualized learning

- ✈ Maintain high expectations
- ✈ Make use of praise, minimize criticism
- ✈ Depend on learning technologies
- ✈ Balance direct instruction with challenging activities
- ✈ Teach learning strategies
- ✈ Accommodate learner learning style
- ✈ Establish an experiential base for learning
- ✈ Teach vocabulary directly
- ✈ Focus on meaningful skills, concepts, and activities
- ✈ Use exemplars and demonstrations
- ✈ Actively involve the learners
- ✈ Encourage cooperative learning
- ✈ Ask and encourage questions
- ✈ Teach self-monitoring and self-management
- ✈ Provide creative opportunities for practice and review
- ✈ Integrate skills and concepts throughout the curriculum
- ✈ Build learner interest and enthusiasm
- ✈ Manage the instructional process efficiently
- ✈ Celebrate cultural diversity in the classroom
- ✈ Facilitate parental involvement with school

Individualized instructions

Individualized instruction means giving suitable instruction to each learner. It is learner-centered education, and its target is to help learners to use their own learning style to learn what they need at their own pace.

a. Areas of individualization

 (i) objectives (ii) method (iii) pace (iv) content (v) level of difficulty

b. Comparison of the kinds

Of the five kinds of individualization, individualizing pace and individualizing levels are relatively easy. In contrast, unless the facilitator has one or more assistants, it is very difficult to individualize content, objectives or methods in the ordinary language classrooms.

c. The role of the facilitator

Facilitators and their assistants have the responsibility to help each learner find the best way to learn, to help them with their work, and to guide them to have more effective learning. Individualization involves letting individuals decide, in consultation with the facilitator what is best for them. As facilitators, we need to find the best methods for managing and administering courses that uses individualized instruction works in different kinds of classes and with different kinds of learners.

The major advantage of individualized instruction is that each learner learns according to his/her needs, interests, learning style, and English proficiency and at his/her own pace. Using computers, a facilitator can establish a learning environment where there is one tutor with one learner. As computers are becoming cheaper, and more instruction materials are developed for the computers, individualized instruction will become even more economical and efficient.

Computers were considered ideal for individualized instruction. In the 1980s, personal computers were much more widely available and less expensive, and many schools purchased them for their use in classes. In Japan, personal computers became more widely available in the latter half of the 1980s. Foreign language CAI became more common. However, it is questionable whether computers are being used effectively to meet individual learners' needs

Necessities for individualized instruction with CAI

a. Facilities: To use CAI, special classrooms with computers are necessary.

b. Materials: There should be materials for various targets, such as reading, writing, listening, speaking, grammar, standardized tests, business English, and conversations, depending on the target of the class and the goals that learners have set for themselves, the interests and levels of learners. All materials should have clear, concrete targets so that learners can choose the material they need or want.

Content: a variety of content areas.

Levels: different levels of difficulty.

Important characteristics: clear instructions and good exemplars.

c. Personnel: learners, facilitators, assistants and administrators need to understand what learners are studying, how well they are doing, and how fast they are working. It is therefore useful to keep old computer records. When learners are working outside of class time, there should be someone in the computer room who can help them.

Principles guiding the use of computers in individualized learning:

a) The instruction/learning context: The context in which learning is carried out is extremely important. For instance, a CAI programme was utilised in Vadodara district in order to improve the mathematical skills of the learners. The programme was relatively simple and contained some easy games to play, which were liked by the learners. The CAI programme was a huge hit and the performance of the learners increased by a standard deviation of 3.75. Similarly, the instruction context also needs to be kept in mind. If a facilitator is instruction English, it is better to use audio in CAI programme, so that the pronunciation is correct. On the other hand, if a facilitator is instructing about science, then he/she should make use of a CAI programme with three dimensional images.

b) The aims/objectives of education: The aim of education is equally important. If one desires to enhance and support collaborative and cooperative learning, group learning is better. In classes with high learner-facilitator ratio, individualized learning does not really work. It becomes difficult for the facilitator to give attention to every learner; as a result, the educational aims are not achieved. On the other hand, individualized learning is better for schools with low learner facilitator ratio. In such schools, the facilitator is able to give attention to every learner, and hence the educational aims are achieved. This is a very important factor. This is the primary reason why private schools, which have larger number of learners as compared to government schools, prefer group learning/instruction to individualise instruction. The same goes for the use of computers in individualized learning. If the aim is to evaluate and test the learner, an individualized CAI programme can be used as an effective strategy. On the other hand, if the aim is to introduce a fresh and new lesson and/or topic, it is better that facilitator introduces the concept first and it is followed by remedial classes through the aid of a CAI programme.

c) The cognitive level of the learners: Appropriate instruction techniques should be used keeping the intellectual and cognitive level of the learners in mind. In case the learners are weak and need extra attention, individualized learning is better. It enables the facilitator to focus on every learner and give personal attention. On the other hand, in case the class comprises of a heterogeneous group, whole group learning is better. The facilitator can engage in whole group learning, keeping in mind the Vygotsky principle about learners as active constructors of knowledge. Similarly, a CAI programme should be used keeping in mind the cognitive level of the learner. In case, the learners are cognitively bright, CAI programmes which test and evaluate them can be used. On the other hand, if the learners are not cognitively bright, a CAI programme with images, audio and sounds can be utilised. As discussed earlier, in case the learners are cognitively not so bright, the use of individual CAI programme should be minimised as there would not be much scope for the facilitator to personally assess the learners and adopt effective remedial strategy.

d) Cultural appropriateness of the media: This is closely linked to the cognitive level of the learners. A CAI programme should be devised keeping in mind the specific cultural context in which the instruction/learning process is carried out. In case one is instruction in a government school, then it makes more sense to have a CAI programme with exemplars which the learners can connect to. The same goes for a CAI programme to be used in a private school. This is same in case of instruction without a CAI programme. The learners should be able to connect to the CAI programme; or else the target of instruction will be lost.

e) The infrastructure of the school

Requisites and conditions for individualized learning:

The requisites for individualized learning and conditions for their achievement are necessary.

Requisite	Conditions for achievement
Perception of need	Motivation, external stimuli, synchronization, time
Identification of an objective for fulfilling it.	Self-confidence and confidence in their setting, interaction with others, collection, analysis and organization of information, enterprises.
Implementation of the strategy for reaching the objective	Behavioural attitudes, problem solving capabilities, psychological attitude

The table given below presents the conditions for individualized learning and kind of activities:

	Personal activities	Social activities	Target
Perception of need	Diagnostic systems	Diagnostic systems micro worlds simulation environments	School facilitators and company managers
Identifying the objective that will satisfy the need	Multimedia tools web browsing	E-mail discussion lists collaborative working support systems	School facilitators, school-leavers and the unemployed
Implementation of the strategy for reaching the objective	Multimedia tools web browsing	Teleconferencing systems e-mail discussion lists charts	Company management and staff

Factors affecting individualized learning related to learner—
There are several factors which affect individualized learning. A few of them are:

→ Level of intelligence
→ Aptitude
→ Goals
→ Interests
→ Readiness & maturation
→ Motivation
→ Self-concept(how one perceives himself / herself)

+ Attitudes & values
+ Level of aspiration
+ Learning style
+ Socio-cultural determinants

Advantages of individualized learning
There are several advantages of individualized learning. A few of them are:

+ The more one learn, the smarter one get - being smarter helps one to be more successful and make one more likely to achieve the dreams.
+ The more one learn, the more one can learn - the brain is just like the muscles, and exercising it helps one to increase the brain-power.
+ The more one learn the more knowledgeable one become and know how to do.
+ The more one learn how to learn, the easier it is to learn fresh and new things - a lot of schoolwork and homework is practice to teach one how to learn, and once one get the hang of learning, one will just get better and better at it
+ The more one learn, the better one will get along with others - prejudice comes from fear of the unknown, and the more one learn, the less unknown there will be, so one won't be afraid of it.
+ The learners will get more attention of the facilitator when they learn individually; learners with special needs gets benefitted more.
+ Good for introverts and shy learners.
+ Builds self-confidence.

Limitations of individualized learning

+ Insufficient interaction with peers and adults socially
+ Neglect of norms and values
+ Loneliness
+ Can be boring
+ Requires self-discipline
+ Difficult to test synthesis
+ Can lead to single perceptive
+ Focus on self-interest and personal success
+ Can ignore the success/ failure of others
+ No support system from peers
+ Insufficient knowledge to draw from oneself

5.4 COMPUTER-ASSISTED INSTRUCTION
Most proponents of individualized instruction saw the computer as a way to further improve the design and delivery of individualized instruction - now in an electronic environment. With the advent of the computer came the potential to deliver individualized instruction in a more powerful way. This potential was anticipated long before the proliferation of the home computer. 'A modern computer has a characteristic that is closely parallel to those needed in any educational system and wishes to provide highly individualized instruction.

The specific advantages that the computer could provide:

→ It has a very large memory capacity that can be used to store instructional content material or to generate such material.

→ The computer can perform complex analyses of learner responses.

→ The computer can make decisions based on the assessments of learner performance, matching resources to individual learner needs.

A self-learning technique, usually offline/online, which involves interaction of the learner with programmed instructional materials. Computer-assisted instruction (CAI) is an interactive instructional technique whereby a computer is used to present the instructional material and monitor the learning that takes place. CAI uses a combination of text, graphics, sound and video in enhancing the learning process. The computer has many targets in the classroom, and it can be utilized to help a learner in all areas of the curriculum. CAI refers to the use of the computer as a tool to facilitate and improve instruction. CAI programs use tutorials, drill and practice, simulation, and problem solving approaches to present topics, and they test the learner's understanding.

Coburn defines computer assisted interactions as 'computer applications applied to traditional instruction methods such as drill, tutorial, demonstration, simulation and instructional games'. In CAI, the computer itself selects and presents the right kind of programmed materials for a particular learner with the help of an instruction machine attached. Under CAI, the learner even has the options of putting questions to the computer. There is no single instructional design methodology for developing a CAI programme.

Computer assisted instructional packages are important as the learners learn lessons at their own pace. It takes into account the Piagetian differences across learners rather than treating them as a homogenised entity with the same intellectual and cognitive level. Moreover, children obviously learn differently and better with computers, compared to the traditional facilitator method. Computers motivate children to learn collaboratively, rather than competing with other children. Computer-assisted instruction was first used in education and training during the 1950s. Early work was done by IBM and such people as Gordon Pask and O. M. Moore, but CAI grew rapidly in the 1960s when federal funding for research and development in education and industrial laboratories was implemented.

Four phases in computer assisted interaction

→ Presentation of information
→ Guiding learners interaction with the learning material
→ Practising the learning material
→ Testing their performances in the subject taught.

The four phases are self-explanatory, and the computer may serve any combination of the above said phases of instruction. It is, therefore, important that all the four phases be included in computer assisted interactions. Information can be presented through computers through the aid of pictures, cartoons, documentaries as well as the conventional strategies of a visual descriptive exposition of the said lesson. Learners can be familiarised with the learning material by providing access to the same along with back ground knowledge about what would be taught. Finally, one can test their performance in the subject test by making them practise the learning material through online assignments, games and quizzes.

Computers can be used at every level, beginning from the kinder garden to higher studies. However, one must possess the discretion to teach age appropriate topics while at the same time using age appropriate techniques for its testing. For instance, computer games would be an appropriate technique to test a learner in the seventh or eighth standard. However, it would be a redundant technique in the twelfth standard.

Computers in various educational areas
Computers in preschools and primary schools

- ✈ In primary schools across the globe, facilitators are using many maths instruction and language instruction programmes.
- ✈ This would also involve logic games that aim at instruction problem-solving techniques.
- ✈ The use of computers is comparatively lesser in India than USA, though there have been some E.L.T (English language instruction) software programmes that teach basic forms of sentences.

Computers in secondary and senior secondary classes

- ✈ There is greater flexibility in higher classes as the learners are cognitively brighter and well equipped with computers, which facilitates quizzing and various other forms of educative communication on line. (our use of wikispaces can be seen as an instance of this)
- ✈ Computers present information, ask questions and also evaluates the learners.
- ✈ Poetry is often taught through the use of computers in higher classes. Using a power point presentation, the kids can be made aware of what a 'frown' is along with various other difficult words in the poem.

Computers in vocational education

- ✈ In India, computers are used to present a three dimensional reconstruction of magnetic resonance imaging techniques to understand the anatomic complexity of operative brain lesions and to improve pre-operative surgical planning.
- ✈ A flight training programme in England teaches trainee pilots about the landing procedure for a private light plane.

Computers in non-formal education

- ✈ This involves the use of computers in entertainment and/or education. Documentaries and videos are an important medium through which the masses can be sensitised and educated. Computers play a huge role in this regard.
- ✈ Computers are extensively used in the workplace for maintaining accounts, processing information, writing letters, communicating with others and so on.

Two phases in CAI

CAI comprises of two phases
i) Pre-tutorial phase
ii) Tutorial phase

In the former, the computer gives instructions according to the behaviour of the learner. Some pre-set techniques as well as instructions are there in the computer which must be followed by the learner to get the desired results. There is no feedback in the pre-tutorial phase. In the latter, there are a set of instructions along with a feedback system. There is also a selection unit that accepts the entry behaviour. Following this, there is a control unit. The tutorial phase has a feedback system which pre-tutorial phase does not have.

To conclude, one can say that computers have permeated every facet of human life including education. Computer assisted interaction should not and cannot replace the role of a conventional facilitator and people who think it can fall into the trap of over simplifications. A computer merely acts as a facilitator which aids the facilitator and makes his/her job relatively easy. Similarly, to uncritically dismiss the role of computers in education as superfluous is another oversimplification. The various exemplars demonstrate that its effect is far from superficial. Computers possess immense potential, and the need of the hour is to utilise this potential without being either over critical or over dependant on the same.

CAI and systems approach

Computer is a hardware approach of educational technology, while system approach is a software approach. In CAI, there is a relationship with cognitive skills while in system approach or programmed instruction, there is a development of cognitive as well as psychomotor skills.

Advantages of computer assisted instruction (CAI)

→ Immediate feedback: the immediate feedback provided by interactive terminals keeps learners interacting and eager to keep trying.
→ Active participation: even weaker learners are obliged to participate actively. They often remain passive in lectures.
→ No annoyance: the computer will wait patiently for an answer and does not express annoyance with wrong response.
→ Graphics facility: interactive graphics make it possible to sample many more illustrations.
→ Mathematical calculations: mathematical calculations can be done as fast for realistic exemplars and can be solved analytically.
→ Accurate data: large volumes of data can be handled with accuracy.
→ Enrichment of course: this technique provides enrichment of course through added variety.

5.5 SIGNIFICANCE OF 'SIMULATIONS' AND 'EDUCATIONAL GAMES' AS FACILITATORS IN LEARNING

Simulation is a language learning model which allows learners to express themselves to their peers in a group setting, groups comprising usually three or four. It is related to role play, but in simulation learners retain their own personas and are not required to pretend to be someone else. In role play one learner might be told that she is a supermarket checkout assistant whilst another is a customer. Learners might also be given fairly tight guidelines outlining the nature of their exchange or the language points they are expected to cover.

In simulation the group members would not be expected to place emphasis only on a given set of language points. Effective communication should be the outcome, rather than strictly correct use of vocabulary and structures. The group is given a task which may last a single period or stretch over a number of sessions. These tasks may range from fairly short to long-term, more wide-ranging as well as complex .The length of the simulation need not be connected to the complexity of the language required to carry it out, as the language skills which learners bring with them to the exercise are what determines its linguistic complexity. At the end of the exercise the group will have arrived at some decision or series of decisions and choices which they will be expected to explain and justify. However, the process of the exercise is of at least as great importance as the product in the sense that the linguistic interaction among the learners will determine its effectiveness and success. In order to succeed; a simulation should be underpinned by a sense of reality or should create a brand fresh and new reality. Ideally, it should be relevant to the lives and interests of the learners who are in charge, with the facilitator unobtrusively monitoring the proceedings. This feature of simulation increases learners' autonomy and motivation, and lowers their anxiety levels since they are interacting as equals within a small group of their peers rather than performing for the facilitator and class as a whole.

Importance of educational games in learning

Educational computer games for middle school learners can help them understand the basic concepts in a fun filled way. We often observe that learners are totally bored of attending the lectures of facilitators and learning there without much practical exposure. Educational computer games will provide them with the much needed recreation. However, these games cannot be a substitute for classroom learning and that the lectures and games should be arranged as per the convenience of learners and facilitators. Many of the educational pc games are thought provoking and help learners learn logical and analytical thinking effectively. Since logical thinking is required in all streams and branches of formal education, these games can prove to be very useful in the years to come. The facilitators can organize educational games, competitions so that the children take these games seriously. However, there are some suggestions on which educational computer games should be introduced to the kids. The games which have violence or some stuff which is harmful for the learners should not be recommended at all. This is because these games will be misguiding the learners instead of helping them. The facilitators should check for the quality and utility of the games before they encourage the learners to try them. Therefore, playing game can be fun but playing educational game can not only bring one a lot of fun, but also help one develop some useful skills which are good for one.

We believe that to address these challenges, we should look towards developing:

+ Fresh and new models for designing relevant curricula: We envisage a system that encourages the mass participation of experts, facilitators and learners in shaping and updating curricula in a timely manner.
+ Fresh and new models for authoring training material and instruction aids: We envisage a system that allows facilitators and learners to comment

and discuss sections of textbooks, link supplementary material for further study, share lectures, exercises, assignments, tests and so on. We also see the participatory development of training material for helping facilitators and administrators update and enhance their skills.

→ Fresh and new models for providing access to instruction aids: We envisage a system in which every facilitator is able to access and used instruction aids developed anywhere and by anyone.

→ Fresh and new models for instructing learners: We envisage a system that can provide flexible ways of instructing learners in the face of socioeconomic pressure that make it difficult for learners to attend regular classes and systemic pressure that have resulted in a shortage of qualified facilitator.

5.6 ROLE OF VARIOUS AIDS PROVIDED BY EDUCATIONAL TECHNOLOGY IN THE CLASSROOM ACCORDING TO VYGOTSKY

Cognitive development means trying to grow and exercise thinking skills not acquire information. Academic activities like 'brain quest' help child get smarter, but they do not necessarily grow their cognitive skills, although some of the spatial games and riddles are an exception. Real cognition is not adding more content, but more structure. It is not information but the neural infrastructure that makes the content come alive- connections, conclusions, etc. So one want games which encourage comprehension (what and why?), analysis (breaking information down), synthesis (putting information together), and evaluation (so what? Or is it good?). Don't confuse making the kid 'smarter' with exercising their brain. Of course the two go together, but there are specific ways to get the thinking skills to stretch and grow that strategy games/toys force, while academic learning does not. One doesn't have to buy stuff if one doesn't want to, but if one doesn't, one will need to make up for it with even more verbal one-on-one time. Kids this age thrive on skill-building.

Most cognitive development takes place in tandem with language so that the talking to the child with more reasoning-based or refined analysis will teach the child how to reason/analyse. But don't confuse this with the child's talking (expressive) ability, which may not match their cognitive ability. Three year old boys are ready to learn this stuff, even if they can't talk. This is easy to forget. Talk through whom/what/where/when/why/how as if they understood it all. One will be amazed how much it will start coming back to one by the time they're four and five.

Classroom applications of Vygotsky theory

Vygotsky's concept of the zone of proximal development is based on the idea that development is defined both by what a child can do independently and by what the child can do when assisted by an adult or more competent peer (Daniels, 1995; Wertsch, 1991). Knowing both levels of Vygotsky's zone is useful for facilitators, for these levels indicate where the child is at a given moment as well as where the child is going. The zone of proximal development has several implications for instruction in the classroom.

According to Vygotsky, for the curriculum to be developmentally appropriate, the facilitator must plan activities that encompass not only what children are capable of doing on their own but what they can learn with the help of others (Karpov & Haywood, 1998).

Vygotsky's theory does not mean that anything can be taught to any child. Only instruction and activities that fall within the zone enhance and support development. For an instance, if a child cannot identify the sounds in a word even after many prompts, the child may not get benefitted immediately from instruction in this skill. Practice of previously known skills and introduction of concepts that are too difficult and complex have tiny positive impact. Facilitators can use information about both levels of Vygotsky's zone of proximal development in organizing classroom activities in the following ways

→ Instruction can be planned to provide practice in the zone of proximal development for individual children or for groups of children. For an instance, hints and prompts that helped children during the assessment could form the basis of instructional activities.

→ Cooperative learning activities can be planned with groups of children at different levels who can help each other learn.

→ Scaffolding (Wood, Bruner, & Ross, 1976) is a tactic for helping the child in his or her zone of proximal development in which the adult provides hints and prompts at different levels. In scaffolding, the adult does not simplify the task, but the role of the learner is simplified through the graduated intervention of the facilitator (Greenfield, 1984).

For an instance, a child might be shown coins to represent each sound in a word (e.g., three coins for the three sounds in 'man'). To master this word, the child might be asked to place a coin on the table to show each sound in a word, and finally the child might identify the sounds without the coins. When the adult provides the child with coins, the adult provides a scaffold to help the child move from assisted to unassisted success at the task (Spector, 1992). In a high school laboratory science class, a facilitator might provide scaffolding by first giving learners detailed guides to carrying out experiments, then giving them brief outlines that they might use to structure experiments, and finally asking them to set up experiments entirely on their own.

The following activities were chosen with particular criteria in mind: they should be easy to implement; they should provide a loose structure for learner practice with readings, lecture material, or their own writing; they should not require group grades; and they should require learner preparation, not for a grade, but in order to participate in the class community. In addition, each of these activities involves various possible sizes of groups and various amounts of in-class, group activity. For this reason, the collaborative activities listed here are suited to classes of varying size and format. The first activity is highly recommended for the first day of class to accustom the learners to active participation; the other activities can be implemented at any time.

a) First day of class: Groups of 4-5 learners discuss and develop questions they have about the class, its structure, content, requirements, and so on. The syllabus is distributed, and groups review their questions in light of the syllabus. The class reconvenes to discuss any existing questions and to review groups' preconceptions and thoughts about the course (activity from Kadel & Keehner, 1994)

b) Encouraging reading outside the classroom: A reading review sheet of 3-12 questions is distributed before a given reading assignment. The day the reading is to be discussed; small groups begin the class by comparing their answers to the review questions. Groups might be asked to pinpoint a particularly difficult question and to reach a consensus on the answer to report to the class.

Alongside this activity's primary goal of increasing the number of learners completing reading assignments in a timely fashion, the collaborative group work gives more learners' confidence to participate in class-wide discussion. Learners are given intrinsic motivation for coming to class prepared lest they be unprepared for the small group discussion with their peers. These activities can be used for ensuring preparation for any in-class activity (activity from Kadel & Keehner, 1994; Hawkes 1991).

5.7 SMALL GROUP LEARNING

Small group learning is a useful educational approach. The group work has to be carefully planned and frequently requires a facilitator to ensure group progress. In addition the group function and the learning that takes place needs to be assessed and evaluated. The material learned is just as important as the group's ability to achieve a common goal. Facilitator skills are important and require the facilitator to ensure that both the task is achieved and the group functioning is maintained.

Small group learning allows learners to the develop problem solving ability, interpersonal, presentational and communication skills, thus are all beneficial to life outside the classroom. These generic skills are difficult to develop in isolation and require feedback and interaction with other individuals, as well.

Principles related to small group learning strategy

+ Learner ownership of learning activities;
+ Learner understanding, relevance & significance (of both content & process);
+ Learner developing specific interactional skills;
+ Active participation among group members;
+ A faculty leader who facilitates rather than dominates discussion;
+ A focus on application of knowledge or problem-solving;

Overall: Creating a stimulating & enjoyable learning environment that is perceived by learners as beneficial for their future.

Advantages of small group learning in class

If we divide the large class into small groups then it can give learners more opportunities to participate, work as a group, and receive more personalized instruction. Here are several advantages of starting small group learning or workshops

+ Hands-on learning opportunities: Small group stations afford learners the chance to work with their hands in labs, small experiments, puzzles, and even physical activities. A smaller group means that each learner will have more of a chance to take an active role in the activity, and the station becomes a hands-on challenge for the learners, rather than a demonstration by the instructor. Learners will generally remember what they learn through these stations better than if they had learned the same concepts from a demonstration because they are actively involved.
+ Group focus: Small group learning is heavily focused on group work, which is very different than the traditional lecture-based format of the classroom.

Because of this setup, learners will feel more motivated to involve themselves in their education, ask questions, and participate.

➤ Peer learning: Often, learners who have enjoyed certain workshops in the past will revisit the class in later years and assist in leading a small group station, giving the fresh and new learners a chance to learn from their peers. This kind of learning can sometimes be more effective, as many learners feel more comfortable asking older peers for help or more detailed explanations. The older learners also have the opportunity to learn better instruction skills as a result.

These aspects of small group learning will ultimately provide learners with a fresh and new and different approach to learning that could be highly beneficial.

The small group activities in class room
a) Case studies

Case studies are commonly used with business learners. Case studies are descriptions of common management problems. Often a case study is modelled after a real incident but with the names changed and other identifiable elements altered. Using real exemplars from company history can lead to participants listening to the actual outcomes once they have provided their solution to the situation. Choosing case studies that explore the topic by working through issues leads participants to learn actively and retain key concepts.

b) Role playing

Role playing is when participants experience the different roles to play in a scenario. This kind of activity works well while practicing communication style and techniques such as interviewing skills, performance management, conversations or customer service techniques. Creating a scenario that mimics an actual situation that the learners will experience in the job allows participants to practice reacting and acting in a safe setting.

c) Timed group challenges

Assigning a timed challenge as a small group activity can create a buzz of energy as groups have to solve a difficult issue in a crunch. Clearly define the issue and the time allotment so that participants understand that quick decisions are expected. Ask the groups to record their action plan to resolve the issue and discuss it with the larger group to gather feedback on their approach.

d) Debates

Debates are great activities to understand the advantages and limitations of complex subjects especially ones with potential ethical dilemmas such as conflict of interest scenarios or customer service exemplars, where the customer's actions are questionable.

e) Simulations

Simulating a work environment to test product knowledge or understanding of processes is a great way to keep learning active. Simulations can be as elaborate as an exact replica of a store or processing plant or as simple as a mock-up of a work environment. To keep training active it is important to use techniques that challenge the learners to use their experience on the job to direct the learning. Case studies, role playing, timed group challenges, debates and simulations are some of the ways to engage learners in the topic.

5.8 WHOLE GROUP LEARNING

Whole group learning is whole class instruction in which facilitators present a lesson to the whole class with tiny differentiation in either content or assessment for learner's ability.

It has been recognized that diversity in culture, experience, and learning style fosters in every learner a unique set of educational needs. The ideal response would be to provide every learner with a totally individualized curriculum; but economic and other considerations have historically made this model impractical. Most of us grew up with the more common model: one facilitator presenting content and practice activities to learner group of ten or more all at once, typically with knowledge acquisition and skill building as the primary outcomes and lecture as the primary means of delivery. This scenario and a number of variations of it are often referred to as 'whole-class instruction'.

- ✦ Whole group instruction is designed to involve all learners at all times with limited available technology
- ✦ The learners are immersed in the technology-connected curriculum.
- ✦ The facilitator is the only one with hands-on technology.
- ✦ As the facilitator uses software that is shared with the learners through the use of a scan converter, the learners demonstrate interaction with the technology.
- ✦ Learner interaction may be achieved by using some kind of data collection or fact gathering form.
- ✦ Simply watching does not demonstrate that all learners are interacting with the technology or the curriculum. During the whole group, all learners must show interaction with the technology that is used by the facilitator.
- ✦ Use the whole group activities modelled during the in tech classes to guide the planning of lessons with this requirement

Whole group learning

Target of whole group learning

The target of whole class instruction is that all learners are presented with a series of learning tasks to allow them to acquire and/or practice their learning. The pace of instruction is such that all learners can master it. Learning is then assessed using standardised measures such as graded assignments or topic tests.

Guiding principles of whole group learning and instruction

- Every learner has the right to learn.
- Instructions must be rigorous and relevant.
- Targeted assessment drives instruction and affects learning.
- Learning is a collaborative responsibility.
- Learners bring strength and experiences to learning.
- Responsive environments engage learners.

For learners

- Learner's prior knowledge can help or hinder learning.
- How learners organize knowledge influences how they learn and apply what they know.
- Learner's motivation determines, directs, and sustains what they do to learn.
- To develop mastery, learners must acquire component skills, practice integrating them, and know when to apply what they have learned.
- Goal-directed practice coupled with targeted feedback enhances the quality of learner's learning.
- Learner's current level of development interacts with the social, emotional, and intellectual climate of the course to impact learning.
- To become self-directed learners, learners must learn to monitor and adjust their approaches to learning.

For facilitators

- Effective instruction involves acquiring relevant knowledge about learners and using that knowledge to inform the course design and classroom instruction.
- Effective instruction involves aligning the three major components of instruction: learning objectives, assessments, and instructional activities.
- Effective instruction involves articulating explicit expectations regarding learning objectives and policies.
- Effective instruction involves prioritizing the knowledge and skills we choose to focus on.
- Effective instruction involves recognizing and overcoming expert blind spots.
- Effective instruction involves adopting appropriate instruction roles to support learning goals.
- Effective instruction involves progressively refining course based on reflection and feedback.

Different instructional strategies for whole group learning

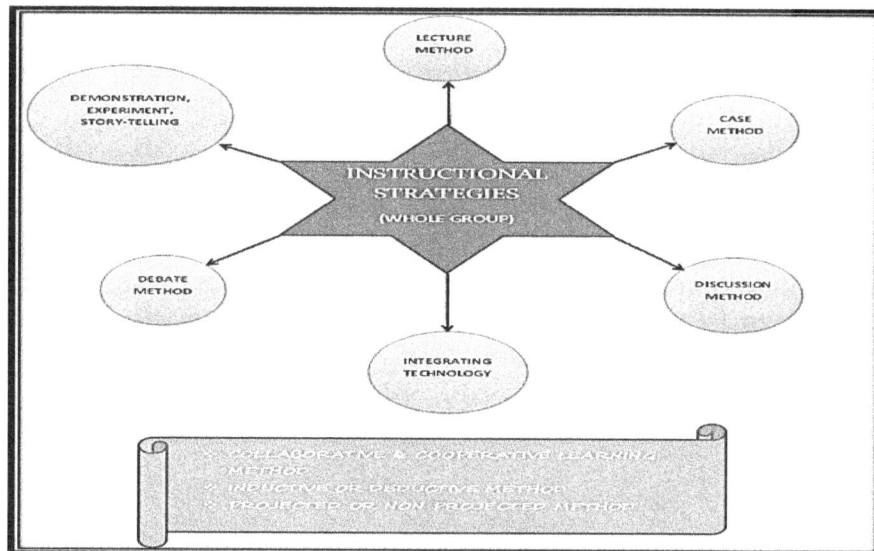

a. Lecture: For many years, the lecture method was the most widely used instructional strategy in college classrooms. Nearly 80% of all US college classrooms in the late 1970s reported using some form of the lecture method to teach learners. Although the usefulness of other instruction strategies is being widely examined today, the lecture still remains an important way to communicate information.

Used in conjunction with active learning instruction strategies, the traditional lecture can be an effective way to achieve instructional goals. The advantages of the lecture approach are that it provides a way to communicate a large amount of information to many listeners maximizes instructor control and is non-threatening to learners. The limitations are that lecturing minimizes feedback from learners, assumes an unrealistic level of learner understanding and comprehension, and often disengages learners from the learning process causing information to be quickly forgotten.

The following recommendations can help make the lecture approach more effective

- Fit the lecture to the audience
- Focus the topic - remember one cannot cover everything in one lecture
- Prepare an outline that includes 5-9 major points one want to cover in one lecture
- Organize the points for clarity
- Select appropriate exemplars or illustrations.
- Present more than one side of an issue and be sensitive to other perspectives.
- Repeat points when necessary.
- Be aware of the audience and notice their feedback
- Be enthusiastic - one don't have to be an entertainer but one should be excited about.

b. Case method

Providing an opportunity to learners so that they can apply what they learn in the classroom to real-life experiences has proven to be an effective way of both disseminating and integrating knowledge. The case method is an instructional strategy that engages learners in active discussion about issues and problems inherent in practical application. It can highlight fundamental dilemmas or critical issues and provide a format for role playing ambiguous or controversial scenarios. Course content cases can come from a variety of sources. Many faculties have transformed current events or problems reported through print or broadcast media into critical learning experiences that illuminate the complexity of finding solutions to critical social problems. The case study approach works well in cooperative learning or role playing environments to stimulate critical

thinking and awareness of multiple perspectives.

c. Discussion

There are a variety of ways to stimulate discussion. For an instance, some faculty begins a lesson with a whole group discussion to refresh learner's memories about the assigned reading(s). Other faculty finds it helpful to have learner's list critical points or emerging issues, or generate a set of questions stemming from the assigned reading(s). These strategies can also be used to help focus large and small group discussions.

Obviously, a successful class discussion involves planning on the part of the instructor and preparation on the part of the learners. Instructors should communicate this commitment to the learners on the first day of class by clearly articulating course expectations. Just as the instructor carefully plans the learning experience, the learners must comprehend the assigned reading and show up for class on time, ready to learn.

d. Integrating technology

Today, educators realize that computer literacy is an important part of a learner's education. Integrating technology into a course curriculum, when appropriate, is proving to be valuable for enhancing and extending the learning experience for faculty and learners. Many faculties have found electronic mail to be a useful way to enhance and support learner/learner or faculty/learner communication between class meetings. Others use on-line notes to extend topic discussions and explore critical issues with learners and colleagues, or discipline-specific software to increase learner understanding of difficult concepts.

e. Debate

Classroom debates are based on controversial issues—issues that have advantages and limitations. Debates are learner-centred; facilitators take on the role of active facilitators. This strategy requires higher-level thinking. Learners learn information about an issue or idea, take a position, relate their position to others, and defend it. Learners must learn to listen to the opposing side and refute the arguments proposed in a convincing manner. They must learn to manipulate knowledge to appeal to both the factual and emotional needs of their audience. Debate is a strategy that requires a high level of thought, but it is effective only when there is quality classroom management in place. Facilitators must be active facilitators, monitoring for appropriate conduct until learners have learned to function within the guidelines of classroom debate.

f. Demonstrations, experiments, story-telling

Demonstrations, experiments place the facilitator in the role of 'expert' providing knowledge or skills by demonstrating a step-by-step method. Demonstrations are a form of 'show and tell.' Story telling is a method used for instruction language and can be used for instruction history.

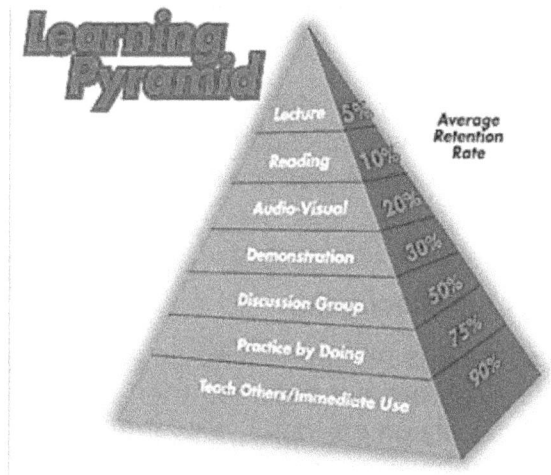

Learning Pyramid

Criteria for choosing an appropriate media for a whole group

The following criteria should be kept in mind while selecting an appropriate media for instruction to the whole group:

+ The subject taught.
+ Cultural appropriateness.
+ Availability of infrastructure.
+ Cognitive level of the learners.
+ Awareness of the facilitator

Recapitulation

The facilitator needs to- select one strategy that fits best, have complete preparation for successful implementation, train learners in appropriate conduct and response, implement the strategy, and monitor for the success during implementation, make adjustments as needed, and check learner comprehension after completion. Interestingly enough, the level of classroom management is quite varied. As the level of learner involvement increases, so does the need for quality classroom management. Of course, anytime learners are working with materials that might be dangerous, the level of management increases as well, and strategies that include 'hot topics' require closer monitoring. At all times, learners need a safe environment in order to make comments and ask questions. The willingness to select strategies wisely; monitor, adjust, and change strategies when needed; and consistently check for quality of understanding are all options that enhance the facilitator's effectiveness.

Advantages of whole group discussion

+ Whole group discussions provide for greater interaction between facilitator and learners.
+ Instructors maintain a greater control over what is being taught because they are able to steer the discussion.
+ Auditory learners find them appealing to their learning styles.
+ Facilitators can check on what learners are retaining through questions posed.
+ Whole group discussion is comfortable for many facilitators because it is a modified form of lecture.
+ Learners have a tendency to stay focused on the lesson because they might be called on to answer questions.
+ Learner may feel more comfortable asking questions during whole group discussions.

Limitations of whole group discussion

+ Whole group discussions require setting up and enforcing ground rules for learners. If these rules are not enforced then there is a possibility that the discussion could quickly go off-topic.
+ Learners who are weak in note-taking skills will have trouble understanding what they should remember from group discussions. This is even more so than in lectures in many cases because not only the facilitator but fellow learners are talking about the lesson.
+ Some learners may not feel comfortable being put on the spot during a whole group discussion.

5.9 COLLABORATIVE LEARNING VERSUS INDIVIDUALIZED LEARNING

Dewey described learning as an interactive cycle of invention, observation, reflection and action (Scion, 1992). Individualized learning may be defined as the capacity to build knowledge through individual reflection about external stimuli and sources; and through the personal re-elaboration of individual knowledge and experience in the light of interaction with others and the environment. In modern day society, the rapid change brought about by innovation, increased levels of competition, and unsuitability of other forms of training emphasize that this ability needs to be developed much more than in the past. In educational technology, instructional strategies are made for learning through computer also. Computer assisted instructions are for whole group learning as well as small group.

Collaborative learning and individualized learning: Individualized learning is viewed as the capacity to learn, how to learn and knowledge acquisition as an active and continuous process that results in changes in behaviour and a different perception of the world around us. It is therefore necessary to provide tools and methodologies that stimulate the development of these capacities. The potential that multimedia and network technologies provide for the development for individualized learning skills are within four different adult populations- facilitators, trainers, company employees and public servants.

The constructivist theory of learning holds that learners construct knowledge by understanding fresh and new information and assimilating fresh and new information with previously obtained information which is an active process. Each learner arrives at a learning site with some pre-existing level of understanding. Although the constructivist model encourages learning by doing, which one might argue is a group learning dynamic, but individualized learning is a large part of the constructivist model. Individuals within the group are exercising their own learning and contributing whatever they learn, to the group.

Segall said that knowledge is deconstructions, reconstructions and co- constructions that emerge as a result of the interaction between what is already known and what is yet to be known again, in a fresh and new form i.e. when a person is learning individually they take all the information they already have and connect it to what they are experiencing at that moment in time to form fresh and new knowledge. The requisites for individualized learning are perception of a need, identification of an object that may satisfy that need; and identification of a strategy for reaching that objective. Generally speaking, a few people have an innate capacity for individualized learning. The strategy for reaching the objective may call for strong commitment and radical change in normal behaviour.

5.10 INDIVIDUALIZED LEARNING VERSUS WHOLE GROUP LEARNING

The relative importance of 'individualized' and/or 'group learning' depends on the context in which the learning is carried out along with the aim and objectives of instruction. In case one needs to engage in collaborative learning, where the learners are active constructors of knowledge, group learning is better. On the other hand, if the concept in question is a difficult one and group instruction would not be feasible for it then, individualized learning is better.

Individualized learning is a person relying on himself/herself for a knowledge base. Contrast this with whole group learning where multiple knowledge and stimuli (from the group) can give the individual opportunities to learn fresh and new things or inspire that individual with 'hints' to help him/ her learn. Individuals can learn with three modalities/styles of activity, the ear or audio processing' the eye or visual processing and the hand or kinetic processing. Usually, individuals have a proclivity for one or two of these learning styles. The computer is an excellent sample of the use of all three learning styles and is therefore very engaging to most learners. The individual is the building block of the group, and knowledge base of one, that is where he/she is limited. The knowledge base of the group is only limited by the size of the group.

At present, group learning is preferable to individualized learning. But individualized learning provides opportunity for authentic learning based on cognitive style and self-learning approach.

EXEMPLARY QUESTIONS

1. (a) What are the learning theory underpinnings of collaborative learning?
   (b) Describe the elements of true collaborative learning.
   (c) Describe at least two strategies of collaborative learning which one can use for instruction the subject. Illustrate with suitable exemplars.

2. Do you think individualized learning is better than whole group learning? Justify the answer. What principles does one think would guide for using computer in individualized learning?

3. What is necessary for individualized instruction with CAI?

4. (a) Discuss the significance of 'educational games' and 'simulations' as facilitators in learning.

   (b) As a facilitator, how would one address the challenges of using education technology in a typical Indian classroom?

5. Vygotsky emphasizes the role of social interaction in the cognitive development of learners. In this context, what is the role of various aids provided by educational technology in the classroom?

UNIT - 6

SYSTEM APPROACH IN EDUCATION

This unit deals with concept, components and scope of system approach in education

'There can be infinite uses of the computer and of new age technology, but if teachers themselves are not able to bring it into the classroom and make it work, then it fails.'

— **Nancy Kassebaum**

Unit 6
System Approach in Education

6.1 SYSTEM

A system is expressed as an active and independent group of items forming a unified whole. It can also be understood as a methodically arranged set of ideas, principles and methods. From a systems approach view, instruction with technology involves four major components: the learners, the instructor, course content, and technology tools. An examination of each component raises a set of issues that we need to consider in order to make technology integration as successful as possible. For example, content can be examined in terms of learning outcomes and the discipline being taught. Instructors can think of their own experience with technology, the amount of time they have for planning and instruction, and their view of their role in the instruction and learning process. We need to think carefully about our learners, their exposure and access to technology as well as their preferred learning styles. Finally, we can turn to the technology itself and analyse it according to its functions. This approach to instruction and learning with technology assumes that the four component parts are integrated and that changes in one part will require adjustments to the other three in order to achieve the same goals.

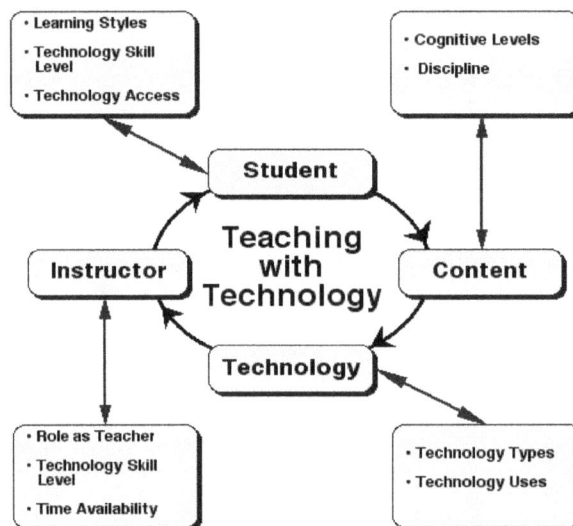

Fig. 1. A model of instruction with technology

Meaning of the term 'system'

A system may be defined as a dynamic, complex, integrated whole consisting of self-regulating pattern of inter-related and interdependent elements organised to achieve a set of pre-determined and specified objectives.

System thinkers consider that :

↣ A system is a dynamic and complex whole, interacting as a structured functional unit;

↣ Energy, material and information flow among the different elements that compose the system;

→ A system is a community situated within an environment;

→ Energy, material and information flow from and to the surrounding environment via semi-permeable membranes or boundaries;

→ Systems are often composed of entities seeking equilibrium but can exhibit oscillating, chaotic or exponential behaviour.

A holistic system is any set (group) of interdependent or temporally interacting parts. Parts are generally systems themselves and are composed of other parts, just as systems are generally parts of other systems.

Types of system

→ Physical or abstract system
→ Open or closed system
→ Man made
→ Formal information system
→ Informal
→ Computer based information system
→ Hard or soft system
→ Evolutionary system

An explanation of hard, soft and evolutionary system

→ Hard system— involving simulation, often using computers and the techniques of operations research/management program. Useful for problems that can justifiably be quantified. However it cannot easily take into account unquantifiable variables (opinions, culture, politics, etc.), and may treat people as being passive, rather than having complex motivations.

→ Soft system— for systems that cannot easily be quantified, especially those involving people holding multiple and conflicting frames of reference. Useful for understanding motivations, viewpoints, and interactions and addressing qualitative as well as quantitative dimensions of problem situations. Soft systems are a field that utilizes foundation methodological work developed by Peter Check land, Brian Wilson and their colleagues at Lancaster University. Morphological analysis is a complementary method for structuring and analysing non-quantifiable problem complexes.

→ Evolutionary system —Benathy developed a methodology which is applicable to the design of complex social systems. This technique integrates critical systems inquiry with soft system methodologies. Evolutionary system, similar to dynamic system is understood as open, complex systems, but with the capacity to evolve over time. Benathy uniquely integrated the interdisciplinary perspectives of systems research (including, chaos, complexity, and cybernetics), cultural anthropology, evolutionary system and others.

Parameters of systems

→ Input-refers to what is put into the system
→ Process-is what goes on in the system
→ Output-is the product of the system

+ Control
+ Environmental context-refers to all those conditions, factors and constraints related with the physical and social environment in which the system operates.
+ Feedback-process of comparing a sample of the output with the input

Characteristics of a system

+ General term: a system is a general term applicable to various fields including instruction and education
+ Self-governing structure: is self-regulating, self-maintaining structure
+ Dynamic and whole: is a dynamic complex and integrated whole
+ Systemic organization: system represents a complex but systematic organization of interrelated elements or parts.
+ Specified role: all elements in system have respective roles which have to be specified in relation to each other and with respect to the purpose.
+ Effective functioning: system as whole functions more effectively and achieves better results than any sub system or combination of effects of individual's parts.
+ Interactions: all parts of systems interact in a way that all contribute to the achievement of the overall goal of the system.

Following are the characteristics of an educational system:

+ The concept of a system: It refers to a dynamic order of parts and processes in mutual interaction, e.g. Human body as a physiological system. Our body has various parts like heart, brain, liver, kidney, pancreas etc. All these parts called components are inter-related and interact with each other.
+ A system is a relative concept: Classroom as a system can be studied as a subsystem of a bigger system (suprasystem) termed as school. But if consider school as system then classroom will be its subsystem and community will be its suprasystem. A facilitator or a learner can be studied as a subsystem of a class or an independent system. Thus the terms, micro or macro, subsystem or suprasystem are always used in relation with each other.
+ A system can be closed or open: Closed system does not accept fresh and new information and which has become detached from interfering with other system which is dependent upon it, e.g. presently available auto driver or cars are closed system, as they will not change their route or direction is case of traffic or blockage. It means it is not at all interacting with its environment. On the other hand an open system is one which accepts information from its interfering system and is capable of adapting to fresh and new circumstances. E.g. A refrigerator with thermostat is a relatively open system compared to a motor car as it can change its adjustment as per changing voltage and current supply i.e. its environment. A facilitator should always be an open system, ready to take input from its surrounding. He can change the presentation style of a content to suit the best abilities of his learner. He/she should always be ready to take feedback from the learner and himself/herself to bring a change to make the presentation such that it is best for its learner.

- ✈ All systems have goals: The goals may be of different degrees. The dynamics of the system, the transformation of the input into output- the processes, the function, the operation of system are geared toward achieving these goals.
- ✈ All systems have constraints: A system does not work in a vacuum. It has an interface- is surrounded by other system- environment. Some of these external system or their components may facilitate, while some may inhibit the processes within a given system. Under consideration, a facilitator in a college in Mumbai, who has just returned from US and is quite well versed in his subject finds that learners are not listening to him. Later he discovered that his Yankee pronunciation was his main constraint in interacting with learners.
- ✈ A system can have alternatives: When a system analyst designs a system he is usually aware of the fact that under different conditions, different processes, different interrelationships of the components would produce the desirable result, if nothing else, he always has to battle against the time and cost constraints. Under this situation he provides alternatives, which are different configuration of components of a system.
- ✈ A system is based on feedback: One of the very important contributions of educational cybernetics is a science of control and coordination that helps to see and evaluate the instruction learning process. In educational cybernetics there are provisions to actually experience what was considered as black box by the followers of behaviouristic approach (e.g. B. F. Skinner). Here there are specific algorithms for both the facilitator and the learner which defines the process in its own ways, in the sense, that what should be the first step and what will follow it and how it will end. It here refers to learner or facilitator. The process of instruction and learning can be evaluated based on these instruction learning algorithms. For a system to work efficiently it is very essential to have periodical feedback if regular feedback is not possible.
- ✈ Revisability of the system: All open systems have procedures for feedback and revision of the course (midcourse correction). As seen before cybernetics as a science gives importance to corrective value of the feedback. The revision could be in terms of repeating the steps, changing the sequence, changing the components and their interrelationships. In other words, a system designer never considers his design as the final or eternal one. Evaluation and revision is an integral part of being the system designer.

6.2 EVOLUTION OF THE SYSTEM APPROACH

The systems approach integrates the analytic and the synthetic method, encompassing both holism and reductionism. It was first proposed under the name of 'general system theory' by the biologist Ludwig von Bertalanffy. Von Bertalanffy noted that all systems studied by physicists are closed: they do not interact with the outside world. When a physicist makes a model of the solar system, of an atom, or of a pendulum, he or she assumes that all masses, particles, forces that affect the system are included in the model. It is as if the rest of the universe does not exist. This makes it possible to calculate future states with perfect accuracy, since all necessary information is known.

However, as a biologist Bertalanffy kfresh and new that such an assumption is simply impossible for most practical phenomena. Separate a living organism from its surroundings and it will die shortly due to lack of oxygen, water and food. Organisms are open systems: they cannot survive without continuously exchanging matter and energy with their environment. The peculiarity of open systems is that they interact with other systems outside of themselves. This interaction has two components: input, that what enters the system from the outside, and output, that what leaves the system for the environment. In order to speak about the inside and the outside of a system, we need to be able to distinguish between the systems itself and its environment. System and environment are generally separated by a boundary. For example, for living systems the skin plays the role of the boundary. The output of a system is generally a direct or indirect result from the input. What comes out needs to have got in first? However, the output is usually quite different from the input: the system is not just a passive tube, but an active processor. For example, the food, drink and oxygen we take in, leave our body as urine, excrements and carbon dioxide.

Thus, over the years as research continued and many other thinkers gave their ideas; the theory of Bertalanffy emerged as the 'system approach'.

Foundation of system approach

The concept of system approach is very simple. It is a wholesome method to deal with any planning be it of a institute or organization or a school .it takes into account several features important for the system to work ,e.g. When a patient suffering from a stomach ache goes to a doctor for taking medicine, doctor does not give medicine just like that, he first asks the previous history of the patient to check if he has the same problem earlier and also if he is allergic to any medicine, then whether he has some other ailment along with that, then age and physiological state of that patient and his genetic background. After looking at all these factors a doctor prescribes a medicine; and that is the system approach of the doctor for the patients.

With respect to any institution the system approach works towards development of all areas like manpower, finance, beneficiaries, place, area or location, materials and machines input, technologies needed, technicians required, profit, loss, etc. So system approach is an integrated wholesome approach for any system (small or big). System approach is the latest concept in the technology of education.it was initially developed in the areas of industry and management, but subsequently it was introduced in education for managing its different aspects. Historically, the concept of system approach emerged during the world war (second) as a result of research and development in problem-solving efficiency, analysis, and most significantly the development of complex machine system in the industry. Thus, system approach is an operational planning concept.

Recently, system approach has been introduced in the field of education to manage, control and improve the process and products of education. It focusses first upon the learner and the performances required of him. Only then it makes decisions regarding course content, learning experiences and the most effective media and instructional technologies. It is concerned with all elements of instruction including media.

The systems thinking approach incorporates several tenets

+ Interdependence of objects and their attributes - independent elements can never constitute a system
+ Holism - emergent properties not possible to detect by analysis should be possible to define by a holistic approach
+ Goal seeking- systemic interaction must result in some goal or final state
+ Inputs and outputs- in a closed system inputs are determined once and constant; in an open system additional inputs are admitted from the environment
+ Transformation of inputs into outputs- this is the process by which the goals are obtained
+ Regulation- a method of feedback is necessary for the system to operate predictably
+ Hierarchy- complex wholes are made up of smaller subsystems
+ Differentiation- specialized units perform specialized functions
+ Equifinality- alternative ways of attaining the same objectives (convergence)
+ Entropy- the amount of feedback necessary for the system to operate predictable
+ Multifinality - attaining alternative objectives from the same inputs (divergence)

A useful way to understand the behaviour of groups of people in a school is to use a systems approach. A whole school or a department within a school or even a team within the school can be considered a system. The approach encourages us to see people not as isolated units but as functioning within a wider social system. We begin to see how change in one part of the system will affect all other components.

In a school system, every part is linked, like the working of administrative department has to function in sync with the instruction staff and other parts of the school. For proper functioning of the school it becomes necessary that all parts function in perfect co-ordination. If any one of the part is not in tandem with others then this creates randomness and may hinder the effectiveness of the school.

The following table shows how systems approach thinking differs from the usually followed person centred approach.

Individual centred approach	Systems approach
Individuals who make errors are careless, at fault, reckless	Poor organisational design sets people up to fail
Blame and punishment	Focus on the system rather than the individual
Remove individual is equal to improving the safety	Change the system is equal to improving the safety

We always work in a system. Even if we are alone our body is a perfect example of a system, there are several body organs in us which coordinate at different levels within themselves as well as in cooperation with other body organ systems.

There are three types of system approach

- → Technical system approach
- → Behavioural system approach
- → Socio-technical system approach

6.3 SYSTEM APPROACH TO EDUCATION

Different views given for system approach to education are

In view of Keshav and Michean, it is defined as techniques which aim at finding the most efficient and economically intelligent method for solving the problems of education scientifically.

As per Neil's view it is defined as a particular method of exploration to find effective ways of talking about designing and organising learning situation in practices.

As per Kaufman's view it is defined as a tool developed to make educational adventure more responsive, responsible, logical, orderly and self-correctable and flexible rather than wholly intuitive, orderly, undefinable and doubtful.

As emphasized earlier, system approach refers to a well-thought technique or rational approach for designing, controlling and using a system for realizing the system objectives in the best possible ways. Its application in the field of education will surely make the system of education self-maintaining with its basic parameters operating scientifically on the principle of feedback and equilibrium.as a result, the systems approach to education is likely to solve various educational problems related with the organization and management of the process and products of education.

Meaning of system approach to education

- → It is one of the techniques, which aims at finding the most efficient and economically intelligent methods for solving the problems of education scientifically.
- → It is defined as a particular method of exploration to find effective ways of talking about, designing and organising learning situations in practice.
- → It is a tool developed to make the educational endeavour more responsive, responsible, logical, orderly, self-correctable and flexible rather than wholly intuitive, unordered, undefinable and doubtful.

In the light of the above definitions, it can be concluded that system approach is concerned with the systemic planning, designing, construction and evaluation of education system.it is applied to develop, implement the educational system, curriculum or even for designing an individual lesson.it is a rational, problem-solving method of analysing the educational process.it is a process taken as a whole incorporating all of its aspects and parts, namely pupils, facilitators, curriculum, instructional strategies, physical environment and the evaluation of instructional objectives.

System approach to education implies

- → Standards of output performances
- → Planned input and processes involving organised learning material and methods

- ✦ Monitored output, which is to revise, improve and evaluate the instructional system providing feedback to the learner and facilitator
- ✦ A degree of inbuilt flexibility to adjust to individual situations

Parameters of system approach to education

- ✦ Input - it involve learners (their age, minimum entry qualification and their aptitude and attitude, facilitators, curriculum, administrators. context and instructional material
- ✦ Process- it implies formal, non-formal and informal education process. It includes curriculum, institute i.e. Physical environment, furniture, library books and journal etc., facilities i.e. Laboratory, society services centres, recreational activities and facilitators.
- ✦ Output - in terms of product of system, performance of learner, monitored output which is used to revise, improve and evaluate the instructional system.
- ✦ Analysis and feedback- monitored environment provide feedback to learner and facilitators. A system operates in a physical and social environment. A system cannot operate beyond the limits and boundaries of its environmental content and constraints.

Purposes of system approach to education

- ✦ Improvement in instructional system: system approach can effectively improve the instructional system .system approach in instructional system helps in understanding ,controlling and improving the structure and functions of the system in view of the effective realization of instructional objectives .it helps in providing best possible solution to hot problems related to learning, process and product of instruction
- ✦ Utilization of resources: system approach can help in optimized uses of human and non-human resources connected with the process of education .it can utilize more effectively the school personnel by controlling, coordinating and evaluating continuously the activities of the personnel.
- ✦ Increased control and co-ordination: in system approach, effective school management techniques are used to control the various component of instructional process .co-ordination between different parts is exercised as a result of achievement of specific objectives at the level of operation.
- ✦ Improvement in school affairs: system approach may help in managing and improving the school affairs by bringing efficiency in the school management and administration.
- ✦ Improvement in planning: our schools do not have systematic planning of short or long range goal of education .system approach in education can help in systematic educational planning in terms of long range goals and specific short range objective.
- ✦ Improvement in co-curricular activities: system approach in education may help in bringing improvement in the organization of co-curricular activities and other education aspects for maximum development of personality.
- ✦ Improvement in evaluation : system approach in education may help in bringing improvement in the examination and evaluation system

- ✈ Improvement in training: system approach in education may help in improving training and development programmes. Both preserving and in-service facilitator training may be effectively improved with the help of system approach.
- ✈ Improvement in guidance: system approach in education can help in organizing and improving the guidance services of the schools.
- ✈ Improvement in non-formal and adult education: system approach in education can prove an effective means for designing, controlling and improving the systems of non-formal and adult education.
- ✈ Improvement in quality of education: system approach in education can provide valuable services in improving the quality of education in all its aspects. It does so by solving various problems related to education and thereby improving the quality of education.
- ✈ Application of cybernetics in education

Difficulties in implementation
- ✈ Difficulty in saying good bye to old methods
- ✈ Time consuming
- ✈ Hard work
- ✈ Not suitable for all problem

Recapitulation

In spite of certain difficulties or limitations ,system approach can be applied for the development of educational administration or organization, examination system ,instructional system, models of facilitator education ,models of curriculum and educational and vocational balance system .it provides opportunities to modify and improve the educational system as best as possible in the light of the evaluation of the outcomes relation to input, processes, environmental constrains and stipulated objectives. Thus system approach has full potentiality to provide effective control to the process and products of education by solving the various problems inherited in it.

Importance of system approach for education
- ✈ Provides framework for planning, controlling decision making and problem solving
- ✈ Throws light on dynamic nature of management
- ✈ Institution is viewed as an adaptive system, which adjusts as per environment changes in order to survive.
- ✈ Provides a unified focus to institutional efforts.
- ✈ Helps to look at institution as a whole and not as parts.
- ✈ Helps the manager to identify the critical sub systems and their interaction with each other. The practicing manager learns to see the phenomenon not in isolation but in its relation to other phenomenon and elements due to constant interactions.
- ✈ Helps in improving institution
- ✈ Helps in bringing efficiency in school administration and management
- ✈ Helps in systematic educational planning
- ✈ Maximum utilization of resources

- ✈ Helps in improving examination and evaluation system
- ✈ Maintaining, controlling and improving the guidance services
- ✈ Designing, controlling and improving non-formal and adult education system
- ✈ In improving the quality of education
- ✈ In improving the facilitator training programmes- in-service as well as pre service

Recapitulation

In spite of certain difficulties, system approach can be applied for the development of educational administration and organisation, examination system, instructional system, models of facilitator education, models of curriculum and educational guidance system.it provides opportunities to modify and improve the educational system as best as possible in the light of evaluation of outcome in relation to the inputs, processes, environmental constraints and stipulated objectives. Thus system approach has full potentiality to provide effective control to the process and products of education by solving the various problems related to education.

6.4 SYSTEM APPROACH TO SCHOOL SYSTEM
Steps involved in system approach

- ✈ Identification of problem
- ✈ Specification of objectives
- ✈ Analysis of the task involved in achieving the objectives
- ✈ System analysis
- ✈ System design and development
- ✈ Identification of the preferred solution
- ✈ Operation and implementation of preferred solution
- ✈ Evaluation of preferred solution.
- ✈ Providing feedback in the light of the evaluation for bringing necessary improvement and modification.

The various stages in the systems approach in school curriculum making:

(a) Consider target population characteristics and topic area, the range of backgrounds, interests, knowledge, attitudes and skills of learners coming on to the course will have a strong influence on course design. Pre-knowledge and any common misconceptions will have to be catered for in the design of the course (these may, for example, affect sequence, structure and support mechanisms).the broad thrust of the course content will also have to be considered. Consideration will be given to the sort of people whom the course is trying to develop. The subject area may have traditional aims and directions, but one may wish to consider the justification of these and/or preparation for future change.

(b) Estimate relevant existing skills and knowledge of learners there may be minimum standards of entry to the course, but this will not always be so. For example, the increasing numbers of non-standard and mature learner entrants to higher education will not necessarily have conventional paper qualifications, but may possess skills and qualities which will have an influence on course design.

This may have implications for instruction methods, bridging courses; support systems etc.

(c) Formulate objectives/learning outcomes'. The objectives and learning outcomes of the course or curriculum element will attempt to encapsulate the fresh and new skills, knowledge or attitudes which it is intended that the learners will acquire. They may be formulated by the learners themselves, by employers, by instruction staff, by a validating, examining or professional body, or by some combination of these and other sources.

(d) Select appropriate instructional methods: having specified the objectives and learning outcomes (i.e., what we are trying to achieve in the course), we should be in a better position to select appropriate instruction/learning methods through which these have a reasonable chance of being achieved. There are far more instruction methods available to choose from than most people realise - one recent book describes no less than 303 different instruction/learning methods! The process of attempting to match appropriate methods, to given objectives and learning outcomes, are normally done on the basis of a combination of research and experience.

(e) Operate course or curriculum: the next element in the system is the actual implementation of the course. This involves all the logistical arrangements associated with running the course, including overall structuring, pacing, implementing the chosen instruction strategies, using appropriate supportive media and materials, and ensuring that all aspects of the course run as smoothly as possible. Later booklets will provide detailed guidance on how this can be done.

(f) Assess and evaluate: the combined result of the preceding stages is that learners are involved in a learning experience that is planned to develop their knowledge, skills and attitudes, taking into account the individual needs and experience of the learners. Just how effective the pre-planning and subsequent operation has been can be measured by studying learner's performance during and/or post-course assessments. These assessments should be closely related to the specified course objectives and learning outcomes. Poorly-achieved objectives or learning outcomes should lead the course designers to examine the entire system in order to identify places where improvements might be made. This could involve a change in the objectives/learning outcomes, a revised assessment of learners' pre-knowledge, a critical review of the instructional methods used, an examination of the course structure and organisation, a consideration of the assessment methods used, or a combination of some or all of these. These deliberations, together with feedback on the course from staff, learners, employers, etc., can be used in an evaluation of the entire concept of the course, which should, in turn, form the basis of an on-going cyclical course development process.

Role of facilitator in the system approach

- → Assessment of input
- → Data collection: should collect data possible for subject matter.
- → Alternatives: should think of alternative processes for achievement of objectives.
- → Analysing objectives—should analyse all the objectives
- → Discussion— should make discussion regarding processes and components of the optimum means for further processes.

- ✦ Activation: should activate the system by putting plan into action.
- ✦ Feedback data: should provide feedback data accordingly and systematically.
- ✦ Modification of components and processes: based on feedback carry out modification.
- ✦ Assessment of system—should assess the entire system.
- ✦ Modification of system—should modify the system, wherever required, based on the assessment.

6.5 THE SYSTEMS APPROACH TO EDUCATIONAL TECHNOLOGY

The systems approach to the design and analysis of instruction/learning situations is the basis of the great majority of modern educational technology-related developments. However, the terms system and systems approach are themselves jargon terms that can have a variety of interpretations. Let us therefore take a look at these terms in order to define the way in which we are to use them.

In general systems theory, a system is any collection of interrelated parts that together constitute a larger whole. These component parts, or elements of the system are intimately linked with one another, either directly or indirectly, and any change in one or more elements may affect the overall performance of the system, either beneficially or adversely. A simple system is illustrated schematically in fig. 2.

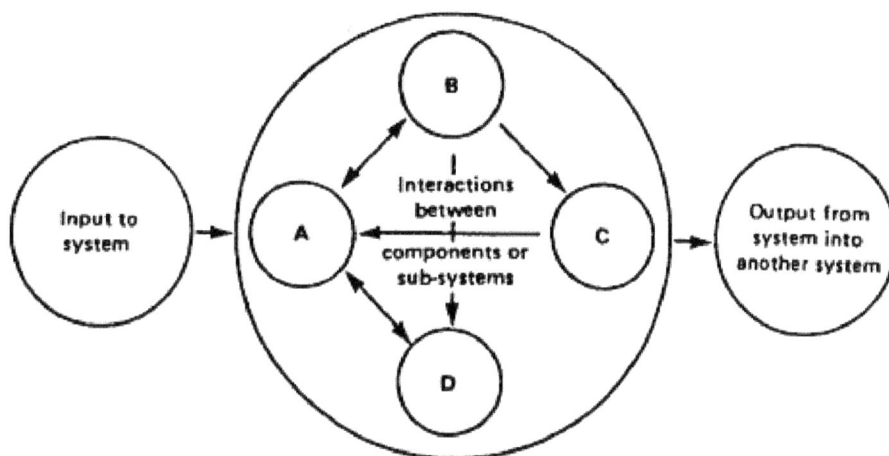

Fig. 2. A typical system

In figure 2, the system consists of four distinct elements a, b, c, d, which are related to or dependent upon each other as indicated. Note that some interrelationships may be two-way, while others may be one-way only. These elements may themselves be capable of further breakdown into other smaller components, and may thus be regarded as sub-systems of the overall system.

The processes of instruction and learning can be considered to be very complex systems indeed. The input to a given instruction/learning system consists of people, resources and information, and the output consists of people whose performance or ideas have (it is to be hoped) improved in some desired way. A schematic representation of systems of this type is shown in figure 3.

Input	The System	Output
target students; human resources; technical resources; financial resources; information	teaching/ learning process (black box)	students whose performance or ideas have improved in specific areas

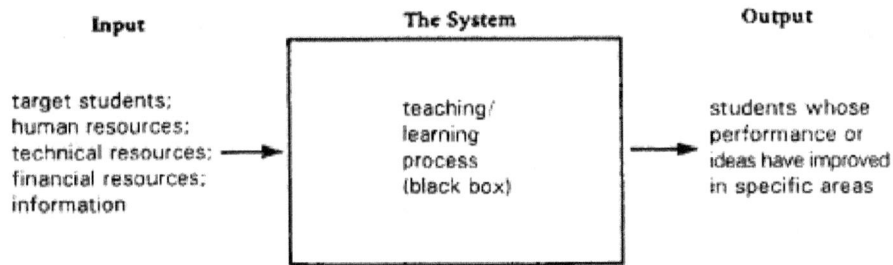

In a system, the instruction/learning process may be so complex that it can only be considered as a 'black box' whose mechanisms are not fully understood. However, research into the nature of the learning process has thrown some light on what happens inside the 'black box'. This has enabled educational technologists to structure the input to systems of this type in such a way as to try to improve the output through increasing the efficiency and effectiveness of the learning process, thus leading to a systems approach to course and curriculum design based on current knowledge of how people learn. Such a systems approach attempts to mould the input to a course in such a way as to enable the optimal assimilation of knowledge and skills to take place during the learning process, and hence maximize the quality of the output.

Glenn immigrant has observed that the system has following properties :

- ✦ It is goal oriented and has a purpose
- ✦ In designing the system an input is allocated, processed and output is taken
- ✦ All systems tend toward a state of randomness.
- ✦ All systems have boundaries
- ✦ All systems have factors that affect the structure and function of the system

6.6 SCOPE OF SYSTEM APPROACH

System approach is related to whole process of educational system such as instruction method, evaluation of educational system, curriculum organization and management, physical and human resources etc. System approach makes instruction and learning more effective. The system approach is vast term in modern world. Its scope is seen in the success of many educational institutes, industries and other organizations.

Instructional system

Improvement in instructional system - In instructional system, system approach provides more and more effective ideas and situation that facilitates instruction learning process. It helps in understanding and controlling the instructional system to make the learners learn in best effective way. System approach also helps in improving the structure and function of an instructional system in the best possible way. In instructional system, there is a systematic operation within instructional element to gain some desired instructional objective.

After analysing the instructional system, Robb (1973) has marked three major phases in system approach to instructional system

- ✦ Planning

→ Execution
→ Evaluation

Now this number has been increased to six (Jalaludin, 1981), as outlined below:

→ Formation of objectives: specify as to exactly what is to be taught and the type and kind of learning experiences the learners will be expected to encounter. Also identify the knowledge of the skills which the learner will be required to demonstrate as outcome.

→ Pre-assessment of learner previous or entering behaviour: define the entry levels of learners; identify the knowledge of the skill which the learner already equipped with.

→ Designing and development of the system: identify the learners, design the various role of facilitators, select material and media involve in the instrumental system to help the learners achieve predetermined objectives.

→ Operation and implementation phase: integrate the selected approaches, methods, media and tasks into a system model, work out the task to be carried out by each variable in the system and conduct a try-out of the instructional system with a small sample of learners under specified condition.

→ Evaluations of outcomes: validate the outcome of original learner's objective. Measure the learner performance competency and examine the same against the stated objectives.

→ Improvement of the system: on the basis of feedback of evaluation results, modify the system to improve its effectiveness in terms of learner learning.

In order to ensure effective planning, it is essential to identify the instructional problems, development of organisational structure, the delineation of instructional needs, the specification of goal - state the formulation of learning objectives, the development of an evaluation mechanism, the determination of learning experiences, the selection of instructional strategy, development of inventory of resources, the selection and development of instructional contents, the sequencing and implementation of instructions, follow-up and feedback. All these elements should be covered while planning instructional system. Witch and Schuler, in their book 'Instructional technology: Its nature and use', described the various steps or operations of system approach to improve instructional system.

The application of system approach early in the conceptual phase helps one to reduce the chances of oversight, or the occurrence of so called appraisal gaps. And this is achieved by using a structured technique of continuously identifying and assessing the impact of changing objectives, constraints, and design criteria on the required resources and the available resources: technologies, personnel, and facilities. Education according to system approach is the process in which a facilitator presents subject matter to a learner so that he responds to it in a way that enable the facilitator to determine the halt of information to be presented. A program is a coherent body of knowledge presented in such a fashion that in the absence of facilitator a learner for whom it is intended, it consist of a sequence rather than small steps followed by questions to which the learner gives the sufficient number of correct answers to feel motivated to continue. It exploits the process of differential reinforcement.

The following are the main activities (ADDIE model: Analysis, Design, Development, Implementation, Evaluate) undertaken in system approach to instruction

Analysis

+ Determine business outcome or linkage.
+ Analyse system (department, job, etc.) To gain an understanding of it.
+ Compile a task inventory of all tasks associated with each job (if needed).
+ Select tasks that people need to learn to become performers (needs analysis).
+ Build performance measures for the tasks to be learned.
+ Choose instructional setting for the tasks to be learned, e.g. classroom, eLearning, on-the-job, self-study, blended, etc.
+ Estimate cost and assess the advantages gained.

Design

+ Develop the learning objectives, to include both terminal and enabling objectives.
+ Identify and list the learning steps required to perform the task.
+ Develop performance tests to show mastery of the tasks.
+ List the entry behaviours that the learner must demonstrate prior to entering the learning program.
+ Sequence and structure the learning objectives.

Develop

+ List activities that will help the learners learn the task.
+ Select the delivery methods (media).
+ Review existing material so that one does not reinvent the wheel.
+ Develop the instructional courseware.
+ Synthesize the courseware into a viable learning program.
+ Validate the instruction to ensure it accomplishes all goals and objectives.

Implement

+ Create a management plan for conducting the training.
+ Conduct the training.

Evaluate

+ Review and evaluate each phase (analyse, design, develop, implement) to ensure it is accomplishing what it is supposed to.
+ Perform external evaluations, e.g. Observe that the tasks that were trained can actually be performed by the learners in their working environment.
+ Revise training system to make it better and to meet future challenges.

In short, ADDIE model can be understood as:

+ Analyse the performance environment in order to understand it and then describe the goals needed in order to correct any performance deficiencies (identify training requirements).
+ Design process to achieve the goals, that is — corrects the performance deficiencies.

- Develop the initial discoveries and process into a product that will assist the learners into becoming performers (in training, this product is often called course ware).
- Implement by delivering the course ware to the learners.
- Evaluate the performers, course ware, and audit-trail throughout the four phases and in the working environment to ensure it is achieving the desired results.

Steps in the system approach as applied to instructional development system

- Identify the task or the problem
- Analyse the situation
- Arrange for good management
- Identify the objective
- Specify the materials and method to be used
- Construct a prototype design
- Test the prototype design with a sample group
- Analyse the result
- Implement and recycle

Lesson planning

This approach for improving lesson planning involve working for an all-round development of the learner .it involve Addie that is analysis , development, design ,implement and evaluate. It also involves training at the end. A lesson is planned keeping in mind the points like the kind of school, background of learners attending a school, the age group of the learner, the strength of the class, the general attendance, the books being followed, table instruction, the concerned chapter, the content, the time for presentation, use of suitable instruction aid. The different learning abilities of the learner and special cases like visually challenged learners. Evolving a fresh and new system of education - a system which sees every aspect of education and the system in totality where a learner is an educant, where each learner is taken as special and his needs are prime and this is applied to all educant, which benefits the system.

Advantages of lesson planning

- It provides conceptual framework on which plan are built for implementing change for education.
- Helps to identify suitability or otherwise of the resources material to achieve specific goals
- Helps to access the resources and facilities as per need in terms of quantities, time and other factors.
- It could be used to provide integration of man, machine and media to develop the education system.
- It permits an orderly instruction of components demonstrated for system success in terms of learner learning.

Limitations of lesson planning

- Developing a system education programme is time consuming process.

- It need trained personnel
- Problems in changing and adapting something fresh and new are sometimes very difficult.
- Sometimes it is cost effective also and it, too, becomes a limitation.
- It spreads institutional racism as few who can have better facilities in terms of using learners friendly and helpful technologies like smart class etc. will definitely be seen as superior as and better than others in comparison to who don't have these facilities.

Scope of system approach to education can be summarized as

- Utilisation of resources– system approach can help in improving utilisation of physical and human resources in education
- Increase control and co-ordination
- Improvement in school affairs
- Improvement in planning
- Improvement in evaluation
- Improvement in co-curricular activities
- Improvement in training
- Improvement in guidance
- Improvement in non-formal and adult education
- Improvement in quality of education

6.7 SYSTEM APPROACH AND DIFFERENTLY-ABLED LEARNERS

When we refer to a class of differently abled learners, it means learners which are not like other learners but have specific challenges that may be related to their physical, mental set-ups .these learners are in no way less than other learners but have in them certain different abilities. Previously, this term differently abled learner was used for learners who were handicapped or challenged in one way or the other., in a class, it is very important to take into consideration these specific learners not thinking of them as helpless or miserable or by feeling sorry for the them but by treating them and giving equal opportunities and ground to work on and do things at the same time providing them all the faculties which help them to be self-reliant and independent. When we talk of learner, we have to be little sensitive as they have lots of emotions and thoughts, flourishing in their small minds. One has to reach to their level, understand their true potential, needs etc. to realise the true goals of education. System approach is needed here to realise the true goals of education and to help these special learners. Our government had also thought about this and to meet this, certain plans and policies had been devised like national policy for persons with disabilities which ensure equal opportunity to them. Inclusive education means inclusion for all groups in society.in fact, each learner in a class is different from another in one way or the other and it is sometimes difficult to manage a class with such differently abled learners.to manage these group of differently abled learner is a challenging task. For this, we need a system approach to these learners.

System approach means an approach where various components of a system are worked upon. The processes are analysed and based on the analysis, evaluation and feedback the processes are revised, improved and applied again to that system to have a better product which is refined and monitored. As such there is not any specific end to this process but of identifying, planning, analysing, designing, organising, implementing evaluating and taking feedback and then again planning leads to repetition of the above steps.

Following are the various steps being taken to help the learner by the methodology of system approach.

a. *Identification of the problem-* the first step towards system approach to differently abled learner is the identification of the specific problem of the particular learner. This will require an in-depth study of the learner and his difficulty.

Government of India has found seven categories of differently abled learner. These are :

- ✈ Blindness
  Low vision
- ✈ Leprosy cured
- ✈ Locomotors disability
- ✈ Hearing disability
- ✈ Mental weakness
- ✈ Mental illness

So first we have to see the kind of disability the person might be suffering from and then accordingly we have to proceed.

b. *Specification of objectives-* the next step is to ascertain what is our specific objective with respect to a specific learner or a group of learner. It will vary according to our learner or group of learners, for example for a learner with visual impairment our objective will be to facilitate him with the right kind of help to enhance his learning by overcoming his disability, and for a person with mental weakness can be to motivate her/him enough so that he feel enthusiastic about learning. The objectives can be various and different also depending upon the type of disability that one might be facing and the specific problem one is having with his disability, like problem in interest, problem in motivation, problem in right kind of facilities. Depending upon these we will proceed further.

c. *Analysis of the task involved in achieving the specific objective*s- after setting our specific objective we need to analyse our task as a facilitator, guide, friend or facilitator and to help that learner in achieving the specific objectives. This involves study of the learner, his/her own system, his/her classroom in which he/she is studying, his school for the facilities and other things they had for that specific category of learner, study of the suprasystem i.e. His community in which he/she will is living. As a facilitator one has to be very specific when dealing with the differently abled learner so that they can bring out an all-round development of the child.

d. *System design and development-* this will involve designing and organising the specific system in which the learner is going to get the maximum advantage. This will need an elaborative study of the constraint of the system and suprasystem.

e. *Implementation of the system being developed for the learner.*

f. *Assessment and evaluation of the system being developed-* by assessing the performance of the learners.

g. *Feedback-* this involves taking the feedback of the learner by taking into consideration his evaluation and then again revising and improvising the changes as felt necessary for the system.

A case of system approach to differently-abled learners

As one facilitator shared, every school has few learners who belong to some specific category of differently abled learner. Even in her school, such learners were there. One such learner in her class was Ina. She was a nice girl, but a mentally challenged learner. Due to her weakness most of the facilitators didn't pay attention to her or ignore her. As a result of which, her interest in studies and attending classes was reducing. When this facilitator taught her first class, Ina was not there as she was scared of a fresh and new facilitator. But after sometime when she came to know about this facilitator and got assured that she could help her, she started attending her classes. First few days were difficult for her as a facilitator as she never participated in any group activity nor answered any of the questions being asked. So she first tried to find out her problems which were- difficulty in remembering things, hesitation and fear in speaking as her fellow mates were not cooperative to her, and a lack of interest in science class. Then this facilitator set her objectives to improve Ina's learning. So, at first, she talked with her about her family and friends and came to know that her mother's behaviour is not so good with her and so she doesn't like to be at home. She liked school more than home but here also she didn't have many friends. So as a facilitator her objective was to improve her interest in learning and in attending classes and make her happier. Yes it was true that even though she wanted to help her in all possible ways but had her own limitations provided by the system itself, as she couldn't do much about her problems at home. The task was to talk with her parents about her, talk with her classmates, so that they can also be friendly with her and help her in all the best possible way, to make learning interesting for her.

System design and development for her - After this she met her parents and tried to talk to them about Ina's problems and asked them to give her more love and help her in learning. Then one day she talked with her classmates about her and asked them to accept her as their friend. She asked them if they will like if anybody behave in the same way as they did with her. They replied negatively. And, then, all came to consensus that everybody will behave in a good way with Ina and help her in all the ways possible, so that she can develop interest in reading and writing. Though all these things were not very easy to achieve, but this is only suggestive way to precede in such kind spot a problem. This was just one kind of problem which one can encounter in class of differently abled learner. To these learners education can be made much more effective and accessible to persons with disabilities by including assistive technology products. Textbooks can be converted to digital talking books and is available for the print impaired (people with learning and visual impairment); computer aids such as screen reader, adaptive keyboard and desktop magnifier can have a major impact in education of persons with disability.

ICT tools for tracking education of intellectually challenged children. The Clevy clipboard that features attractive playful colours for vowels, consonants, numbers and function key etc. Using computers to write, read, view and check text alongside human sound voice etc. Just like a person with mild disability can use spectacle to correct his/her vision, we envision a world where a non- verbal person can have access to a portable solution like ava2 to help them speak, each disability requires a different kind of technology and there can be many such technologies which are being developed that will revolutionize the world of person with disability.

In its broadest and all-encompassing meaning, inclusive education, as an approach, seeks to address the learning needs of all children, youth and adults with a specific focus on those who are vulnerable to marginalization and exclusion. It implies all learners, young people - with or without disabilities being able to learn together through access to common pre-school provisions, schools and community educational setting with an appropriate network of support services. This is possible only in a flexible education system that assimilates the needs of a diverse range of learners and adapts itself to meet these needs. It aims at all stakeholders in the system (learners, parents, and community, facilitators, and administrators, policy makers) to be comfortable with diversity and see it as a challenge rather than a problem.

Researches have shown that inclusive education results in improved social development and academic outcomes for all learners. It leads to the development of social skills and better social interactions as learners are exposed to real environment in which they have to interact with other learners; each one having unique characteristics, interests and abilities. The non-disabled peers adopt positive attitudes and actions towards learners with disabilities as a result of studying together in an inclusive classroom. Thus, inclusive education lays the foundation to an inclusive society accepting, respecting and celebrating diversity. The ministry of human resource development is currently in the process of developing a comprehensive action plan on the inclusion in education of children and youth with disabilities. A statement spelling out the areas of action was made by Minister for Human Resource Development on the 21st of March, 2005. Since then, the ministry has been interacting and consulting with experts, NGOs, disability rights groups, parents groups, government bodies etc. The following framework of the action plan and list of activities has been developed as a result of the initial consultations. The plan covers the inclusion in education of children and young persons with disabilities. The different sectors to be covered in the plan are early childhood care and education, elementary education, secondary education, higher and technical education and vocational education.

EXEMPLARY QUESTIONS
1. What are the characteristics of a system? Give an example of system approach to school system.
2. What is system approach? Illustrate system approach with help of a school system.
3. Suppose that one has a group of differently abled learners in the class. How would one use system approach to solve their learning problem? Discuss by taking a problem from any subject area.

UNIT - 7

COMPUTER AND TECHNOLOGY IN EDUCATION

This unit deals with computer, emerging technologies and issues in educational technology

'Teachers need to integrate technology seamlessly into the curriculum instead of viewing it as an add-on, an afterthought, or an event.'

— **Heidi-Hayes Jacobs**

Unit 7
Computer and Technology in Education

7.1 APPLICATION SOFTWARE

Application software (AS) is computer software designed to aid and support the user to perform specific tasks, e.g. enterprise software, accounting software, office suites, graphics software and media players.

AS is different from system software and middleware that manages and integrates a computer's capabilities, such as interfacing with the hardware, or facilitating the input and output operations indirectly, but typically do not directly apply them in the performance of tasks that benefit the user. The system software serves the application (app) that in turn serves the user. Exemplars of system software are Operating Systems (OS). Exemplars of middleware are the driver software, such as mouse driver, keyboard driver, webcam drivers, etc.

Similar relationships apply in other fields, e.g. a shopping mall does not provide the merchandise a shopper is seeking, but provides space and services for retailers that serve the shopper. Similarly, rail tracks support trains, permit and facilitating the trains to transport passengers. AS apply the power of a specific computing platform, or system software, to a specific aim. A few apps such as Microsoft (MS) office are available in versions for several different platforms; others have narrower requirements and are thus called, e.g. a geography app for Windows or an android app for education or Linux gaming. A few times a fresh, new and popular app arrives, that only runs on one platform, increasing the desirability of that platform. This is called a killer app.

The delineation between system software such as OS and AS is not exact, however, and is occasionally the object of controversy, e.g. MS antitrust trial was whether MS's internet explorer web browser was part of its Windows OS or a separable piece of AS.

In a few kinds of embedded systems, the AS and the OS software might be indistinguishable to the user, as in the case of software that are used to control a printer, VCR, DVD player or microwave oven.

AS fall into two general classes Horizontal applications and vertical applications.

- ✦ Horizontal apps are the most popular and widespread in departments or companies. Exemplars of such apps are office suites, data administration software, etc.
- ✦ Vertical apps are niche products, designed for a specific kind of business or division in a company. Exemplars of such apps are like banking solutions, automation tools, etc.

Kinds of AS

There are several kinds of AS

- ✦ Educational software is related to content access software, but has the content and/or specialities adapted for use in by educators or learners, e.g. it might deliver evaluations (tests), track progress through material, or include collaborative capabilities. Exemplars are eduware educational, educational OS, educational programming languages, interactive geometry, learning management, note taking, pedagogic integrated

155

development environments, renaissance learning, virtual learning environments etc.

✈ Simulation software are computer software for simulation of physical or abstract systems for research, training or entertainment aims. Exemplars are computer simulators, scientific simulators, social simulators, battlefield simulators, emergency simulators, vehicle simulators, flight simulators, driving simulators, simulation games, vehicle simulation games etc.

✈ Product engineering software is used in developing hardware and software products. This includes computer-aided design (CAD), computer-aided engineering (CARE), computer language editing and compiling tools, integrated development environments, and app programme interfaces.

✈ An app suite consists of multiple apps bundled together. They usually have related functions, specialities and user interfaces, and might be able to interact with each other, e.g. open each other's files. Business apps often come in suites, e.g. MS office, openoffice.org and iWork, that bundle together a word processor, a spread sheet, etc.; but suites exist for other aims, e.g. Graphics or music.

✈ Enterprise software addresses the needs of organization processes and data flow, often in a large distributed environment. Exemplars include financial systems, customer relationship management (CRM) systems and supply-chain management software. Note that departmental software is a sub-kind of enterprise software with a focus on smaller organizations or groups within a large organization. Exemplars include travel expense management and IT aid and support desk)

✈ Enterprise infrastructure software provides common capabilities needed to support enterprise software systems. Exemplars include databases, email servers, and systems for managing networks and security.

✈ Information worker software addresses the needs of individuals to develop and manage information, often for individual projects within a department, in contrast to enterprise management. Exemplars include time management, resource management, documentation tools, analytical, and collaborative. Word processors, spread sheets, email and blog clients, personal information system, and individual media editors might aid-in multiple information worker tasks.

✈ Content access software is software used primarily to access content without editing, but might include software that permit and facilitates for content editing. Such software addresses the needs of individuals and groups to consume digital entertainment and published digital content. Exemplars include media players, web browsers, aid and support browsers and games.

✈ Media development software addresses the needs of individuals who generate print and electronic media for others to consume, most often in a commercial or educational setting. This includes graphic-art software, desktop publishing (DTP) software, multimedia development software, html editors, digital-animation editors, digital audio and video composition, and several others.

✈ Mobile apps (mobile apps) run on hand-held devices such as smart phones, tablet computers, portable media players, personal digital assistants and enterprise digital assistants.

→ A command-line interface is one in that one kind in commands to make the computer do a something. One has to learn the commands and what they do, and kind them correctly. DOS and UNIX are exemplars of command-driven interfaces.

→ A graphical user interface (GUI) is one in that one select command choices from several menus, buttons and icons using a mouse. It is a user-friendly interface. MS Windows and Mac OS are both GUI.

→ A third-party server side app that the user might choose to install in his or her account on a social media website or other web 2.0 website, e.g. a Facebook app.

Main focus, here, would be on educational software, that can also be classified on several parameters.

Language: computational linguistics, computer-assisted translation, machine translation

Library and information science: dictionary, digital library, institutional repository, library automation, reference management, bibtex

Sciences:

→ Artificial intelligence, agent-based, chatterbots, computer vision, expert systems, face recognition, natural language, neural network, optical character recognition, speech recognition

→ Astronomy

→ Bioinformatics, molecular modelling, molecular dynamics

→ Cheminformatics, chemistry, computational chemistry, molecular modelling, molecular dynamics, mass spectrometry

→ Computational science

→ Earth science, earth sciences graphics, virtual globes, environmental science, geographic information system (GIS), integrated hydrologic modelling, numerical climate and weather models, remote sensing

→ Geology

→ Laboratory

→ Linguistic research

→ Mathematics, computer algebra, formal methods, model checkers, theorem proving, formula editors, interactive geometry, numerical, finite element, mathematical optimization, pi, statistical, data analysis, econometrics, spread sheets, cryptographic

→ Physics, computational physics, optics

→ Plotting

→ Simulation : computer-aided engineering, geotechnical engineering, interior design, optical, scientific simulation, outer space/space flight.

Advantages and limitations of AS

Advantages

When we compare the advantages and limitations of AS, we find that advantages outweigh the limitations, very easily. These are the advantages of AS that is designed for a specific aim, to be used either by individuals or by businesses.

- The single biggest advantage of AS is that it meets the exact needs of the user. Since it is designed specifically with one aim in mind, the user learns that he has to use specific AS to accomplish his task.
- The threat of viruses invading custom-made AS is very small, since any business that incorporates it can restrict access and can come up with means to protect their network, too.
- Licensed AS gets regular updates from the developer for security reasons. Additionally, the developer also regularly sends personnel to correct any problems that might arise from time to time.

Limitations

There are certain limitations of AS, too. Though these are not spoken about very often, nor are they highlighted, the fact is that they do exist and affect certain users. But people have accepted these misgivings and still continue to use such software as their utility and importance is much more profound than their weaknesses.

- Developing AS designed to meet specific aims can prove to be quite costly for developers. This can affect their budget and their revenue flow, especially if too much time is spent developing software that is not generally acceptable.
- A few software that are designed specifically for a certain business might not be compatible with other general AS. This is a something that can prove to be a major stumbling block for several corporations.
- Developing AS is a something that takes a lot of time, as it needs constant communication between the developer and the customer. This delays the entire production process that can prove to be harmful in a few cases.
- AS that is used commonly by several people, and then shared online, carries a very real threat of infection by a computer virus or other malicious programs.

7.2 FREE AND OPEN SOURCE SOFTWARE

Free and open-source software (f/oss, Foss) or free/libre/open-source software (floss, fl/oss) is liberally licensed to grant the right of users to use, study, change, and improve its design through the availability of its source code. This approach has gained both momentum and acceptance as the potential advantages have been increasingly recognized by both individuals and corporations.

In the context of free and open-source software, free refers to the freedom to copy and re-use the software, rather than to the price of the software. The free software foundation, an organization that advocates the free software model, suggests that, to understand the concept, one should 'think of free as in free speech, not as in free beer'.

Foss is an inclusive term that covers both free software and open source software that despite describing similar development models, have differing cultures and philosophies. Free software focuses on the philosophical freedoms it gives to users, whereas open source software focuses on the perceived strengths of its peer-to-peer development model. Foss is a term that can be used without specific bias towards either political approach.

Free software licenses and open source licenses are used by several software packages. While the licenses themselves are in most cases the same, the two terms grew out of different philosophies and are often used to signify different distribution methodologies.

A few free educational software
Celestia

Celestia is a 3-dimensional astronomy program developed by Chris Laurel. The program is based on the Hipparcos catalogue and permits and facilitates users to travel through an extensive universe, modelled after reality, at any speed, in any direction and at any time in history. Celestia displays and interacts with objects ranging in scale from small spacecraft to entire galaxies in three dimensions using OpenGL, from perspectives that would not be possible from a classic planetarium or other ground-based display. NASA and ESA have used Celestia in their educational and outreach programs, as well as for interfacing to trajectory analysis software.

Celestia is available for Linux, Mac and Windows. Released under the general public license (GPL), Celestia is free software.

Functions

Celestia displays the Hipparcos catalogue of around 120,000 stars. Celestia uses the very accurate vsop87 theory of planetary orbits. This makes it possible for it to provide a solar and lunar eclipse finder and to display the orbital paths of planets (including extra solar planets), dwarf planets, moons, asteroids, comets, artificial satellites, and spacecraft. The user can vary the number of stars that are visible on the screen and have them drawn in different styles.

Celestia users can virtually travel/fly through the Celestia universe using simple keyboard controls, at any speed from 0.001 m/s to millions of light years/s. Viewpoints can be set to look forward, backward or at any angle to direction of travel. Controls permit and facilitate users to orbit stars, planets, moons and other space objects, track space objects such as spacecraft, asteroids and comets as they fly by, or travel to and/or fly through nebulae and irregular, elliptical and spiral galaxies.

The time simulated by Celestia can be set at any point in the future or past, although planetary orbits are only accurate within a few thousand years of the present day.

The names and positions of multitudes of objects in space can be displayed, from galaxies, star clusters, nebula, constellations and stars to planets, moons, asteroids, comets and artificial satellites, as well as the names and locations of cities, craters, observatories, valleys, landing sites, continents, mountains, seas and other surface specialities.

Celestia displays such specialities as detailed atmospheres on planets and moons, planet shine on orbiting satellites, sunsets and sunrises, moving clouds, planetary rings, eclipse and ring shadows, constellation lines, borders and illustrations, night-side lights, detailed surface textures, specular reflections off water and ice, nebula gases and star flares.

Information about the objects that Celestia draws can also be displayed : the radius, the distance, length of the real day and average blackbody temperature of the planets are shown and the distance, luminosity relative to the sun, spectral class, surface temperature and radius of stars are indicated.

The user can change Celestia's field of view from as wide as 120 degrees to a highly magnifying 3.4 seconds of arc, while dividing the window into multiple panes, in order to observe several objects simultaneously and including light time delay if desired.

Graphic screen-shots and movies can be captured in classic or HD resolutions on Windows and Linux platforms. Educational lessons and computer lesson plans are available.

Limitations

+ The default setting for Celestia's earth is a spheroid. The irregular surface of the earth causes low earth orbit satellites to appear to be in the wrong places in the sky when watched from Celestia's ground, even when the earth's oblations is specified.

+ Several kinds of astronomical objects are not included with Celestia. Variable stars, supernova, black holes and nebulae are missing from the standard distribution. A few are available as add-ons. Although objects, that form part of a planetary system move, and stars rotate about their axes and orbit each other in multiple star systems, stellar proper motion is not simulated and galaxies are at fixed locations. Celestia's binary star catalogues only describe a few hundred systems of multiple stars. Most binary star systems cannot be simulated as adequate orbital information is not yet available.

+ Celestia does not include any stars that are more than a few thousand light-years from the sun as the parallaxes of more distant stars are too small to be precisely measured by the Hippocras astrometry satellite. In addition, objects in solar systems are only drawn to a distance of one light-year from their suns and Celestia does not consider the wobbling of a few stars induced by their planets.

+ Wavelength filtering is not implemented in Celestia's engine. The actual rendering tries to match as closely as possible human vision at the observer's position. This means false-colour maps, multi-colour nebulae and over-exposed galaxies are not part of the official distribution. Camera lens artefacts like lens flare and glare are not rendered, either. Also, in a total lunar eclipse, the moon is completely dark.

+ Celestia also does not simulate gravity. That means, e.g. that a near-earth object approaching the earth would not collide with the planet after being caught by the earth's gravity unless the person who defined the Neo's trajectory for Celestia included that effect.

+ A few of Jupiter's moons do not cast a shadow on Jupiter during eclipses. This is as irregularly shaped objects do not cast shadows in the current version of Celestia.

+ In the real world, constellations gradually change shape as stars would move over time that Celestia does not take into account.

Avogadro

Avogadro software is a molecular editor designed for cross-platform use in computational chemistry, molecular modelling, bioinformatics, materials science, and related areas. It is extensible through a plug-in architecture

Specialities

- ✈ Molecular builder/editor for Windows, Linux, and Mac OS.
- ✈ All source code is available under the GPL.
- ✈ Translations into Chinese, French, German, Italian, Russian, Spanish and several other languages.
- ✈ Supports multi-threaded rendering and computation.
- ✈ Plug-in architecture for developers, including rendering, interactive tools, commands, and python scripts.
- ✈ Open babel import of files, input generation for multiple computational chemistry packages, crystallography, and biomolecules.

Geogebra

Geogebra is interactive geometry software for education in schools. Most parts of Geogebra are free software. Geogebra is written in java and thus available for multiple platforms.

Dynamic geometry, algebra and calculus

Geogebra is dynamic geometry software. Constructions can be made with points, vectors, segments, lines, polygons, conic sections, and functions. All of them can be changed dynamically afterwards.

Elements can be entered and modified directly on screen, or through the input bar. Geogebra has the ability to use variables for numbers, vectors and points, find derivatives and integrals of functions and has a full complement of commands like root or extremum. Facilitators can use Geogebra to make conjectures and prove geometric theorems.

Exporting

Constructed projects can be exported in several formats. Dynamic applets can be exported to html, as a single file suitable for use in a virtual learning environment (VLE), such as Moodle. SVG vector images can be further edited using third-party software, e.g. inkscape. EMF vector formats can be directly imported in several office apps. There are also choices for exporting to the system clipboard, PNG and EPS.

Licensing

Most parts of the Geogebra program is licensed under GPL and CC-BY-SA, making them free software. However a few parts, including the Windows and Mac installers, have a license that forbids commercial use and are therefore not free software. In practice, this means that non-commercial use by facilitators and learners is always free of charge, while commercial users might need to pay license fees.

Since July 2010, Debian Linux distribution provides a free version of Geogebra in that all not-free parts of the program were removed or replaced by free software. This version might be used for commercial aims without paying licensing fees.

7.3 AUTHORING SYSTEMS

The term authoring systems to refer to a computer based system that permit and facilitates a general group (including non-programmers) to develop (i.e., author) content for intelligent tutoring systems. It is a program that has pre-programmed elements for the development of interactive multimedia software titles. Authoring systems vary widely in orientation, capabilities, and learning curve.

In the development of educational software, an authoring system is a program that permits and facilitates a non-programmer to easily develop software with programming specialities. The programming specialities are built in but hidden behind buttons and other tools, so the author does not need to learn how to program. There is no such thing, at this time, as a completely point-and-click automated authoring system; some knowledge of heuristic thinking and algorithm design is necessary. Whether one realize it or not, authoring is actually just a speeded-up form of programming; one don't need to learn the intricacies of a programming language, or worse, an API, but one do need to understand how programs work.

Generally authoring systems provide lots of graphics, interaction, and other tools educational software needs. Authoring systems also provide a lot of documentation as to how to use the system in the most optimal manner.

Anyone would want to use an authoring system. It generally takes about 1/8th the time to develop an interactive multimedia project, such as a CBT program, in an authoring system as opposed to programming it in compiled code. This means 1/8 the cost of programmer time and likely increased re-use of code, assuming that one pass this project's code to the next CBT project, and they use a similar or identical authoring system. However, the content creation (graphics, text, video, audio, animation, etc.) is not generally affected by the choice of an authoring system; any production time gains here result from accelerated prototyping, not from the choice of an authoring system over a compiled language.

We can develop all material in the authoring system. Although most packages permit and facilitate one to develop content using their in-built tools, these tend to be rudimentary when compared with those available in dedicated programs. For more professional output, one should use software dedicated to the creation and editing of that medium, and then import/integrate the content into the multimedia program.

Major content-development packages are likely to include
+ Paint programs for still images (photos, original digital artwork)
+ Paint effects programs
+ Illustration (draw) programs for still images (modelled and rendered objects)
+ Modelling/rendering programs (for 3-D objects)
+ Video digitizing/editing programs
+ Video effects programs
+ Audio sampling/editing programs
+ Word processors
+ Text editors
+ Database programs
+ Animation programs
+ Asset-management programs

The best authoring system

This is the most impossible question one could ask. It's like asking what's the best hammer : it depends upon the job one is trying to do, and a few times (like when one is working on plumbing), there is no answer.

Name of a few classes of authoring systems
- ✈ DOS authoring systems
- ✈ Summit authoring system
- ✈ Macintosh authoring systems
- ✈ Next authoring systems
- ✈ Os/2 authoring systems
- ✈ Solaris authoring systems

7.4 ISSUES IN EDUCATION AND TECHNOLOGY: SOCIETAL, EDUCATIONAL, CULTURAL/EQUITY, AND LEGAL/ETHICAL

One reason that instruction is so challenging is that it occurs in an environment that mirrors, and a few times magnifies, a few of society's most profound and problematic issues. Adding computers to this mix makes the situation even more complex. Yet to integrate technology successfully into their instruction, educators must recognize and be prepared to work in this environment with all of its complexities. A few important current issues and their implications for technological trends in education are described below.

Societal issues in current technology use

The economic, political, and social trend have a great impact on whether or not innovations take hold, or have limited acceptance, or are ignored completely. Societal issues that are aid and supporting to shape the current climate for educational technology include the following
- ✈ Economic conditions – recent economic downturns in the economy have meant decreased education funding. Experts predict that funds would not return to previous levels when the economy improves.
- ✈ Anti-technology positions – a few critics say that ubiquitous technology interferes with privacy and complicates daily life. Others feel that instruction/learning advantages have not been clearly established, and that technology is not as important as other programs that are being cut (e.g. music, arts). Still others say that computer use poses potential health hazards and that internet cyber porn and predators pose other risks, especially to young users.

This combination of social conditions means that educators increasingly are forced to set priorities for scarce education money. In light of this and recent attacks on technology by those outside education, it is ever more important to use research results and best practice findings to establish a sound rationale for technology use and justify technology expenses and potential risks to learner users. Increasingly, funding for technology-based strategies would be dependent on these results and findings. In light of increasing accountability requirements, it also seems likely that schools would begin emphasizing the use of computer systems to track learner progress.

Educational issues in current technology use

Trends in the educational system are intertwined with trends in technology and society. The three kinds of educational issues listed below have special implications for the ways technology would be used in instruction and learning

+ Standards movement – all content areas and states have skill standards learners must meet to pass courses and to get degrees and certification. High- stakes tests on standards determine success. This movement might drive a trend toward using technology in ways that aid and support facilitators and learners pass tests and meet required standards.

+ Reliance on the internet and on distance education – increasing numbers of virtual courses are being provided, and virtual high schools are becoming commonplace in education. This means that learners could have increased access to high-quality courses and degrees. However, virtual learning takes special skills not all learners have, and dropout rates from distance courses are higher, that could further widen the digital divide. A few critics say that distance learning is not as empowering as a face-to-face educational experience.

+ Debate over directed vs. Inquiry-based, constructivist instructional methods – educators disagree on the proper roles of traditional, facilitator-directed learning versus learner-led, inquiry-based methods. Long-used and well-validated directed uses of technology have been shown to be capable and influential for addressing standards, but several educators see them as passé. Inquiry-based, constructivist methods are considered more modern, but it is less clear how they could address required standards.

Cultural and equity issues in current technology use

The three factors listed next reflect the complex racial and cultural fabric of our society, and they continue to have a great impact on technology use

+ Digital divide – a phrase coined by Lloyd Morisot, who was former president of the Markel foundation, the digital divide refers to a discrepancy in access to technology resources among socioeconomic groups. The single greatest factor determining access is economic status, although race and gender might also play a role, depending on the kind of technology. Recent studies find that while children from all income levels have greatly increased their internet use, children from underserved populations (e.g. low-income and minority learners) still lag far behind other learners in home and school access.

+ Racial and gender equity – technology remains dominated by males and certain ethnic groups. Studies show that when compared with males, racial or religious majority groups, females and minorities use computers less and enter careers in math, science, and technology areas at lower rates. Several educators believe these two findings are correlated: lower use of technology leads to lower entrance to technical careers. Even where computers are available in schools, there tends to be unequal access to certain kinds of activities, e.g. children might have access to computers, but use them mainly for remedial work rather than for email, multimedia production, and other personal empowerment activities.

+ Special needs – devices and methods are available to aid and support learners compensate for their physical and mental deficits and permit and facilitate them equal access to technology and to learning opportunities.

However, technological interventions that could aid and support learners with special needs are difficult to purchase and implement and often go unused. Parents clamour for the technology resources guaranteed their children by federal laws, but schools often claim insufficient funding to address these special needs.

The power of technology is a two-edged sword, especially for education. While it presents obvious potential for changing education and empowering facilitators and learners, technology also might further divide members of our society along socioeconomic, ethnic, and cultural lines and widen the gender gap. Facilitators would lead the struggle to make sure technology use enhance and supports, rather than conflicts with, the goals of a democratic society.

Legal and ethical issues in current technology uses

In several ways, technology users represent the society in a microcosm. The legal and ethical issues educators face, reflect those of the larger society. The five major kinds of ethical and legal issues discussed next have great impact on how technology activities are implemented

- → Viruses/hacking − illegal activities of two kinds are on the rise: (1) viruses, or programs written to cause damage or do mischief, cause problems ranging from lost files to systems being shut down for weeks. (2) Hackers are breaking into online systems in order to access personal data on learners, accomplish identify theft, and do other malicious acts. To combat these problems, schools are forced to install firewalls and virus protection software to safeguard classroom computers, and to spend larger portions of technology funds each year on preventing and cleaning up after illegal activities.

- → New plagiarism – plagiarism is a Latin word that means kidnapping. Greater online access to full text documents has resulted in increased 'cyber cheating,' or learners using materials they have found on the internet as their own. Websites have emerged to aid and support facilitators catch plagiarizers, and the number of educational organizations and facilitators using them is increasing.

- → Privacy/safety – privacy is concerned with personal information. Increasing amounts of learners' personal information are being placed online and learners are spending more time using online resources. Simultaneously, studies show a high incidence of attempts by online predators to contact learners, and objectionable material is readily available and easy to access. Online privacy issues arise due to insecure electronic transmissions, data trails and logs of email messages, online transactions and tracking of webpages visited. To address these concerns, schools are requiring learners/parents to sign an authorized use policy (AUP) and putting procedures in place to safeguard access to learners' personal information. Schools have also been put on notice to supervise carefully all learner use of the internet, and to install filtering software to prevent access to objectionable materials.

- → Security and integrity of information – confidentiality, integrity and availability of information about an individual or organisation are major issues. In order to cope up with these threats, we would have to focus on awareness, responsibility, timely response, ethics, democracy, risk assessment, security design and implementation, security management and reassessment.

→ Copyright – online availability of full-text publications is increasing, and distance courses are posting more materials in online course management systems. To make sure they comply with copyright laws, schools are making facilitators and learners aware of policies about copyright/AUP and fair use of published materials.

→ Illegal downloads / software piracy – an increasing number of websites provide ways to download copies of software or other media without paying for them, and software and media companies are prosecuting more offenders. Despite the ease of copying or downloading free materials, facilitators are tasked with modelling and instruction ethical behaviours with software and media.

The culture, language, and problems of the larger society also emerge among technology users, and their activities reflect several of the rules of conduct and values of society in general. Facilitators who use technology are faced with addressing the problems that would arise when people try to work outside those values and rules. What we are able to do to apply the power of technology to enhance education would be shaped primarily by how we are able to respond to these major issues.

Suggestive reading: Integrating Educational Technology into Instruction (5th ed.) by M. D. Roblyer.

7.5 ONLINE LEARNING

When one learns one is in the process of acquiring skill or knowledge. Online learning (OL) simply describes the way one access this, where learning content is delivered via the internet and other fresh and new media technologies such as mp3s and iPods.

This educational method is growing in popularity as a cost-capable and influential method of providing access to education for a large population. It is one of the most significant developments to have taken place in the world of education for several years. OL has provided to millions of people a wonderful opportunity to become better qualified, enhance their careers and to experience positive change in their lives. The courses provided through OL cover a wide range of subjects, audiences, and prices.

There are five main reasons behind the growth in OL: access, efficiency, stability, cost, and technology. The explosion in OL tools and the adoption of this method by educational institutions around the world speaks to the fundamental desire for more education. The expanded access to knowledge and information provides the groundwork necessary for several people to start fresh and new careers and gain fresh and new skills.

People already learn online

By using the several functions of the internet, people have probably already done a lot of learning online in an ad-hoc way, e.g. they view videos on One Tube just as would view a lecture online, meet people with similar interests, discuss ideas and form friendships on blogs or on community websites like Facebook. They speak to friends and colleagues via instant messaging services. If people think about, they should be comfortable with the idea of learning online as they're already using the technology that OL uses, to delivery learning.

Kinds of OL course access
There are two kinds of online course access; open and restricted.
- ✦ Open access: It permits and facilitates virtually anyone with an internet browser to view the course material. This kind of OL does not require interaction with an instructor. The material covered can range from very specific instructions to university level courses. This initiative removes the barriers to advanced knowledge and permits and facilitates anyone with the interest to learn.
- ✦ Restricted access: Restricted access is used to limit the class to registered learners. These courses usually provide instructor interaction and are typically the method used by courses that require grades upon completion.

Capabilities and influence of OL

OL is capable and influential, and a few times more capable and influential, than the traditional classroom learning. This is in line with Russell's conclusion in his 1999 meta-analysis 'the no-significant-difference phenomenon'. It was found that learners put as much time, performed as much work, and realized the same outcomes as those in the traditional classroom. Amazingly all those things proved true, in spite of the difference in the medium used for the instruction.

Reasons for the capabilities and influence of OL
- ✦ First reason why OL is capable and influential is its ability to provide just-in-time learner assessment and evaluation. This capability has two effects. First, it provides instructors with data regarding the progress of the class and whether the objectives are being met. Second, it provides reinforcement of the concepts taught and provides opportunity for remediation.
- ✦ Second reason why this kind of learning is capable and influential is that it can provide 24x7 accessibilities. In this way learners can not only study when they are available without interfering with their job or other responsibilities, but they can also study when they are most productive. A few people are more productive in the morning while others are in the evening. Learners appreciate the flexibility that not only open opportunity and reduces the stress of getting to class or to resources on time, but it also can result in extra alertness and the related accomplishments.

Class communication affected by OL

While not originally expected, learner-to-learner and faculty-to- learner communication is enhanced when this medium is used correctly. As per Kubala (1998), online learners are more ready and eager to participate due to a measure of anonymity that serves as a motivator. People feel themselves more empowered. They become daring and confrontational about the expression of idea. The reason for this behaviour seems to be that the tools of the web, including forums, chats, and e-mail, increase learner motivation and involvement in class activities. If dealing with younger learners or avid internet users, they interact freely as they are very comfortable with the medium.

There are several reasons for the increase in learner involvement in online classes; a few of these factors are also an incentive to interact freely.

→ Learners view each other's answers and learn through exposure to differing opinions. This aid and supports them develop critical thinking and their own opinions.

→ In this medium all learners are equal and have the same opportunity to speak. No gender bias or other such issues exist and there is no issue of embarrassment of public speaking. In fact even shy learners excel and interact aggressively in when in forums, chat, or via postings.

→ Learners have time to read, think and then express their ideas backing them with facts and searched information. This makes them feel more comfortable than speaking up in a traditional class without researching and backing their argument.

→ Instructors are more accessible via chat, asynchronous posting, or e-mail. In this medium the instructors is more of an 'equal', a peer with whom one interacts in the search of answers, rather than a class manager.

A few sources for OL
One Tube

Most of the people are familiar with One Tube. It is a video sharing website. One Tube database has millions of educational videos.

Learning languages

Free online language courses: - http://www.word2word.com/course.html
This website has 119 languages courses out of that 13 are Indian

Mathematics, physics and engineering courses

(NPTEL - National Program on Technology Enhance Learning)
The following website contains videos lectures of graduate courses prepares by scientists of Indian institute of science and IIT professors
http://nptel.iitm.ac.in/

There are several more OL sources, such as khan academy website: http://www.khanacademy.org/ with a library of over 2400 videos covering everything from arithmetic to physics, finance, and history

Wolfram math world: - http://mathworld.wolfram.com/ the web's most extensive mathematics resource

Advantages of OL
a. Convenience

Online education is that one can get an education as per the own schedule and can do it from the comfort of the own home, that is, learn anytime, anywhere. The biggest advantage of an online is that the virtual classroom would be available to one for 24 hours, a day, and seven days a week.
OL permit and facilitates one to revisit the course content, documents, and discourse forums as often as one like. One seldom misses a thing in an online course.
b. Richer class discourse

People get more out of OL as they find that there is richer class discourse. In a lecture theatre, the shy, less confident learners tend not to contribute to class discourse. When one is online, one has time to think about a meaningful contribution and therefore one is more confident about sharing the views. One also ends up talking with more people as it is easier to approach people online.

c. Deeper interaction with learning content

Another reason people prefer OL is that one can absorb information at the own pace and be more thorough about engaging in the learning content, e.g. when one is in a lecture hall, if one misses what the lecturer said, it's gone forever. However, online learners can rewind over lectures, or research points that the lecturer has made before moving on to their next point.

d. Different learning styles can be accommodated

Learning materials can be developed for different learning styles e.g. A lecturer can provide both visual representation of an idea he is trying to convey along with actually describing it, to satisfy both visual and auditory learners.

e. More friendships developed

It is easier to interact with people online, one end speaking up with more learners, and making more friendships at a deeper level. Also, there is a good chance of meeting with them down the line at a class reunion, or one might be able to organize an informal meet-up with the local classmates.

f. Diversity of views

As learners can be located anywhere, one would most probably be studying with people from different states or countries. This means that one would encounter a rich diversity of views held by people from completely different walks of life.

OL would change the world

More people would receive education

→ People who traditionally wouldn't have access to high-quality education are provided with an opportunity to improve their knowledge and skills. The greater the number of people who are educated, the better the standard of living for the world's citizens, specifically in third world countries

→ OL provides a more learner-centred approach for people who tend not to flourish in a classroom setting and can bring them the important advantages of education that they would not otherwise receive.

→ OL means that more people in work are able to study at their convenience. They can improve their skills to do their jobs better. This in turn aid and supports to improve productivity and innovation, leading to better performing economies and higher standards of living.

Limitations of OL

a. Potential for less interaction

While the flexibility of OL might permit and facilitate for one to work from home, one limitation is the lack of interaction one would get with classmates and the instructor. OL limits the amount of public speaking practice one gain from in-class presentations and discourses, something that is naturally built into a traditionally structured class.

b. Access to facilitator

Sitting down with an instructor to discuss a topic from class or reasons for a certain grade is difficult to do when one can't visit them during office hours. True, one can still email or chat online with an instructor for an online course, but there is a something to be said for a regular conversation instead of words on a screen.

c. Missing out on non-verbal communication

Non-verbal communication is as important, if not more important than verbal communication, and it's hard to see non-verbal communication online. Similar to the need for face-to-face conversations with a facilitator, non-verbal cues are impossible online, and can be just as communicative as actual words.

d. Potential for fewer networking opportunities

Being a member of institutional organizations is a good way to network and a something one can place on the resume, but the organization choices are limited in the OL environment. While one might have an online discourse board with discourse threads with fellow classmates, one have not placed a name with a face, and one might be from different parts of the state, country, even the world, making networking less likely.

e. No facilities

Most traditional institutions provide their learners facilities to use such as libraries, gyms, learner stores, computer labs, research labs, study areas and more. OL can't always provide these aid and supportive tools.

f. Future of OL

A few years ago Chambers of cisco systems once made this prediction about OL that the next big killer app for the internet is going to be education. Education over the internet is going to be so big that it is going to make email usage look like a rounding error in terms of the internet capacity, it is going to consume.

7.6 NETWORKED LEARNING

Wikispaces is a popular exemplar of networked learning (NL). As per Wikipedia, NL is a process of developing and maintaining connections with people and information and communicating in such a way that it supports one another's learning. The central term in this definition is connections. It takes a relational stance in that learning takes place both in relation to others and in relation to learning resources.

NL can be practiced in both informal and formal educational settings.

+ In formal settings, the learning achieved through networked communication is formally facilitated, assessed and/or recognized by an educational organization.

+ In an informal setting, individuals maintain a learning network for their own interests, for learning 'on-the-job', or for research aims.

It has been suggested that NL provides educational institutions more functional efficiency, in that the curriculum can be more tightly managed centrally, or in the case of vocational learning, it can reduce costs to employers and tax payers.

However, it is also argued that NL is too often considered within the presumption of institutionalized or educational learning, thereby omitting awareness of the advantages that NL has to informal or situated learning.

7.7 ETHICAL AND SOCIAL ISSUES IN USING THE INTERNET MATERIAL

The internet has emerged in the last decade as an extremely important conduit for information and communications. The objective of schools is to prepare learners for active and effective participation in the society. The information and communication resources of the internet have become an essential component for this preparation.

Schools are uniquely positioned to serve as the primary vehicle through which young people can develop their knowledge, skills, and motivation to use the internet in a safe, responsible, and effective manner. Many schools have placed primary reliance on filtering software to address online safety concerns. It has always been recognized that filtering software is imperfect : it neither blocks all material that should be blocked, and it frequently blocks access to perfectly appropriate material. There is a growing recognition of the fact that it is simply not possible to protect children with technological tools that are neither infallible, nor present on every internet access device.

No technology protection measure is or ever will be 100% effective in protecting young people from exposure to material that is potentially harmful. There is simply too much material on the internet, with more material posted every second, for any technological system to be truly effective. Virtually every young person will, at one time or another, have unsupervised access to the internet through an unfiltered, unblocked, and unmonitored system. Any time a technology is created that seeks to block access to material; another technology will emerge to get around such blocking actions. Technically proficient young people can easily obtain information on effective strategies to get around these systems.

Schools have become the universal location where young people are learning about the internet. Certainly, then, schools should have an important obligation to help young people learn to use the internet in a safe and responsible manner regardless of the presence or absence of any kinds of protective technologies. Schools are also an important conduit of information for parents : many of whom are not as technically literate as their children. Interestingly, when the NRC committee asked educators about the advantage of having filters, in virtually every school the committee visited the primary reasons provided for filters were to avoid controversy in the community and to avoid liability for exposing children to inappropriate material. Essentially, it appears that the primary reason schools have filters is not to protect kids- but to protect the school. This is unacceptable.

Focussing the educational target

Use of the government internet system should direct to those activities which support education, enrichment, and career development, with the option of limited 'open access' times. Administration must support the educational use of the system through professional development, technical and instructional support, internet-based lesson plans and an educational web site. The best way to enhance and support the safe and responsible use of the internet is to ensure that facilitators are prepared to lead learners on exciting, educationally enriching learning 'adventures' on the internet. When the computers are being used for such activities, the opportunity for misuse is significantly limited.

Education about the safe, secure and responsible use

Facilitators, administrators and learners should receive instruction related to the safe and responsible use of the internet. Education for learners should be appropriate to their age and understandings. Young people should be empowered to independently handle a wide range of interactions and activities on the internet that could be harmful to their safety and well-being. Safety concerns include being the target or recipient of sexual predation, hate group recruitment, gaming and gambling, invasion of personal privacy, internet fraud and scams, harassment, stalking, harmful speech, and access to inappropriate material. We also must address other issues related to the responsible use of the internet by young people. In addition to the intentional access of potentially harmful material, these issues include copyright infringement, plagiarism, computer security violations (hacking, spreading viruses), violation of privacy, internet fraud and scams, harassment, stalking, and dissemination of harmful speech or other violent or abusive material. We must prepare young people to understand their responsibilities as 'cybercitizens.'

Well-communicated clear policy

Learners and staff should have a clear understanding of the kinds of activities that are and are not considered acceptable. Learners and staff should be aware that they have a very limited expectation of privacy when they use the internet at school. They should have a full and complete understanding of the degree to which their activities will be monitored, how this monitoring will occur, and the circumstances under which a specific investigation of their online activities will occur. The policy should address access to inappropriate material, the safety and security of learners when using electronic communications, unlawful and inappropriate activities, and the protection of learner personal information. The policy should address responsibilities of both staff and learners. The policy should serve as the foundation for the government's education program regarding the safe and responsible use of the internet: not simply just another document included in the start-of school informational packet.

Supervision, monitoring and appropriate discipline

Learner use of the internet should be supervised by facilitators in a manner that is appropriate for the age of the learners and circumstances of use. The kind and level of monitoring is somewhat dependent on the circumstances in the school. Supervision and monitoring must be sufficient to establish the expectation that there is a high probability that instances of misuse will be detected and it will result in disciplinary action. When learners are fully aware that there is a high probability that instances of misuse will be detected and result in disciplinary action, they are unlikely to take the risk of engaging in any misuse. The existence of effective monitoring, and learner knowledge of such existence is generally sufficient deterrent for misuse. In small schools with a limited number of learners, limited number of computers, and low level of internet traffic, an approach that involved staff supervision and staff review of internet records will likely be sufficient to establish the expectation of high probability of detection of misuse. With larger schools, more learners, more computers, and a higher level of traffic, supervision and staff review of internet usage logs will likely not be sufficient to achieve a high probability that instances of misuse will be detected. This is where the use of a technology tool becomes an appropriate consideration. Technology tools allow for the more effective and efficient review of internet usage and significantly enhances the probability that instances of misuse will be detected.

It is not possible for administration to enforce a wide range of individual family values when learners are using the internet in school. Administration can address parent concerns and support learner internet use in accord with personal family values by allowing parents to have access to their child's internet use records upon request. Misuse of the internet by learners should be addressed in a manner that makes use of the 'teachable moment' both for the individual learner and other learners in the school. The focus of such instruction should be on the reasons for the rule: the issues or concerns regarding the potential harm the rule is designed to address rather than a focus on disobedience and the power of the facilitator or administrator to impose discipline. No learner should ever discipline for incidents that have occurred that are outside of the control of the learner, such as the unintentional access of inappropriate material. No learner should ever be disciplined for reporting that they have gotten into a dangerous or concerning online situation.

7.8 A brief note on Intellectual Property Rights

Intellectual property (IP) refers to creations of the mind: inventions, literary and artistic works, and symbols, names, images and designs used in trade and commerce. The intellectual properly is created by using sophisticated man power and precious time.

The World Intellectual Property Organization gives the following list of subject matter protected by intellectual property rights

- Literary, artistic and scientific works
- Performances of performing artists, phonograms, and broadcasts
- Inventions in all fields of human endeavour
- Scientific discoveries
- Industrial designs
- Trademarks, service marks, and commercial names and designations
- Protection against unfair competition
- All other rights resulting from intellectual activity in the industrial, scientific, literary or artistic fields

Intellectual property is divided into two categories

- Industrial property: includes inventions (patents), trademarks, industrial designs, geographic indications of source;
- Copyright: includes literary and artistic works such as novels, poems and plays, films, musical works, artistic works such as drawings, paintings, pictures and sculptures and architectural designs.

Intellectual property rights (IPR) are related to copyright. Copyright does not continue indefinitely. The law provides for a period of time during which the rights of the copyright proprietor/generator exist. The period or duration of copyright begins from the moment, when the work has been created, or, under some national laws, when it has been expressed in a tangible form. It continues, in general, until some specific time after the death of the developer/inventor/generator. The purpose of this provision in the law is to enable the successors to benefit economically from misuse of the work after the developer's death.

Way in which rights are protected

The most important feature of any kind of property is that the proprietor may use it exclusively, i.e., as he wishes, and that nobody else can lawfully use it without his authorization. This does not, of course, mean that he can use it regardless of the legally recognized rights and interests of other members of society. Similarly the proprietor of copyright in a protected work may use the work as he wishes, and may prevent others from using it without his authorization. Rights granted under national laws to the proprietor of copyright in a protected work are normally exclusive rights to authorize a third party to use the work, subject to the legally recognized rights and interests of others.

There are two types of rights under copyright

→ Economic rights allow the rights proprietor to derive financial reward from the use of his works by others.
→ Moral rights allow the developer to take certain actions to preserve the personal link between him and the work.

Most copyright laws state that the developer or rights proprietor has the right to authorize or prevent certain acts in relation to a work. The rights proprietor of a work can prohibit or authorize its:

→ reproduction in various forms, such as printed publications or sound recordings or digital formats
→ distribution of copies
→ public performance
→ broadcasting or other communication to the public
→ translation into other languages
→ adaptation, such as a novel into a screenplay

These aspects would help learners about using the material available on the internet and IPR issues associated with these.

EXEMPLARY QUESTIONS

1. Discuss the significance of educational games and simulation as facilitator in learning.
2. Describe software that is available as learning aid in any subject area. Design one assignment for the learners using this software. What are a few of the precautions that one would observe while designing the assignment?
3. Write critical note on use of multimedia application software for small children.
4. What are the various social and ethical issues involved in the use of emerging technologies in the class room?
5. 'There are several social and ethical issues involved in the use of material from the internet.' Comment with appropriate exemplars.

UNIT - 8

ICT FOR EDUCATION: WEB 2.0 TOOLS IN PRACTICES

This unit deals with concept of information and communication technologies with a detailed note on web tools along with a special focus on web 2.0 tools in educational practices

'In fact, one of the saddest but most common conditions in elementary school computer labs is the children are being trained to use Word, Excel and PowerPoint. I consider that criminal, because children should be making things, communicating, exploring, sharing, and not running office automation tools.'

— Nicholas Negroponte

Unit 8
ICT FOR Education: Web 2.0 Tools IN Practices

8.1 INFORMATION AND COMMUNICATION TECHNOLOGY (ICT) AND WEB TOOLS

Information and Communication Technologies (ICT) is an umbrella term. BECTA (2002) said that ICT is a means of accessing, storing, sharing, processing, editing, selecting, presenting and communicating information through a variety of media. It involves finding, sharing and restructuring information in its diverse forms. Some major forms of ICT, as elucidated by Cohen, Manion and Morrison (2005), are word processing, spread sheets, databases, graphing, graphics packages, clipart and sound packages, desktop publishing, multimedia, internet, e-mail, games and simulations.

Use of ICT, now-a-days, in the process of instruction-learning, is being thought of as advancement, in this field. Alexander and Potter (2005) depicted it as ICT makes learning environment more flexible by opening up fresh interaction between pupils and educators, parents and the local and wider community. Wragg (2005) discuss about the art and science of instruction and learning and mentions of virtual reality and interactive technology by giving a message about the use of current, fresh and new technology which includes that people would be more liberated than at present from dependence on a facilitator as the only source of knowledge. The huge memory and the highly interactive nature of the newer forms of educational technology permit several different forms of instruction and learning. Hence, it cannot be denied that ICT has several faces and masks, in turn, for several aspects of instruction and learning.

In addition to availability of means and modes, a better approach is required for ICT and its several aspects in education, including applying and incorporating ICT in instruction and learning. ICT, as every other innovative educational technology, has entered in the field of education with a little bit of ups and downs. And, by the time of writing this book, it has already achieved a remarkable place in almost every aspect of the education, through planning to implementation and evaluation. The prominent ICT tools for these purposes, which are in trend, are web tools. There, majorly, are web 1.0 tools, web 2.0 tools and web 3.0 tools, which are gradually developed forms of ICT.

Let us have a look at web 1.0 tools, web 2.0 tools and web 3.0 tools.
Web 1.0 tools

In a few words, web 1.0 can be characterised as read only content, static HTML websites, and navigation through the web. It was the earlier time, when websites were developed and maintained by the contributing agencies/owner for dissemination of the information. Nobody else was allowed to make any change in the content of web pages. Users could just navigate through the web pages, but were not allowed to make any alterations anywhere. These websites, once created, used to stay as it is for a long time period. Hence, web 1.0 was all about static HTML websites and read-only content. Nobody except contributor or owner could make any changes on the website. Users preferred navigating the web through link directories of websites. Here, users were just consumers, not contributors.
Web 2.0 tools

Web 2.0 can be seen as user generated content, read-write web and blurred dividing line between contributor and consumer. Now-a-days, the consumer or user of the web is not merely passive reader of the content, but also has a freedom to generate the content on the webpage. One can write text, content, even pages over pages on some of the websites. Hence, the discriminating line between consumer and contributor is getting blurred day by day. And, in some of the cases like wiki, this gap has been almost diminished. One can play the role of consumer as well as contributor. Consumer participates, acts, shares, discusses, agrees, and disagrees and so on. Decisions are taken by the users. The significant characteristic of Web 2.0 is people are consuming as well as contributing information through blogs or websites or website applications like Facebook, Orkut, Flickr, YouTube, identi.ca, Digg, Google Groups etc. As revealed from several resources, web 2.0 has some of the prominent aspects as being the read-write web, reaching one billion plus global users (2006), focusing on communities, blogs (weblogs), sharing content, grand use of Wikipedia, XML, RSS, incorporating a vast number of web applications, facilitating tagging ('folksonomy'), making Google more user friendly, reducing cost per click and valuing word of mouth, etc.

Web 3.0 tools

Web 3.0 has advancement over the earlier two by characterising semantic web (or the meaning of data), personalization and behavioural advertising. This is the form of meaning making web. Even the same web page, when opened by different people, gets opened in a different manner. In web 3.0, system collects data about the uses and trend of surfing by an individual and then personalises web page, on its own, for that particular page. It actually concludes about the behaviour of the user. Most of the decisions are taken and provided by the user. For an instance, while opening the Google homepage, everybody, now, gets the same page opened with the same links like web, orkut, image, Gmail etc., while we hardly use all of these links. In web 3.0, if a link is not used for a longer period, web concludes that the link is neither useful nor important for one and decides to make that link disappear. And hence, next time when the page is opened, those links, which are seldom used, temporarily would not appear on that webpage. Experts believe that the web 3.0 browser would act like a personal assistant. As one search the Web, the browser learns what one are interested in. The more one use the Web, the more the browser learns about one and the less specific one would need to be with the questions. Eventually one might be able to ask the browser open questions like 'where should I go for lunch?' The browser would consult its records of what one like and dislike, take into account the current location and then suggest a list of restaurants. The semantic web is a 'web of data' which enables machines to understand the semantics, or meaning, of information on worldwide web. It extends the network of hyperlinked human-readable web pages by inserting machine-readable metadata about pages and how they are related to each other, enabling automated agents to access the Web more intelligently and perform tasks on behalf of users. The term was coined by Tim Berners-Lee, the inventor of worldwide web and director of the World Wide Web Consortium, which oversees the development of proposed semantic web standards. He defines the semantic web as 'a web of data that can be processed directly and indirectly by machines.'

8.2 NEED OF WEB 2.0 TOOLS

↠ **Temporal constraints:** In most of the schools or educational institutions, the time of a class/lecture/period is about 35 minutes to 55 minutes. And moreover, generally, learner has a chance to meet a particular facilitator in that particular limited time slot, as other periods are booked for other individual facilitators. So, a learner finds a lack of time to interact with a particular facilitator. Moreover, generally, if the school time is over or it is a holiday, it is almost impossible to communicate with a facilitator. Hence, due to lack of time and such temporal constraints, one feels difficulty in sharing his/her problems with the facilitator.

↠ **Spatial constraints:** In educational institutes, generally, a learner shares academic problems with the facilitator within school premises. If a learner is not in school/class, he/she finds problem in interacting with the facilitators. Even if a facilitator allows learners to visit him/her at his/her place, it is not easier for all the learners to visit facilitator's place, whenever having an academic problem. Hence, spatial constraints play a crucial role in hindering facilitation of the learners.

↠ **Opportunity constraints:** Likewise, within a small duration of 35 to 55 minutes, everybody can't express his/her views. Everybody does not get equal opportunity in the class. Some learners are over active and they 'grab' most of the time and those who feel shy or are unable to speak in public do not get opportunity to express them in the class. It becomes more vulnerable when it is matter of those, who have linguistics and pronunciation problem. Hence, everybody does not get equal opportunity for sharing and expressing in the class, causing, generally, learning on the part of the learner.

→ **Contribution and collaboration constraints:** Collaborative learning is one of the best strategies of learning. But, in the traditional classrooms, the opportunity for collaborative work is very less. Within the classroom and class period, everybody can't contribute and collaborate with each other in the group. Even discipline norms, too, create a sense of obstacle for collaboration, and hence put a check on the contribution by individuals.

→ **Technology and content customization constraints:** A single technology is found not suitable for all the content and class level. Some of the people think that technology should act as a panacea for all the needs. But, technology needs to be customized according to the content and class level. This not only hinders use and application of technology for the instruction and learning, but also affects the vision about its implications.

→ **Democratic and initiative expression constraints:** Learners may not respect others' views in a traditional classroom and there are chances for conflict and face to face confrontation over some issues. Even a more powerful entity may dominate over the other and may debar the others, even to express themselves freely and democratically. Even the initiative ideas may be checked by the other from expression in the classroom. And, until and unless, every learner is not given freedom for democratic and self-initiated expression of ideas, we can't achieve the fundamental aims of the education.

Meeting these constraints

Though these are fundamental constraints, as I see, pertaining to the educational practices but, no ample solutions are found to meet these constraints. These become more important while dealing with the classroom situations. Hence, it is a big question, how to meet the challenges arisen by these constraints. Of course, there is no panacea available for these constraints but, an endeavour can be made to search the solutions through ICT. Web 2.0 tools can be one of the solutions for these constraints in educational practices, rather open educational practices.

8.3 EXEMPLARY WEB 2.0 TOOLS

Let us know some web 2.0 tools in this regard.

→ **Gmail:** Gmail is one of the most popular web 2.0 tools used for mailing purposes. Using Gmail files like word, ppt, excel etc. can, too, be shared with others. One can send email to an individual or a group of people altogether. One can reply, forward, archive, too, the mails. There is a facility to send blind carbon copy, too, to recipients. Now-a-days people are using the additional integrated functions too like gtalk and chatting. One can make a phone call as well as a video call, using Gmail.

→ **Google applications:** Google provides a platform for so several applications using just a single user account. A number of Google applications are blogger, scholar, books, and video and so on. One can personalise most of these applications for scholarly use. Using scholar, one can find journal papers. Using books, one can find preview and full text of books on several subjects. Google docs can be used to preserve and share several sorts of files. One can control whom to allow viewing particular file and whom to allow editing.

→ **Gtalk:** Though this particular application can be integrated with Gmail, but one has to install it separately after entering Gmail. One can make voice as well as video call using this application. For voice call a headphone is required, while for video call a camera is a must.

- **Google groups:** This application gives freedom to a group of people to organise some discussion, share some files and so on with the security and privacy from others. The advantages of this application are, members can share their views free of time constraints and spatial constraints, they can have equal opportunity as others to create, to share, to collaborate, to discuss, to debate, to agree or disagree and so on.
- **Elluminate and Elluminate live:** Elluminate and elluminate live gives a platform to organise online seminars and classes. Now it has merged with classroom 2.0 for scholastic activities.
- **Classroom 2.0 and classroom 2.0 live:** Classroom 2.0 is a superb sort of tool for online lectures, classes and discussions. This tool is, in fact, a vase of several applications for forums, videos, e-material or e-resources, blogs etc. Classroom 2.0 live is just like a virtual classroom. One can do almost all the activities like raising hands, speaking, agreeing, disagreeing, applauding, using board, sharing documents and texts, and so on. Text can be written in several forms and pictures, too, can be drawn. It is the freedom of the participant, whether he/she wants to share a particular matter with all at a time or just to the presenter.
- **WizIQ:** WizIQ is an equally good tool for facilitators, facilitators or presenters and learners. One can organise a class on any topic which he/she thinks of planning a class. People, at their choice, can search and attend the class. This platform gives facility for free as well as paid classes. WizIQ admin organises free classes for planning and organising a class on WizIQ.
- **Scope:** Scope is, basically, meant for organising seminars. One can organise or attend seminars on this platform. As it says, scope brings individuals who share an interest in educational research and practice. One can attend online workshops and courses. It organises webinars, too. It provides platform for chatting, forums, wikis and resources.
- **Learncentral:** Web conferencing can be pursued using this tool. In addition to forums, resources, groups and events, it provides recordings of earlier webinars. One can use learncentral for connecting, sharing and inspiring.
- **Blackboard and Blackboard Collaborate:** Blackboard provides several platforms BB learn, collaborate, connect, transact, analytics and mobile. By using BB collaborate one can collaborate with others from anywhere, at any time and on any system.
- **Identica:** Identica is a tool for microblogging. One can create a group. One can share something to members of a particular group or with the general public. One can see tags available or popular notices.

We see that web 2.0 tools give freedom to express which can be seen as a fundamental requisite for better educational practices and process of instruction and learning. Hence, there is a need to shift from web 1.0 to web 2.0 tools in educational practices, which in turn can make an effort to bestow equality, justice and value to the work of facilitator as well as learner.

Recapitulation

We have to change ourselves with changing times, for progress, development and better future of the field of education. But, it is equally important to make it clear that ICT tools should not be seen as a replacement of traditional tools and practices. Moreover, it should not be seen as a panacea for all the problems. As a conclusion, ICT-integrated practices should be supported and traditional practices should be BLENDED with ICT for rationalized approach both for educational practices, in general and instruction and learning, in particular.

8.4 AN EXEMPLARY LESSON FROM MATHEMATICS BASED ON WEB 2.0 TOOLS

Topic: Cube
Level: Upper Primary/Secondary
Duration: As per the need (may vary from 3 to 5 days)
Content Outline
- → Early concept of a cube
- → Characteristics of a cube
- → Concept of a cube
- → Cubical objects around us
- → Drawing a cube

Specific procedural objectives
- → To apply Skype as noticeboard tool for initiating the thought process for the cube.
- → To apply TypePad for blogging the views about cube as a previous knowledge.
- → To apply Yammer as a micro-blogging tool for summarizing the views.
- → To apply Photostory for sharing the photos collected, consisting of cubical objects/figures.
- → To apply Classroom 2.0 for collaborating over all common characteristics of a cube from the photos.
- → To apply Glogster for summarizing common characteristics of a cube.
- → To apply Xtranormal for creating videos of photos shared.
- → To apply Xtranormal for sharing videos.
- → To apply Classroom 2.0 for class-discussion.
- → To apply Geogebra for creating several cubes of different size.
- → To apply FacilitatorTube for uploading the videos developed by the facilitator or facilitator for drawing a cube and explaining concept of edges and surfaces.
- → To apply Delicious for tagging these videos.
- → To apply R-campus for creating e-portfolio and attaching individual video for drawing a cube alongwith a presentation, for evaluation.

Procedure
i. Facilitator or facilitator would ask an interesting question using Skype to motivate the learners to recollect the understanding; they currently have, about the cube. The question may be like, 'Yesterday I found somebody talking about a cube. Can anybody tell me what a cube is?' or, 'Hey, have you seen the dice or chalk box? What about its shape?', or, 'I had enjoyed small uniform cheese pieces in mutter-paneer vegetable, just this noon. I wonder how their shape is different from that of a match box. Can anybody help me finding these answers?'
ii. Learners would share their views for responding to the question with freedom of word-limit using TypePad. Some learners may share some incidences, while others some events. Some may simply share their guessing about the cube. Some may share even examples of cubical objects in spite of writing about the concept of the cube. As a whole, learners at this platform are free to share whatever ideas they have about the cube and moreover, they can share in whatever number of characters as they think appropriate.

iii. For summarizing and comprehending their views learners would use Yammer with a prescribed word limit. Here, the learners would be told to summarize their ideas and views, drawn from the above views provided by all, in a character limit. It means, here, learners would be wiser and judicious to share their understanding drawn from above mentioned views. Here, facilitator, too, alongwith others would be able to know about the previous knowledge of the learners.

iv. Learners would be told to collect photos from their surroundings which consist of cubical objects/figures. Learners would collect several sorts of photos and pictures. They may collect photos either already available with them and their relatives or they may create some fresh and new photos, specially generated for this particular concept. The photos may contain pictures of dice, chalk box, typical-book, etc. This exercise would help them to associate themselves with their environment for the learning and concept formation about the cube.

v. Photostory would be used to share these photos with peers and facilitator. Learners would be motivated to share the collected photos with their peers and facilitator on a common platform. Everybody would be thought to be delighted and eager to know about photos collected by others. Moreover, this may help them to come closer to each other.

vi. Learners would discuss common characteristics of cubes based upon these photos on Classroom 2.0 platform. Learner can be told to have a common discussion by sharing several views about common characteristics, which can be found in the photos shared. They would be motivated in such a way that none of the photos is left unmarked. Moreover, it is the liability of the facilitator that almost all the common characteristics are covered.

vii. Glogster would be used by the learners for summarizing these common characteristics to frame their own definition of a cube. Here, learners would be motivated to frame their own definition of the cube individually. While one has shared his/her definition with the others, others may be suggested to compare that definition with his/hers. Moreover, it can be pointed out by other learners if any important common characteristic is left without getting included in the definition.

viii. Learners would be divided into a group of five members each. They would create videos selecting and using at least ten photos from the photos shared at Photostory. Xtranormal would be used to create the videos. Each group would use at least ten photos to develop a story and later on a video. Group may discuss about meaningfulness of that video. Group may suggest for several quotes to be used in the video. They can discuss over the relevance of the quotes used for particular photo of the video. Finally a meaningful, interesting video accepted by the entire group would be the output.

ix. These videos would be shared with all using Xtranormal. Videos developed, thereafter, can be shared on a common platform, so that other peers from all the groups can observe, enjoy and appreciate the video. They can discuss several dimensions of the video pertaining to the concept of the cube, social background of the photos, etc.

x. A classroom discussion would be held using Classroom 2.0 for discussing, sharing, deliberating, raising, exploring the problems, doubts and solutions. Thereafter, learners can be motivated to frame several problems, comprehending their doubts and enlist other related queries. Once, this work would be done, an online class can be planned and organized using classroom 2.0, where all can discuss, share, deliberate upon, raise and further explain their problems, doubts, queries and possible solutions.

xi. Learners would create cubes of several sizes using Geogebra. They can draw some interesting diagrams, too, like gift-box using Geogebra. Geogebra is a mathematical tool which can be used efficiently and interestingly to create cubes of several sizes. Learners would be motivated to create several cubes and to look for commonalities in these cubes. They, further, can be motivated to create a variety of shapes using cube, like dice, gift-box, etc.

xii. As an additional activity, for a need-based discussion about shapes, diagrams etc. Facebook can be used. Moreover, learners can discuss anything pertaining to the topic, anytime throughout the process on a common popular platform, the Facebook. Here, they can share problems, pictures, videos, links, events, applications, etc. pertaining to the topic, here, the cube.

xiii. Facilitator would upload videos on FacilitatorTube showing the process of drawing a cube using ruler and pencil alongwith explaining the concept of radii and circumference. A number of videos either self-created or collected from other resources, would be shared by the facilitator with all the learners. These videos would explain the steps of drawing a cube using ruler and pencil. While drawing cubes of several sizes, the video may introduce the concept of the edges and surfaces of a cube. Further, it can be explained what the volume of a cube is. The video may leave some interesting questions pertaining to relationship about several sides, several surfaces, angles at several vertices, etc.

xiv. Delicious would be used for tagging these videos. Several videos can be tagged in a variety of manners. The tagging can be in such a way that it directs a sort of insight among the learners.

xv. Learners would be suggested to develop their own individual video for developing a cube describing its edges, surfaces, vertices and the process of drawing. They would further prepare their slide-presentation for the learning so far. Learners, motivated by the videos shared by the facilitator, would be provided with a set of lengths, breadths and heights. Each learner would select a number of sides and draw his/her individual cube. A set of cubes drawn by one learner may differ from the set of cubes drawn by other. Learners, while drawing these cubes, would develop videos of the process held with the help of peers or others. Each leaner would be supposed to present the entire concept of a cube including process of drawing his/her cube, so he/she would prepare a slide-presentation. They can plan to present it in front of the peers, as the time and space do permit.

xvi. Learners would create an e-portfolio using R-campus and attach all the generated learning objects to this e-portfolio. This can be used for the evaluation purpose. Each learner would create an individual e-portfolio, mentioning each and every aspect of the entire process and the product, generated so far. They can enrich it more and more as they think suitable. They, alongwith documents and videos already created by them, can share further important and relevant links to the resources, repositories, texts, blogs, etc. pertaining to the topic in this e-portfolio. This e-portfolio can be used by the facilitator for continuous and comprehensive evaluation.

Tools used

S. No.	What?	Who plays the key role?	What for?
I	Skype	Facilitator	Sharing notice

II	TypePad	Learners	Sharing detailed views
III	Yammer	Learners	Summarizing with limits
IV	Photostory	Learners	Sharing photos
V	Classroom 2.0	Learners	Collaborating common characteristics
VI	Glogster	Learners and Facilitator	Summarizing the concept
VII	Xtranormal	Learners	Creating videos using photos
VIII	Xtranormal	Learners	Sharing developed videos
IX	Classroom 2.0	Learners and Facilitator	Classroom discussion
X	Geogebra	Learners	Creating cubes and shapes
XI	Facebook	Learners	All time discussions
XII	FacilitatorTube and Delicious	Facilitator	Sharing procedural videos and tagging
XIII	R-campus	Learners and Facilitator	Comprehending and evaluation

Advantages

→ This is a learner-centred approach.

→ This is a learner-environment-centred approach.

→ It provides temporal and spatial freedom to the learner.

→ It inculcates the values of co-operation and collaboration among the learners.

→ It develops democratic values and respect for others' views among the learners.

→ It provides equal opportunity to all learners involved.

→ It covers all domains of learning.

→ In this approach, learner's reflection and understanding bags the central place

Caution

→ Tools used in this lesson are merely suggestive.

→ Facilitators or facilitator educators can use one, several or all tools as per the need and the rationale.

→ Other tools can also be used, if facilitator finds them more suitable.

→ Finally, facilitator should be wise, free and justified to select, prefer, decide and apply the tools.

→ Facilitators or facilitator educators, while facing any problem in applying ICT in pedagogy of mathematics, may feel free to contact the author through email, as and when required.

These and several other web tools for instruction and learning can give better insight to facilitators for instructions and pave the way for better interaction with their learners.

EXEMPLARY QUESTIONS

1. What do you understand by ICT?
2. How web 2.0 tools are different from web 1.0 tools?
3. Can web 2.0 tools be better used to create a learner-centred learning environment? How?
4. Explain applications and advantages of any two educational web 2.0 tools.

UNIT - 9

OPEN EDUCATIONAL RESOURCES: OPENING UP THE NEW TREND IN EDUCATION

This unit deals with concept, classification, development cycle, exemplary cases and repositories of open educational resources

'"... digitised materials offered freely and openly for educators, students and self-learners to use and reuse for teaching, learning and research.'

— OECD

Unit 9
Open Educational Resources: Opening up the New Trend in Education

9.1 INTRODUCTION

The current unit endeavours to explain the conceptual underpinnings of open educational resources (OER). Initiating from introducing the concept and providing superficial knowledge about OER, it approaches to develop a deeper understanding of it. It tries to explain further the concept of free followed by describing the blurred line between free and the open. OER is a broad term including in it the content, platform and the licences. Classification of OER is a current concern. Various ways of using and applying OER and OER life cycle are discussed. And finally, some exemplars of OER are given in order to facilitate facilitators and learners for applying these in their instruction and learning.

Introducing the 'Open'

The 'open' is a symbol of freedom. The 'open' means with no 'closed chamber' or with no 'curtain' or without 'barrier' or 'restriction-free'. In case of education, the term has evolved out of the basic concept 'access' and 'reach'. Computer and internet, in the beginning, at the time of their inception, have been thought to be means that can be used by elite class only, especially economic and educational elite.

Later, with the ease of access to public, at mass level, to the hardware, software and internet facility, the concept of 'free' evolved which was later followed by the concept of 'open'. The concept of 'open' is a need based concept. If the access is a matter of economic prerogative, how can the society develop as a whole? Hence, it arose into the minds of a group, if the development of the society, as a whole, is a matter of concern, everybody, in other words even the last learner, has to be equipped with the access of these facilities.

As far as 'free' is concerned, there are two points of view – one comprehends the idea of 'free' as 'economically free' while the second takes it as 'liberty' (fees are usually charged for distribution on CDs and USB drives, or for services of installing or maintaining the operation of free software, not for its use).

This further gave rise to the refinement and further clarification between the concepts of 'free' and 'open'. Though the two terms seem to be the same, but both of these are not equivalent. While the concept of 'free' is pertaining to the idea of proprietary hold over the resource, and the permission being provided to others for its use, the concept of 'open' is pertaining to the right to re-use or modify. Hence, it can be understood that where 'free' is more of a financial point of view, the concept of 'open' is evolved from educational and licensing point of view. A 'free' thing may be popular, but may or may not be suitable as per the needs of learners at various places i.e. a tailor-made package cannot suit learners at all levels. In layman's words, in case of 'free' the source cannot be copied or modified without the permission of the proprietor or the author. This is the other aspect that the author of the resource or software bestows opportunity for 'free' use of the resource or the software to the public or a group of specific people.

The idea of the 'open' is entirely different than this concept. 'Open' inherits the paradigm shift over the authority or the proprietorship of the resource or the software. 'Open' means anybody can share, copy or modify the source file/script/code. While in case of 'free', the authority of the content generated by the user lies with the author of the resource, but, in case of 'open' this authority is bored by the user. As a consequence to current discussion, it can be inferred that 'open' is more accessible and reachable to the public, while 'free' still have some implied provisions of 'unreached'. It is worth to be mentioned here that 'open' may or may not be free. One may have to bear the partial or full financial liability for its use. Moreover, an 'Open' may change to a proprietary or vice versa, at any point of time. For an instance, Docebo, which earlier was 'open', now has become a proprietary platform. Hence, whenever the 'open' is planned to be used, its current status should be verified.

9.2 CHARACTERISTICS OF OPEN SOURCE

Now, while we are having a brief overview of the 'open', it is appropriate to talk about deeper understanding of this concept. Open source doesn't merely mean access to the source code. Open-source software, while concerned about more of distribution terms, must fulfil with the following criteria:

a. Free Redistribution

Redistribution is at the heart of 'open'. The license should not restrict any party, involved, from selling or giving away the software - application, utility or system, as a component of an aggregate software distribution containing programs from several different sources. The license shall not require a royalty or other fee for such sale. Means, the financial liability should not be a compulsion, though asking for donation to help is permissible.

b. Free and Unbound Source Code

For modification in the software, the source code is the necessary requirement. The program must include source code, and must allow distribution in source code as well as compiled form. If some form of a product is not distributed with source code, there must be essentially a well-publicized means of obtaining the source code for no more than a reasonable reproduction cost preferably, downloading via the Internet without charge. The source code must be available at one or the other source. The source code must be the preferred form in which a programmer would modify the program. Deliberately obfuscated source code is not allowed. Intermediate forms such as the output of a pre-processor or translator are not allowed i.e. the source code must not require further assistance of a third party for installation or further use.

c. Derivative or Derived Works

When a new product is developed by using a component or set of components, the output is called as the derivative or derived work. The license of software must allow modifications and derived works, and must allow them to be distributed under the same terms as the license of the original software. It can be understood as the license of the derivative must be either same or more flexible as that of the original software.

d. Integrity of the Author's Source Code

Sometimes, the author does not want change in the original source code keeping the same name as that of the original, though derivation is not restricted. The license, in that case, may restrict source-code from being distributed in modified form only if the license allows the distribution of 'patch files' with the source code for the purpose of modifying the program at build time. The license must explicitly permit distribution of software built from modified source code. The license may require derived works to carry a different name or version number from the original software.

e. Equality of Persons or Groups

The license must not discriminate against any person or group of persons. Here the concept of equality gets in. The license of the software must be coherent with the spirit of the equality. As a layman, it can be understood as; the license of the software should not discriminate among the people on any basis, until and unless there are ample/sufficient legitimate reasons.

f. No Discrimination against Fields of Application

No field must be debarred from using the software or the program. The license must not restrict anyone from making use of the program in a specific field of endeavour, e.g. it may not restrict the program from being used in a business, or from being used for genetic research. Though, this may be another aspect that the license may restrict the user from its commercial use for earning the money through selling it.

g. Distribution of License with Freedom of Version

The same license must be spontaneously effective to the distributed software or the program. The rights attached to the program must apply to all to whom the program is redistributed without the need for execution of an additional license by those parties. The same license may have different available versions. Hence, this is another aspect that the license version may be changed by the author under the same license category.

h. License not Specific to a Product

The software or the program must be an independent distinct entity. The rights attached to the program must not depend on the program's being part of a particular software distribution. If the program is extracted from that distribution and used or distributed within the terms of the program's license, all parties to whom the program is redistributed should have the same rights as those that are granted in conjunction with the original software distribution. In simple words, all the copies of the software must have the same license as that of the original.

i. License not Restrict Other Software

The software must be free from imposing restrictions of being 'open' or 'free' for allowing other programs to run using that platform. The license must not place restrictions on other software that is distributed along with the licensed software, e.g. the license must not insist that all other programs distributed on the same medium must be open-source software. The software must permit interaction with other software irrespective of their licenses.

j. Technology-neutral License

The license of the software must not demand pre-availability of a specific technology for its use. No provision of the license may be predicated on any individual technology or style of interface. This is to bar the compulsion of using technology, with other license or with an economical motive, for the application and implication of the 'open' software.

(Source: http://www.opensourcescripts.com/help.html)

9.3 BETWEEN THE 'OPEN' AND 'FREE'

Though conceptually 'open' and 'free' are two distinct ideas, but the massive advantage demands the need of both of the concepts, and, software and programs based upon these concepts for further propagation of information and communication technologies, especially computer, internet, etc., for instruction and learning purposes.

Hence, now-a-days, open as well as free software, both, are being treated as important for their use and application. Wherever the 'open' is available, it can be used and wherever 'free' is available, its use can be allowed. 'Open' is mainly required while one is aimed to change or moderate the source file or wishing to create the derivative of the original software. This may need a higher level of technical expertise, while most of the facilitators may not have the high level of expertise, hence may not feel the need of changing the source code. Due, to this one of the very reasons, the use and application of 'free' and 'open' software are welcomed with equal warmth by the academic fraternity. Hence, it would be equally good to talk about 'open' as well as 'free' software in the current scenario.

9.4 CONCEPT OF OER

OER are open (re)sources which are meant for educational purposes and developed with an aim of facilitating instruction and learning. OER are defined by a report to the William and Flora Hewlett Foundation as follows:

'OER are instruction, learning and research resources that reside in the public domain or have been released under an intellectual property license that permits their free use or re-purposing by others. OER include full courses, course materials, modules, textbooks, streaming videos, tests, software, and any other tools, materials or techniques used to support access to knowledge.'

OER can be software, a tool, a program or an e-platform. In education, the chief areas can be thought to be as developing the learners through effective and better learning, facilitating the learner through better instruction and professional development of facilitators. For all these aspects, open resources can help in a fruitful way. All the open resources for these three chief purposes, and other aspects too of education, can comprehensively be labelled as OER.

OER include:

+ Learning content: full courses, course materials, content modules, learning objects, collections and journals, online tools and software to support content creation.
+ Tools: software to support the creation, delivery, use and improvement of open learning content including searching and organization of content, content and learning management systems, content development tools, and on-line learning communities.
+ Licenses: intellectual property licenses to promote open publishing of materials, design-principles, and localization of content.

OER include different kinds of digital assets. Learning content includes courses, course materials, content modules, learning objects, collections, and journals. Tools include software that supports the creation, delivery, use and improvement of open learning content, searching and organization of content, content and learning management systems, content development tools, and on-line learning communities. Implementation resources include intellectual property licenses that govern open publishing of materials, design-principles, and localization of content. They also include materials on best practices such as stories, publication, techniques, methods, processes, incentives, and distribution.

9.5 VARIOUS CLASSIFICATIONS OF OER

Though the idea of universal single classification system for anything is a myth, but it is another aspect that classification helps in learning through categorization. Based upon the various criteria, OER can be classified into several categories. Some of the prominent criteria can be as internet connectivity, aim and target group.

Based on the internet connectivity: This can be the simplest classification of OER. It is a concern of the mass level now, that how can the digital divide between 'connected' and 'non-connected' be made over or how can the technology gap be minimized. Hence, the concept of such a classification came into existence.

a. Online tools: These are the tools which necessarily need the internet connectivity for its use.

b. Offline tools: These are the tools which do not need the internet connectivity for its use.

c. One-time Connection tools: This can be the third type of resources or the softwares which require one-time internet connection for the installation. Once installed, it does not require any further connection for its use.

Based on the target group: Another way of classification may be based upon the target. The target or the user may be an individual or a group.

a. Individual resource: These are the tools which are meant for one-to-one use and one-to-one interaction.

b. Group resource: These are the tools which are supposed to deal with an entire group- smaller or larger, or a subgroup.

Based on the focus: This method of classification keeps in mind the focus while using the software. There are two sorts of aspects as far as demands of learners are concerned. First, the learners need a platform to communicate among themselves and the facilitator; second, the learners need a platform which is full of specific content related processes and activities. The content needs to be subject-specific. A few may be for mathematics, while some other may be for science or humanities, etc.

a. Communication focused software: These software are meant for providing a common platform for discussing, sharing, arguing, communicating, questioning, answering, agreeing, disagreeing, etc. These are the common needs of all the facilitators though may be associated

b. Content focused software: Software under this category are aimed to address the specific subjects such as mathematics, chemistry, physics, biology, social science, language, etc. As soon as a communication platform is accessed, the facilitators and facilitator-educators are willing to focus upon their subjects of concern. These software fulfil this secondary but prominent need.

9.6 USING OER IN VARIOUS WAYS

Though there are numerous ways in which OER can be used by the facilitators, teacher-educators and their learners. And, several others are still being explored. But, here, at this point of time, we are trying to discuss 5 prominent and representative possible ways of using OER.

These ways can be illustrated as:

→ To enhance an existing course or offering by adding OER: A facilitator who is willing to enhance and enrich a course which is already in flow, he/she can add OER to it, in order to better cater the needs of the learners with the changing scenario. The existing course may not be able to address all the needs and changed concepts in the current times as the existing course may have been developed several years ago. In this case adding OER to the current course may help not only facilitators and teacher-educators, but their learners too.

✈ To improve existing content by replacing the existing materials with the OER: Sometimes, the existing materials may be totally outdated or the mode of transaction of existing material, in its existing form, may be obsolete or uninteresting. In this case, the facilitator may like to replace the existing course with OER. The replacement of the existing materials may help in arousing the interest of the learners or helping out with the conflict management in the mechanism of dealing with the outdated and insignificant material.

✈ To create new part of materials by using or re-purposing OER: The domain of content knowledge is increasing almost every day. Hence, the need arises to introduce the learners with this new content knowledge in addition to the existing content. The facilitator can use OER in order to fulfil this need. For this new content, facilitator can develop OER materials, or use the existing OER or use the material generated for some other purpose by others as per his/her specific needs.

✈ To create new courses by using, re-using and repurposing OER: OER can be used for creating new courses too by using, compiling, re-using, linking, re-purposing, modifying, and referring the recently developed OER. Now-a-days, while, every day the keen, devoted and expert people are developing and sharing OER for the mass advantage keeping in the mind the specific needs of specific set of people, OER for almost every aspect are easily available for facilitators. This can help them in creating easily the new courses considering latest advancement- technical and content-based.

✈ Getting learners to generate OER: Facilitators can motivate their learners to develop OER. If not possible at mass level, he/she can identify a group of tech-savvy learners and with the help of them the facilitator can generate OER. The need of the OER can be discussed at length for motivating the learners. When new OER will be generated, these can be discussed in open for feedback and further refinement before distribution at mass level.

(Source: http://col-oer.weebly.com/module-5:using-oer.html)

9.7 DEVELOPMENT CYCLE OF OER

OER development can be better understood as a development cycle. Commonwealth of learning, explicitly, explains this cycle consisting of six steps prepare, search and classify, re-purpose, value addition, publish and deliver, and review. These steps are explained as follows:

a. Prepare

✈ Module Specifications Sheet (Outline, Duration, Learning Outcomes, Assessment Criteria, Learning Units Description).

✦ Context of Use (whether mainstream educational system through programmes of studies or short professional development courses or both).

✦ Identify type of Open Licensing to be used.

✦ Selection of the pedagogical strategy and instructional techniques.

(For a tutorial on how to identify an Open Licence: http://wikieducator.org/Open_Educational_Content/olcos/CHOOSE_a_license)

b. Search and Classify

✦ Identify repositories to be used (e.g. Open learn, Connexions, MIT, OER Commons, Wiki Educator or Wikipedia etc.).

✦ Look for related content – browse metadata, check license type, check content quality, level, format, pedagogical approach, duration etc.

✦ Build a checklist of available content – classify according to the pertinent criteria above or as per one's requirements.

✦ Identify what is missing and what needs to be added, developed from scratch and/or adapted/repurposed/ re-contextualized.

(For a tutorial on how to search for OER: http://wikieducator.org/Open_Educational_Content/olcos/SEARCH)

c. (Re) Purpose

✦ Decontextualize highly adapted learning content.

✦ Rewrite material that is not contextually correct, write new materials to cater for those that are missing, and/or mix materials from different sources.

✦ Add context-related learning activities that meet the pedagogical approach selected.

(For a tutorial on how to produce and remix OER the link given further can be explored: http://wikieducator.org/Open_Educational_Content/olcos/PRODUCE_%26_REMIX)

d. Value Addition

✦ Add new learning/pedagogical scenarios that improve the learning experience of learners.

✦ Provide multiple modalities (such as animations and multimedia) for learning to suit individual preferences of learners (such as learning/cognitive styles).

✦ Provide multiple access/delivery modes to increase accessibility to learners with different constraints such as internet connection, limited bandwidth etc.

e. Publish and Deliver

✦ Publish on e-learning platform, stand-alone websites, and CD/DVD formats.

✦ Deliver the course to target audience.

✦ Monitor the learner progress and achievements and provide tutoring/technical support.

✦ Share in the different OER repositories or simply put the content available on the local website and let others know about it.

f. Review

> ✈ Gather feedback from learners on the course.
> ✈ Review content to improve the course for subsequent cohorts.
> ✈ Restart the cycle if there are changing requirements and/or to keep up-to-date with on-going developments in the area or to check for other OER that have been published or improved.

(Source: http://col-oer.weebly.com/module-6:the-oer-life-cycle.html)

9.8 EXEMPLARY CASES OF OER

Below are some of the best sources, along with their links, for shared educational content, lectures, video, images, academic journals and reference sources. Facilitators can start to find open licensed material to build or enhance their courses.

> ✈ College Open Textbooks: Textbooks are organized by subject, with various open licenses. http://www.collegeopentextbooks.org
> ✈ Connexions: This is a sort of repository for educational content, organized by discipline. Though it is not a user friendly search interface, but worth a look anyway. http://cnx.org/
> ✈ Bepress: http://www.bepress.com/
> ✈ Digital commons scholarly publications: This is searchable repository organized by grade level, subject, type of content and format. http://www.oercommons.org/
> ✈ Moodle: Moodle is an open platform for learning management system (LMS). Courses can be mutually developed and executed using this platform. http://www.moodle.org/
> ✈ Open Stax: Peer-reviewed college textbooks can be found online here. https://openstaxcollege.org/books
> ✈ Global Textbook Project: Open document format for textbooks are available on business, computing, education, health, sciences and social sciences. http://globaltext.terry.uga.edu/books
> ✈ Curriki: All contents are cc licensed and uploaded by educators. http://www.curriki.org/xwiki/bin/view/Main/WebHome
> ✈ Geogebra: Geogebra is a subject based platform devoted to the combination of geometry and algebra in mathematics. Using it one can draw various shapes from simpler line segments to complex tessellations, use co-ordinate geometry to analyse the figures, etc. http://www.geogebra.org/
> ✈ Hippocampus: In Hippocampus digital content is organized by subject. It includes a lot of streaming content. http://www.hippocampus.org/
> ✈ Merlot: This is searchable repository of educational content, organized by subject, grade level, type of content and format. http://www.merlot.org/merlot/index.htm
> ✈ Open Course Ware search: This includes course content from nearly a dozen institutions, including MIT, Yale, UMass and Notre Dame. http://www.ocwsearch.com/
> ✈ Web quest: Web quest is the platform for communicating in a better and more fruitful way for educational purposes. It allows sharing, discussing, commenting, etc. http://www.webquest.org/

- Wikibooks: This is a creation from the founders of Wikipedia. It contains open access textbooks contributed by scholars, educators and others. http://www.wikibooks.org/
- Wikispaces: This is a learning management system (LMS), which is user friendly. In this platform, the content can be developed by the facilitator as well as learners. http://www.wikispaces.com/
- Flat World Knowledge: Free textbooks are available and searchable by subject. http://www.flatworldknowledge.com/
- Academic Earth: Academic earth includes online course content organized by subject. This content is often available in the form of module. http://academicearth.org/
- The Orange Grove: This is Florida's digital repository for educational content. http://florida.theorangegrove.org
- YouTube: Specifically we can search the education site too. See what we can find out about the source of the video (creator/owner/institution). http://www.youtube.com http://www.youtube.com/education
- Critical Commons: Video clips, lectures and articles are available here. It is a sort of 'you tube' for the higher education set. http://criticalcommons.org/
- Vimeo: It is a source for shared videos. It includes non-educational content as well. http://vimeo.com/
- Ted: It contains video links to lectures by notable experts in science, global issues, technology, business and design. http://www.ted.com/
- Creative Commons: One can find images with open licenses over here. http://search.creativecommons.org/
- Slide share: Power points are searchable by tag terms or a search bar. http://www.slideshare.net/
- Directory of Open Access Journals: One can think of this as a free Proquest. Full text, peer-reviewed journal articles in all subject areas are available. http://www.doaj.org/
- Directory of Open Access Books: This is comparatively a new site from the group that gave DOAJ. It includes peer-reviewed and open-licensed titles. http://www.doabooks.org
- Public Library of Science: Research articles in the sciences are available here. http://www.plos.org/
- Scholarpedia: It is open access encyclopaedia, curated by subject experts. http://www.scholarpedia.org/
- Wikimedia Commons: It contains freely usable media files. http://commons.wikipedia.org/wiki/Main_Page

(Source:https://sites.google.com/a/sbctc.edu/opencourselibrary/developer-resources/librarians)

9.9 EXEMPLARY CASES OF 'FREE' EDUCATION RESOURCES

Below are some of the free sources, not necessarily open, for shared educational content. Facilitators can start to find free material to build or enhance their courses. Some of these are entirely free and some other may provide free trial or free level.

- Bigbluebutton: Bigbluebutton is a free platform for video chatting. While the facilitator is interacting with the learners, they can see each other.

There are many user-friendly options available for better interaction. http://www.bigbluebutton.org/

→ Campus Pack Social Software for Learning: It empowers instructors, academic technologists, and instructional designers to build and implement assignments and activities from a palette of re-usable social media tools.

→ class.io : It helps facilitators to share course resources with learners in a simple way. It integrates with Google Apps, Facebook and other web services that facilitators and learners use.

→ Class Pager: Using it one can text his/her classroom.

→ Classroom 2.0: It is a sort of platform which allows the members to interact virtually. Almost all the activities held in a regular classroom can be virtually held using this platform. The additional values achieved by this platform are temporal free, spatial free environment, providing equal opportunity to all, creating democratic environment, etc. http://www.classroom20.com/

→ Cmap: Cmap is a free tool for concept mapping. The significant value of this tool is that it is user-friendly. It automatically provides help for creating links, connections, modifying connections, creating branches, reversing the directions, modifying roots and branches, etc. http://cmap.ihmc.us/

→ Collaborize Classroom: It allows facilitators to extend their classroom discussions to a structured and private online community.

→ Edmodo: It is a social platform for facilitators and learners to share ideas, files, events and assignments.

→ Edublogs: One can simply create, manage and moderate blogs for all the learners with a minimum of fuss (based on Word Press).

→ Eduglogster: One can engage learners in the creative expression of knowledge and skills using this. EduGlogster premium is collaborative online learning platform for facilitators and learners to express their creativity, knowledge, ideas and skills in the classroom.

→ Edutagger: It is a sort of social bookmarking service for school learners and educators, allowing them to store web links online and share them with others, all within an educational context.

→ ePals Learning Space: It is a safe virtual workspace for K-12 communication, collaboration and learning. It contains collaborative communication tools and stores schoolwork and documents for anytime, anywhere use.

→ Gaggle Apps: These tools help support diversity and the development of communities through safe user friendly platforms that encourages dialogue and the sharing of perspectives.

→ Google Apps for K-12: It is a powerful set of communication and collaboration tools branded for collaboration in the classroom.

→ GoSoapbox: It can be used during class to break down participation barriers, keeping learners engaged, and giving the facilitators insight into learner comprehension that was never before possible.

→ Jog the Web: The Simple, ergonomic solution which allows the user to create, read and share a new online media.

→ My Big Campus: It can be understood as a safe, collaborative online learning environment designed for k-12 schools. Some of its features include blogging, group chats (great for back channelling), tests, classroom pages, discussions—and the list goes on.

→ Schoology: It is a fully hosted, fully managed course management system with a social network for K-12 and Higher Education.

→ Socialmediaclassroom: It is a free and open-source (Drupal-based) web service that provides facilitators and learners with an integrated set of social media that each course can use for its own purposes—integrated forum, blog, comment, wiki, chat, social bookmarking, RSS, micro blogging, widgets, and video commenting are the first set of tools.

→ Twiducate It provides a platform for social networking for schools.

(Source:http://c4lpt.co.uk/directory-of-learning-performance-tools/tools-for-the-social-classroom-ages-5-18/)

9.10 STREAM-BASED EXEMPLARY CASES OF OER REPOSITORIES

Below are some of the OER repositories, along with a brief description, for shared educational means and sources. Facilitators can start to find these repositories to enrich or enhance their specific subject areas.

Science

→ ArXiv.org e-Print archive: ArXiv, set up by Cornell University, is an e-Print archive specializing in Physics, Mathematics, Nonlinear Sciences, Computer Science and Quantitative Biology. It contains documents, mainly as Postscript and PDF files. It is addressed to graduate education mainly. No license agreement is published, so full copyright protection has to be assumed.

→ Biomedical Library UNSW: UNSW is a repository specializing in medicine and health resources. Maintained by the University of New South Wales in Australia, it has not been updated since 2000. It contains mainly links addressed to the higher education space.

→ CITIDEL (Computing and Information Technology Interactive Digital Educational Library): A collaboration between Hofstra University, the College of New Jersey, Pennsylvania State University, Villanova University and Virginia Tech, as part of the US National Science Foundation's National Science Digital Library Project, to create a portal to computing education. CITIDEL is a digital library of educational resources for the computing field, harvested from ten different source collections. It contains to a wide variety of resources, addressed to a diversity of educational levels.

→ CSTC (Computing Science Teaching Center) : CSTC is a repository of peer-reviewed instruction resources for college and graduate level computer science education. The CSTC is designed to facilitate access to quality instruction materials developed worldwide. It is endorsed by the US Association of Computing Machinery and funded by the US National Science Foundation. Metadata for materials are created by users. CSTC is one of the source collections for CITIDEL. It contains all types of archives. It has not been updated since 2003.

→ DLESE (Digital Library for Earth System Education) : It is a Community of digital library access to high-quality collections of educational resources, mainly centered on Earth Sciences. It addresses all levels of education and contains a wide range of resource types.

✈ ESCOT Home Page: ESCOT is a test bed for the integration of innovative technology in middle school (K-12) mathematics. The project investigates replicable practices that produce predictably high quality digital learning resources. It contains graphs, tables and simulations, as well as tools for manipulating geometry and algebra, to be integrated in math education software.

✈ DLESE (Digital Library for Earth System Education): Funded by the US National Science Foundation, DLESE provides learners and educators at all levels with access to materials to support Earth system science education. The collection includes lesson plans, maps, images, data sets, assessment activities, curricula and online courses. The site also provides support services to help users effectively create, use and share OER, as well as communication networks to facilitate interactions and collaborations across the field of earth science. Learning objects for the earth sciences are available under a custom open license.

✈ EEVL (Enhanced and Evaluated Virtual Library): Aims to provide access to quality networked engineering, mathematics and computing resources, and be the UK national focal point for online access to information in these subjects. It is run by a team of information specialists from a number of universities and institutions in the UK, led by Heriot Watt University. EEVL's target audience is learners, staff and researchers in higher and further education, as well as anyone else working, studying or looking for information in Engineering, Mathematics and Computing. EEVL Xtra allows users to cross-search a further 20 databases. All rights and all related rights for the content of the EEVL site are reserved by Heriot Watt University or individual authors. Resources are available for engineering, mathematics and computing. Users may be charged a fee to access some content.

✈ Exploratories: A project of Brown University's Computer Graphics Research Group to create a set of exemplary Web-based learning objects (Java applets); those teach concepts in introductory computer graphics at the college and graduate level. Learning objects are characterized by their flexibility, interactivity, hyper textual curriculum frameworks, and use of explorable 2D and 3D worlds. Users can download complete Java applets, or build their own from the components collection. The project also publishes the results of its research into creating useful learning objects, and is working toward the creation of a complete Design Strategy Handbook. A number of java applets for science and mathematics are available.

✈ Geoscience Data Repository: The collection of Earth Sciences Sector geoscience databases that is managed and accessed by a series of Information Services (GDRIS). This site allows for you to discover, view and download, free of charge, thousands of maps since the mid-1800's, hundreds of digital maps from the Geological Survey of Canada, data related to fossil fuels (oil, gas, coal) in Canada, geochemical surveys, etc.

✈ HEAL (Health Education Assets Library): Part of the US National Science Foundation's National Science Digital Library Project, the goal of the project is to create a collection of digital instruction and learning resources for medical learners, and professionals. Users can search the main Reviewed Collection, a collection of materials awaiting review and 12 affiliated collections. Users can submit materials for review and possible inclusion in the main collection. HEAL is hosted by the University of Utah, UCLA and the University of Oklahoma. Huge number of resources for medicine is available.

+ iLumina: Part of the US National Science Foundation's National Science Digital Library Project, iLumina is a digital library of sharable undergraduate instruction materials for chemistry, biology, physics, mathematics and computer science. Resources range from small learning objects, such as individual images and video clips, to entire courses and several virtual collections. Metadata captures both technical and education-specific information about each resource. Users may contribute their own resources. iLumina was developed by the University of North Carolina at Wilmington, Collegis, Inc., Virginia Tech, Georgia State University, Grand Valley State University and the College of New Jersey. A large number of resources for science, mathematics and computing are accessible.

+ Intute (Science, Engineering and Technology): A free online service providing access to the very best Web resources for education and research evaluated and selected by a network of subject specialists. It covers the physical sciences, engineering, computing, geography, mathematics and environmental science.

+ Intute (Health and Life Sciences): A free online service providing access to the very best web resources for education and research evaluated and selected by a network of subject specialists in the health and life sciences.

+ The Math Forum @ Drexel University: The Math Forum is a leading online resource for improving math learning, instruction, and communication since 1992, created by facilitators, mathematicians, researchers, learners, and parents. It offers a wealth of problems and puzzles, online mentoring, research, team problem solving, collaborations and professional development.

+ Math World: Math World is a mathematical specific repository, created by Wolfram Research. Contains web based (HTML) resources about algebra, applied mathematics, calculus and analysis, discrete mathematics, geometry, history, number theory, probability and statistics, and topology, among others. No educational range is given, but subjects start mainly at the high school level and reach graduate level. Materials are copyrighted by Wolfram Research. One interesting kind of resource is the classroom, which provides a set of pop-up 'capsule summaries' for more than 300 mathematical terms. The HTML headers of each page contain Dublin Core and Mathematics Subject Classification metadata.

+ NEEDS (National Engineering Education Delivery System) : NEEDS is a digital library of learning resources for engineering education. NEEDS provides web-based access to a database of learning resources where learners and instructors can search for, locate, download and comment on resources to aid their learning or instruction process. It is possible to search for resources suitable for mobile devices (so-called 'Learning Everywhere' resources). NEEDS also supports a multi-tier review system for resources, from an industry-sponsored national award competition to user-based reviews of individual learning resources. Materials are mainly at the undergraduate level. There are a lot of resources for science, engineering and mathematics at the higher education level. Users may be charged a fee to access some content.

↛ NSDL (National Science Digital Library): Created by the US National Science Foundation to provide organized access to high quality resources and tools that support innovations in instruction and learning at all levels of science, technology, engineering, and mathematics education. NSDL provides an organized point of access to content that is aggregated from a variety of other digital libraries, NSF-funded projects, and NSDL-reviewed web sites. It also provides access to services and tools that enhance the use of this content in a variety of contexts. NSDL is designed primarily for school-level educators, but anyone can access and search the library at no cost. Access to most of the resources is free; however, some content providers require a nominal fee or subscription to retrieve their specific resources. Resources for science, technology, engineering and mathematics are arranged in many collections. Users may be charged a fee to access some content.

↛ OAISTER: OAISTER is a project of the University of Michigan Digital Library Production Service. Our goal is to create a collection of previously difficult-to-access, academically-oriented digital resources. It contains a huge number of records from vast number of institutions.

↛ SMETE: The SMETE Digital Library is a dynamic online library and portal of services by the SMETE Open Federation for facilitators and learners, specializing in science, mathematics, engineering and technology education, addressing all levels of education. It contains around 20.000 resources. It is partially supported by the National Science Foundation, National STEM Education Digital Library program. There are a huge number of resources for science, technology, engineering and mathematics.

Social Sciences

↛ Intute (Social Sciences gateway): A free online service providing access to the very best Web resources for education and research evaluated and selected by a network of subject specialists in the social sciences fields. Each subject area within Intute has its own collection development policy (available on request). Only covers information of relevance to social science HE and FE learners, academics, researchers and practitioners. The social sciences are broadly defined, as well as core subjects the gateway covers areas such as law, business, hospitality, sport and tourism.

↛ Learning Objects LA Exchange: Learning Objects LA is the home to an Information Literacy Learning Object collection of the Wesleyan University (Connecticut) of around 40 objects. It is also a common environment of learning objects that staffs of this university are developing. Learning Objects LA allow staff to discover materials developed by other faculty, and provide opportunities for collaboration within the academic disciplines on the Wesleyan campuses that have begun to develop and use Learning Objects. Learning Objects LA is also the home to a collection of

Information Literacy Learning Objects that we are developing as part of a collaborative Information Literacy Project that Wesleyan, Trinity, and Connecticut College are working on. They are, at the moment in beta version.

Humanities

➤ Digital Scriptorium: The Digital Scriptorium is an image database of medieval and renaissance manuscripts, intended to unite scattered resources from many institutions into an international tool for instruction and scholarly research. It contains enormous number of images and large number of manuscripts and documents. All rights reserved to The Regents of the University of California.

➤ Humbul Humanities Hub: The Humbul Humanities Hub is a service of the Resource Discovery Network funded by the Joint Information Systems Committee and the Arts and Humanities Research Council, and is hosted by the University of Oxford. Humbul is dedicated to discovering, evaluating and cataloging online resources in the humanities for higher and further education. Resources include educational materials, and links to institutions, academic research projects and companies offering educational software. Materials are submitted by users and reviewed and cataloged by on-site staff. Humbul also maintains a Virtual Training Suite of subject-based self-learning Internet skills tutorials.

➤ Intute (Arts and Humanities): Free online service providing access to the very best Web resources for education and research evaluated and selected by a network of subject specialists in the Arts and Humanities fields. Many web resources, listed here, are freely available by keyword searching and browsing.

(Source: http://wikieducator.org/Exemplary_Collection_of_Open_eLearning_Content_Repositories)

Reflection

OER is not merely a concept now, but a dream come true. It is the need of the hour that we should not only use but also propagate its use in instruction-learning processes for the massive advantage of facilitators and learners, and hence the betterment of entire educational system. The OER having a vast number of varieties with numerous functions can be fitted in all the situations of instruction-learning processes. In other words, one can always find an OER for every aspect of classroom or learning scenario. At the heart of OER lie core ideas of inclusive education, development of all, learning of all and education for all. This has become almost indispensable to use and promote the use of OER for the development of the society as a whole. Hence, in the current century, keeping the future of education in the concern, OER must be used and supported for massive use.

EXEMPLARY QUESTIONS
1. What are open educational resources?
2. How OER are useful for access, reach and quality of education?
3. Discuss in detail the characteristics of open educational sources.

4. Why review is necessary while developing an OER?

UNIT - 10

OPEN EDUCATIONAL RESOURCES FOR TEACHING-LEARNING AND PROFESSIONAL DEVELOPMENT OF TEACHERS AND TEACHER-EDUCATORS

This unit deals with open educational resources for in-service training programmes, academic collaboration, journals, statistical analysis and web conferencing for webinars, conferences and workshops

'We are all inventors, each sailing out on a voyage of discovery, guided by a private chart, of which there is no duplicate. The world is all gates, all opportunities.'

— **Ralph Waldo Emerson**

Unit 10
OER for Teaching-Learning and Professional Development of Teachers and Teacher-Educators

10.1 INTRODUCTION

Teacher-educators deal with teachers (facilitators), teachers deal with learners and teaching-learning through school subjects. Therefore, everybody deals with school subjects. It is the sense of fear, failure, disappointing curriculum, crude assessment, inadequate teacher preparation and support in school teaching (NCF, 2005; NFG, 2006), which makes school teaching a little bit more challenging and more demanding task. The role of facilitator, so teacher-educator, in current era, has shifted from 'the sage on the stage' to 'the guide by the side' which means the role of the facilitator has transformed to be more challenging, resourceful, demanding, updated, sensitive, concerning, humanistic, attentive, facilitating and above of all more professional.

After inception of computer in the field of learning, learner's quest and problems have evolved with fresh and new dimensions. It demands more efficiency and professionalism on the part of the facilitator and the people educating the facilitator. Today's facilitators and teacher-educators need to be skilful, up-to-date and enriched enough with the knowledge and aware of fresh and new curriculum, fresh and new materials and policies in the respective field and its pedagogy. Hence, professional development of facilitators and teacher-educators, have evolved to be an important and vital aspect for better teaching and learning. In this respect, there are in-service training (Inset) programmes, facilitators' associations, forums, journals, research projects, conferences and webinars, etc. that can be seen as some of the agencies for professional growth of teacher-educators.

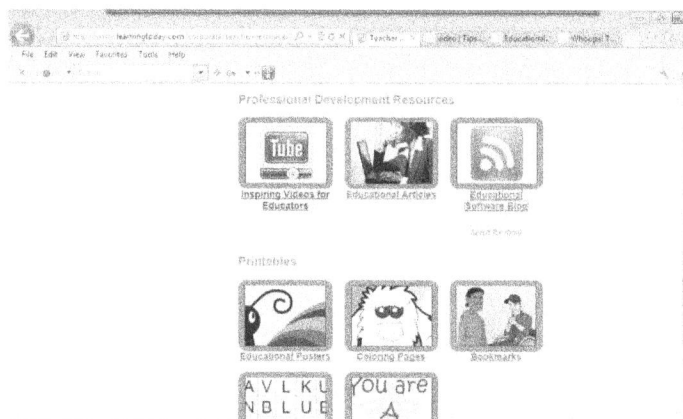

(Source: http://www.learningtoday.com/corporate/teacher-resources.asp)

Though, the facilitators may be equipped with computer and internet skills, the lack of resources and restriction from modification of tailor-made resources may handicap them using these skills in their day-to-day classroom activities. Facilitators may not find suitable the available resources in their original form. Moreover, the workshop or programme material developed should be available to facilitators, for later use and modified as per their needs. All these aspects belong to a sound approach of professional development of teacher-educators. Hence, the professional development should be done in such a way that spirit of 'open' is developed. Here, comes the concept of OER for professional development.

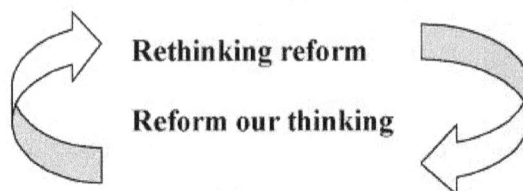

Rethinking reform

Reform our thinking

Learning objectives

After going through this unit and its modules, the teacher-educator is being looked forward to:

✈ develop the understanding of in-service programmes and get acquainted with suggestive OER for these programmes.

✈ get acquainted with the Wikispaces, as one of the OERs, for the purpose of academic association, collaboration and forums.

✈ develop the understanding of role of OER in journal's directory.

✈ learn about OER statistical tools for teaching, learning and research.

✈ develop the understanding of the various aspects pertaining to web conferencing for participation in conferences, seminars, webinars and workshops through OER.

10.2 IN-SERVICE TRAINING PROGRAMME (INSET PROGRAMME)

In-service training programmes are the programmes, which are meant for in-service teacher-educators. These programmes supplement the skills learnt in pre-service facilitator programmes. Behari (2008), while talking about facilitator education programme, pointed out some parameters for facilitators, which are equally good for teacher-educators too, which can help in knowing a high quality facilitator at entry level having experience of teaching, some generic skills of teaching, some personal characteristics, the knowledge and understanding of his/her subject, and understanding of the educational function of his/her subject.

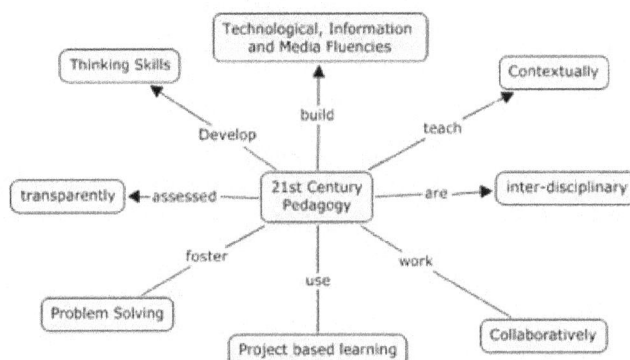

(Source: http://esheninger.blogspot.in/2011_08_01_archive.html)

After entry in the teaching profession, If any of these parameters is lacked up to any degree, there is a need to focus on it in in-service training itself by attending the unattended needs and equipping the facilitator and teacher-educator with the lesser developed aspects. Helsing, Howell, Kegan and Lahey (2008), while talking about professional development of educational leaders, expressed some views, which are equally good for teacher-educators, in the words, 'for meaningful change in their school environments, demands often require a level of personal development many adults may not yet have, and there is a need for professional development programs that are genuinely developmental.' Ramadas (2010) focused on the use of teleconferencing in in-service training programmes for facilitator trainers, which can be seen as a good directive for inset programmes for teacher-educators too. He concludes, 'The two-way audio-video interactive technologies used in the teleconference helped not only to train a large number of target participants but also brought about positive attitudinal change in them.' It can be seen as advantageous as discussion on a single platform and on a real time basis. Further time constraint in these programmes can be overcome by using e-mail technology and telephonic contacts.

Main business in an in-service programme, as revealed from various sources, may include motivation for topics in school subjects, application of school subjects, strategies for involvement of learners physically, emotionally and intellectually in the learning process of school subjects, use of school subjects laboratory, knowledge of school subjects competitions viz. mathematical Olympiad, exploring alternative methods of solutions and proofs, discussion of various problems of school subjects teaching and learning with sharing their classroom experiences, discussion on historical references and anecdotes in school subjects and their use in teaching and learning of school subjects, projects in school subjects, strategies for problem posing and problem solving as foci of mathematical teaching, discussion of school subjects curriculum including school subjects books and various evaluative techniques in school subjects.

National Curriculum Framework for Teacher Education (NCFTE, 2009), by National Council for Teacher Education (NCTE), gives the broad aims of continuing professional development programmes for facilitators as to explore, reflect on and develop one's own practice, strengthen one's knowledge of and update oneself about one's academic discipline or other areas of school curriculum, research and reflect on learners and their education, understand and update one about educational and social issues, prepare for other roles professionally linked to education/teaching, such as facilitator education, curriculum development or counselling, break out of intellectual isolation and share experiences and insights with others in the field, both facilitators and academics working in the area of specific disciplines as well as intellectuals in the immediate and wider society.

In-service programme for teacher-educators
Various in-service training programmes for teacher-educators can be categorized into three types: Skill enhancement programme, Updating and enrichment programme, and Introductory programme for fresh and new policy and the curriculum.
Skill enhancement programme
Now a day, the knowledge of computers and skills like developing PowerPoint presentations etc. are thought to be very important for teacher-educators. Most of the learners feel comfortable and are becoming more habitual of submitting their assignments and projects through computer texts and

presentations. If a facilitator is not equipped with the skills of using and evaluating these, how she/he can do justice to the learners' work. So skill enhancement programme are very important in this regard.

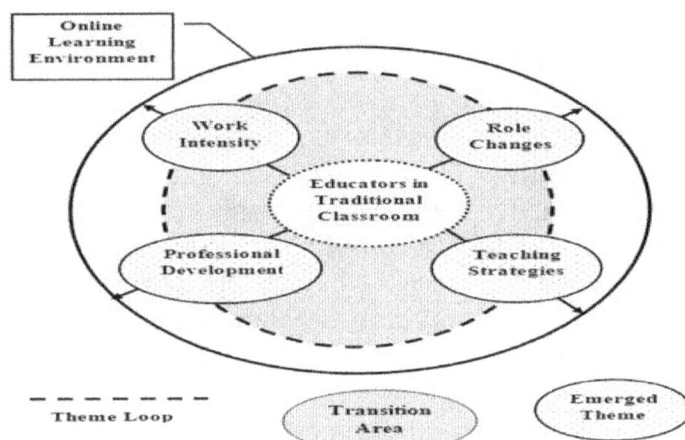

(Source: http://jolt.merlot.org/vol5no4/degagne_1209.htm)

Updating and enrichment programme

Updating and enrichment in existing practices and content is an essential sector for better teaching-learning of school subjects on the part of teacher-educators. There are in-service training programmes meant for this purpose. These programmes are mainly organised by SCERTs of most of the states of India. These programmes are of various durations which are continuously varying from time to time.

Introductory programme for fresh and new policy and the curriculum

Sometimes a fresh and new policy is introduced or fresh and new textbooks are introduced. Since these were not in trend earlier, it becomes important that facilitators should be involved in the application process of these. Moreover facilitators may be given participatory role in the feedback for these fresh and new policies, curriculum or textbooks. It becomes essential to introduce these concepts to the teacher-educators for the betterment of learners and the process of teaching-learning.

10.3 ACADEMIC ASSOCIATION, COLLABORATION AND FORUM

For various purposes, teacher-educators may require academic collaboration. This may be for writing a joint paper or writing a book in collaboration. Or, in order to solve some problem arisen in the academic and professional field, they may require some academic discussions.

For this purpose, Wikispaces, etc. may be used very effectively. Though, it is a learning management system for learners, but it is equally good for academic collaboration of teacher-educators for various purposes. By exploring and exploiting this tool, teacher-educators can collaborate in any possible manner, up to the length of any number of pages, any number of members, with controlled and uncontrolled rights for editing, reviewing, reframing, etc.

10.4 JOURNALS

Journal, in any academic field, is the mirror of the current and most recent research activities in that field to give the acquaintance of the progress in the field to the concerned persons. This is the most powerful tool to give directions for further research at mass level. This gives a name, fame and recognition to not only the researcher but also to a fresh and new line of action, area, methodology, ideology in the academic field. There are journals at regional, national and international levels.

Now-a-days, a remarkable advantage of these journals is that many journals are available not only as print-journals but also as online-journals and open-journals. While undergoing teaching-learning process, teacher-educator applies various novel strategies, content, methodology; self-prepared text material, and self-made tests etc. to find the solution of problems arising to achieve the goal of better learning by each and every learner. Hence, knowingly or unknowingly, she/he comes up with fresh and new idea or novel solution to the situation in order to reach to the heart of their learners and empathising crux of their problems. This output is also a sort of research output for a teacher-educator. They should try to get it published in the journals. Hence, every teacher-educator should participate in journals in order to reach the academic heart of the learners and in turn for the professional development of the entire teacher-educators' community including himself/herself.

Participation in journals

Different journals have their own format for publishing research papers and research notes. Some of the journals have space for book reviews also. We, here, are more concerned about research papers. Once a school subjects facilitator conducts a research, may be fundamental research or applied research or action research, he/she should prepare a detailed write-up of the research work and arrange this write-up (sometimes called as manuscript) in the required format as directed by the particular journal in which researcher wishes to get published her/his research paper. A suggestive format may be given as: the title page, the abstract, introduction, significance, delimitations, sampling, tools, procedure for data collection, output, analysis and discussion, conclusion and references. This is an important aspect that almost all journals ask for references, not the bibliography. As accepted by wide number of researchers, references contain note of only those documents or websites which are actually mentioned in the text of the paper or research report while bibliography can contain those too which are read and used but not actually mentioned in the text of the paper or research report. Thereafter, if they wish, they may consult experts for feedback and suggestions. After incorporating the rational feedback and suggestions, the research paper is ready to be sent to the editor of the journal. Teacher-educators can send this paper to the editor and should wait to get the response and feedback again from the editors. After incorporating these suggestions too, following instructions from the journal authority and sending back the paper to the editor, the paper can be hoped to be published in the journal whenever the space would be available in the journal. When getting the paper published and receiving the copy, one should not forget to share the paper with every concerned person pertaining to the field of school subjects and school subjects teaching in her/his community for the advantage of all at mass level.

10.5 STATISTICAL TOOLS FOR RESEARCH

While dealing with research analysis teacher-educators may require various types of tools. A few years back, the statistical and analytical tools were available just as proprietary tools or authoring tools. One had to pay directly or indirectly for these tools. But, now a day, various statistical and analytical tools are available as free and open education resource tools.

There are tools available both for qualitative and quantitative analysis. Some of the quantitative tools are available through the OER platforms like Statistics Open For All (SOFA), R-Project, S-Project, etc. Some of the qualitative tools are available through the platforms like Weft QDA (OER), AnSWR (freeware), etc. Some of the paid qualitative research tools are as MaxQDA, Nvivo, Atlas.ti, Nud.ist, Ethnograph, HyperResearch, HyperTranscribe, HyperBundle, CAQDAS, CDC-EZ-Text, Code-A-Text, Kwalitan, QDAMiner, Qual-Software, Qualifiers, Qualrus, Symphony Context Analysis Software, TAMS Analyzer, and Transana, etc.

Participation in webinars using web-conferencing

Due to some of the major delimitations of place, distance, travel, officially allotted assignments within the premises and limited number of seats for participants; most of the professionals are not able to participate in the seminars. Technology tried to impart a solution to this problem. And hence, the concept of webinar evolved. The term 'webinar' has been originated from 'web' and 'seminar,' which clearly indicates about the use of web resources for the seminar. There are some organisations, for instance the Open Education Resource Foundation (OERF), which are using a fresh and new version of audio-video teleconferencing along with help of some other latest technologies for enabling most of the interested people at mass level to attend online seminars removing the constraints of place, time, travel and the distance. For attending or participating in webinar, one should have web or internet facilities at his/her place.

Except the use of web, it is almost same as that of seminar. The only addition is that in webinar we use web facility to conduct the online seminar through web conferencing. Organisation, which holds the webinar announces the theme, subthemes, format, eligibility, important dates, how to apply and make contribution etc. for the knowledge of all. Any mathematics facilitator, agreeing with the norms for the webinar can send request to the concerned authority to participate in the seminar. When accepted, facilitators can follow the rest of the guidelines, conveyed time to time to them, and participate in the webinar. These webinars are conducted through web-conferencing.

Recapitulation

In-service programmes or in-service training programmes enhance skills, help in introducing fresh and new policy and curriculum, supplement in updating and enrichment for teacher-educators. These programmes can be of three types on the basis of their purposes: skill enhancement programme, updating and enrichment programme, and introductory programme for fresh and new policy and the curriculum. While statistical tools help in analysing data in appropriate manner, educators' associations, journals and webinars through web conferencing provide some of very important means which can help teacher-educators to enhance their professional outlook, qualitatively as well as quantitatively.

10.6 IN-SERVICE TRAINING PROGRAMME: AN EXEMPLAR

OCL4Ed: Content licensing workshop

Open content licensing for educators (ocl4ed) is a free online workshop designed for educators and learners who want to learn about *open education resources*, *copyright* and *creative commons licenses*. The course provides prerequisite knowledge required by educators to legally remix open education materials and help institutions to take informed decisions about open content licenses.

The course materials have been developed as a collaborative project by volunteers from the OER foundation, wikieducator, the opencourseware, consortium and creative commons with funding support from UNESCO. It is a course sponsored by the open education resource (OER) foundation, the commonwealth of learning (COL) chair in OER at Otago polytechnic, the UNESCO-COL chair in OER at Athabasca University and Creative Commons. New Zealand celebrated the recent adoption of the 2012 Paris OER declaration at the UNESCO World OER congress.

Significance of the workshop

Access to content in education and affordability is a major concern in most of the countries worldwide. In the words of Sir John Daniel (1996):
'More than one-third of the world's population is under 20. There are over 30 million people today qualified to enter a university who have no place to go. During the next decade, this 30 million would grow to 100 million. To meet this staggering demand, a major university needs to be created each week. '

The need of the hour is to enhance and support open resources in education worldwide. The concept of open education encapsulates a simple but powerful idea that the world's knowledge is a public good and that the open web provides an extraordinary opportunity for everyone to share, use, and reuse knowledge.

In a digital world, the cost of replicating knowledge is near zero hence favours open learning. Thus the open web combined with open content licensing provides us the technology to freely distribute learning materials in support of all national curricula. Moreover, we are able to manipulate and transform digital data for a variety of delivery technologies, including print for those learners who do not have access to the internet at virtually any additional cost. Thus the workshop aims at the following objectives
Ocl4ed workshop:
✛ reflects on the practice of sharing knowledge in education and the permissions educators consider fair and reasonable;
✛ defines what constitutes an open education resource (OER);
✛ explains how international copyright functions in a digital world;
✛ introduces the creative commons suite of licenses and explain how they support open education approaches;
✛ connects educators around the world to share thoughts and experiences in relation to copyright, OER and creative commons.

Utility of the workshop
Through this workshop
✛ Every facilitator, lecturer and trainer has the opportunity to make a difference, to widen access free learning materials for all learners, by sharing their teaching materials drawing on the power of collaboration now possible with

social software. This workshop serves as a rare occasion where individual contributions can transform the world.

✈ Free online courses usually attract hundreds of participants worldwide thereby providing a platform to make fresh and new friends and share our thoughts, ideas and experiences.

Detailed description

The workshop has been divided into a 5 sessions. The workshop enlightens the issues like-

- ✈ Why does open matter in education?
- ✈ What constitutes an open resource? What are their advantages?
- ✈ What is copyright and how can an educator legally copy in an online world?
- ✈ How can educators refine their copyright for sharing knowledge freely?
- ✈ What licenses are used to copy the content legally?

The learning materials for the workshop can be accessed from the following sites (participants have to register in any of these sites):

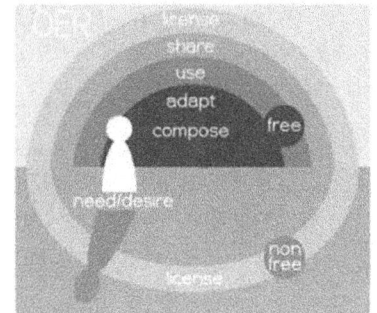

- ✈ Moodle-presents content in an organised format
- ✈ Wiki educator- for participants who navigate using Wikipedia
- ✈ Ask OERU

The participants can provide/give/post their views, opinions and feedback on micro blogging sites like twitter, WE groups, identi.ca or create a discussion forum on Moodle.

The workshop focuses on three major aspects which are: (A) open education resources, (B) copyright and (C) creative commons licenses

A. Open Education Resources

The term Open Educational Resources (OER) was coined at UNESCO's 2002 forum on open courseware. It was expressed as 'teaching, learning and research materials in any medium, digital or otherwise, that reside in the public domain or have been released under an open license that permits no-cost access, use, adaptation and redistribution by others with no or limited restrictions. Open licensing is built within the existing framework of intellectual property rights as defined by relevant international conventions and respects the authorship of the work.'

The Organisation for Economic Co-operation and Development (OECD) mentions OER as '...digitised materials provided freely and openly for educators, learners and self-learners to use and reuse for teaching, learning and research. OER includes learning content, software tools to develop, use and distribute content, and implementation resources such as open licences. This report suggests that OER refers to accumulated digital assets that can be adjusted and which provide advantages without restricting the possibilities for others to enjoy them. '

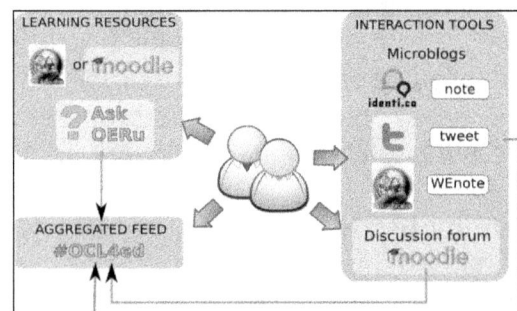

In nurturing the development of a sustainable open education ecosystem, there is growing consensus that a definition of OER ideally needs to incorporate three interrelated dimensions which are as follows:

I.   Educational values: OER should be free

The free in OER means OER must be accessible at no-cost to the user. To qualify as OER, there must always be a version of the materials freely accessible at no-cost to the user. This does not necessarily imply that distributors of OER content may not charge for packaging, distribution or value-added services. Educators should be able to edit or copy the content at no additional cost. Also they should be able to download the content freely from the website.

OER should respect the freedoms of the users.

The freedom of OER users are derived from the essential freedoms of the free software movement i.e. the freedom or permission to act without restriction. They are encapsulated in the 4r framework (reuse, revise, remix, redistribute) and decisions about technology and media choices below.

II.   Pedagogical utility: the 4R framework

✦ Reuse - the right to reuse the content in its unaltered / verbatim form (e.g., make a digital copy of the content i.e. Making an e-copy of the content)

✦ Revise - the right to adapt, adjust, modify, or alter the content itself (e.g., translate the content into another language or modify a learning activity, like Wikipedia)

✦ Remix - the right to combine the original or revised content with other content to create something fresh and new (e.g., incorporate the content into a mash up)

✦ Redistribute - the right to share copies of the original content, user's revisions, or user's remixes with others (e.g., give a copy of the content to a friend)

Content is open to the extent that its permissions enable users to engage in the 4r activities. Content is less open to the extent that its permissions restrict users access (e.g., forbidding derivative works or prohibiting commercial use) to the 4r activities.

III.   Technology and media choices

Digital technologies are the enablers for the 4rs above. There are two important considerations pertaining to technology and media choices for OER:

✦   Access to the tools required for editing, and
✦   Ensuring that OER is meaningfully editable.

OER should be stored and distributed using open standards and formats which are easily editable and publicly available with unencumbered rights to use the standards or specification concerned. Educators and OER developers should be encouraged to respect the freedoms of future users by providing open file formats of their creative works. In this way it can be ensured that:

✦   All users would have unrestricted access to the tools required to revise and remix OER content. All users (educators and OER developers) should be free to use the software of their choice, and should not be forced to purchase software licenses (e.g. formats like windows media player) in order to participate freely in the 4rs.

✢   All users have the capacity to edit an OER to suit their local needs, e.g., while the portable document format (pdf) is an open standard for document exchange it is not easy to edit other than minor changes. OER provided in this format only cannot be revised easily for suitable local use.

B. Copyright or IPR

Copyright or Intellectual Property Right (IPR) is a legal concept which grants creators (authors, musicians, artists and other creators) the rights of ownership and protection against unauthorised use of their work for a fixed period. Copyright may provide protections for personal interests called 'moral rights' and attempts to balance exclusive rights of copyright holders with the interests of society at large by providing a number of exceptions and limitations.

Copyright is given to certain content when:

✢   It is used to protect creative works- like literary, art, scientific works
✢   The form and style of the expression is protected, not the underlying idea
✢   Very often, copyright requires an expression in a particular form
✢   The work must be original
✢   No formalities are required

When duration of the copyright ends, the content automatically comes into the public domain.

Public domain

The public domain refers to creative work which is not protected by intellectual property rights at all and available for use by all members of the public. Work enters the public domain when the intellectual property rights have expired or the creator donates work to the public domain by forfeiting all intellectual property rights. Because copyright law is different from country to country, the recognition and meaning of the public domain would vary across national boundaries. Some countries may limit the use of public domain work or may not acknowledge public domain work at all.

C. CC Licenses

Creative commons (CC) is a non-profit organization that enables the sharing and use of creativity and knowledge through free legal tools. Cc tools and licenses give everyone from individual creators to large companies and institutions a simple, standardized way to grant copyright permissions to their creative work. The combination of their tools and their users is a vast and growing digital commons, a pool of content that can be copied, distributed, edited, remixed, and built upon, all within the boundaries of copyright law.

CC licenses are not an alternative to copyright but enable us to modify our copyright terms to best suit our needs. There are hundreds of millions of works — from songs and videos to scientific and academic material — available to the public for free and legal use under the terms of our copyright licenses, with more being contributed every day.

A CC license is composed of three distinct layers legal code - each license begins as a traditional legal tool, in the kind of language and text formats that most lawyers know and like. This is the actual license, which is a detailed legal document.

Commons deed - this is a handy reference that summarizes and expresses some of the important terms and conditions. Think of the commons deed as a user-friendly interface to the legal code beneath, although the deed itself is not a license, and its contents are not part of the legal code itself.

Machine-readable version - the final layer of the license design is a 'machine-readable' version of the license - a brief of the key freedoms and obligations written into a format that can be understood by software system, search engines, and other kinds of technology.

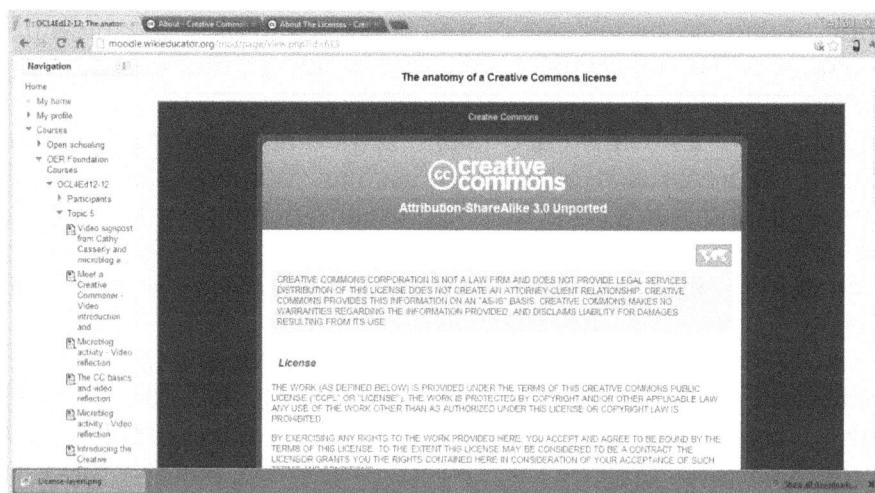

An exemplar of a Creative Commons License

Important features of CC licenses

Every creative commons license:

→ helps creators retain copyright while allowing others to copy, distribute, and make some uses of their work at least non-commercially.

→ ensures licensors get the credit for their work they deserve from the licensees.

→ works around the world and lasts as long as applicable copyright lasts (because they are built on copyright).

These common features serve as the baseline, on top of which licensors can choose to grant additional permissions when deciding how they want their work to be used. A cc licensor has to decide whether he wants to allow it for commercial use or derivative works. If it is for derivative works then the licensee has to 'share alike' the same terms and conditions of the licensor. Licensees must credit the licensor, keep copyright notices intact on all copies of the work, and link to the license from copies of the work. Licensees cannot use technological measures to restrict access to the work by others.

Advantages and limitations of OERs

There are both advantages and limitations associated with using OERs in the classroom.

Advantages of using OERs include

(i) Learners can be benefitted from the following

- Expanded access to learning: learners anywhere in the world can access OERs at any time, and learners can access material repeatedly.
- Scalability: OERs are easy to distribute widely with little or no cost.
- Augmentation of class materials: OERs can supplement textbooks and lectures where deficiencies in information are evident.
- Enhancement to regular course content—e.g., by adding multimedia to text: presenting information in multiple formats may help learners to more easily learn the material being taught.
- Quick circulation: information may be disseminated rapidly (especially as compared to information published in textbooks or journals), which can increase the relevance of the material presented.
- Lower learner costs: instead of traditional textbooks or course packs, etc. the use of OERs can substantially reduce the cost of course materials for learners.
- Showcasing of innovation and talent: a wide audience may learn of faculty research interests and expertise. Potential learners and donors may be impressed, and learner and faculty recruitment efforts may be enhanced.
- Ties for alumni: OERs provide an excellent way for alumni to stay connected to the institution and continue with a program of lifelong learning.
- Continually improved resources: unlike textbooks and other static sources of information, OERs can be improved quickly through direct editing by users or through solicitation and incorporation of user feedback. Instructors can take an existing OER, adapt it for a class, and make the modified OER available for others to use.

(ii) The OER originator can be benefitted from
- Learner/user feedback and open peer review
- Reputational advantages, recognition
- Advantages (efficiency and cultural) of collaborative approaches to teaching/learning

(iii) Institutions can be benefitted from

- Recognition and enhanced reputation
- Wider availability of their academic content and focus on the learning experience
- Capacity to support greater numbers of learners
- Efficiencies in content production
- Fresh and new partnerships/linkages with other institutions
- Increased sharing of ideas and practice within the institution, including greater role for support services
- A buffer against the decline of specific subjects or topics (which may not be sustainable at institutional level but can be sustained across several institutions through shared resources)

(iv) Employers can be benefitted from

- Access to re-purposable content
- Fresh and new potential partnerships with content providers
- Up skilling

Limitations of OERs include

✈   Quality issues: since many OER repositories allow any user to create an account and post material; some resources may not be relevant and/or accurate.

✈   Irregular reviewing of the content: whatever content is uploaded on the internet should be thoroughly checked and verified before bringing it to public domain.

✈   Lack of human interaction between facilitators and learners: OER material is created to stand alone, and since self-learning users may access the material outside of a classroom environment, they would miss out on the discussion and instructor feedback that characterize for-credit classes and make such classes useful and valuable.

✈   Language and/or cultural barriers: although efforts are being made to make OERs available in multiple languages, many are available only in English, limiting their usefulness to non-English speakers. Additionally, not all resources are culturally appropriate for all audiences.

✈   Technological issues: some learners may have trouble using some OERs if they have a slow or erratic internet connection. Other OERs may require software that learners do not have and that they may not be able to afford.

✈   Intellectual property/copyright concerns: since OERs are meant to be shared openly, the 'fair use' exemption from the copyright act of a country ceases to apply; all content put online must be checked to ensure that it does not violate copyright law.

✈   Sustainability issues: since OER creators generally do not receive any type of payment for their OER, there may be little incentive for them to update their OER or ensure that it would continue to be available online.

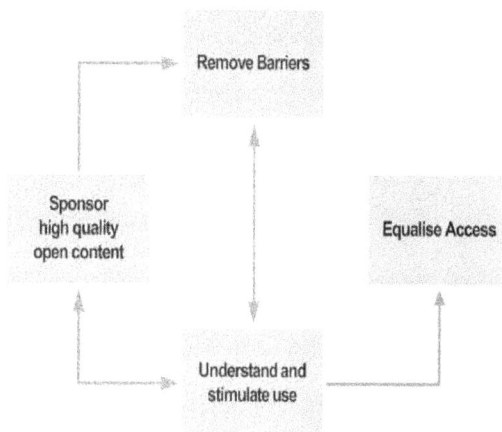

Typical points

✈ Workshop is aimed at promoting resources that can be open access to all.
✈ It aims to create awareness about the open education resources, copyright issues and creative common licenses.
✈ It aims to foster relationship among different educators and institutions across the globe
✈ For any material to become an OER it should take into consideration the educational values, pedagogical aspects and should be based on technology and media.
✈ Copyright once expired comes into the public domain and becomes accessible by all
✈ Creative commons is an agency that helps in creating licenses that help in uploading of free content and its use by a number of users.
✈ Open content resourcing has a number of advantages like enhancement in class curriculum, greater reach, low cost and quick circulation
✈ OER have some limitations as well as quality issues, irregular reviewing of the content and sustainability issues.

Recapitulation

Openness in education is the need of the future. If the problems of developing nations like India and some African countries need to be addressed like affordability of textual material, reach of the content to various remote areas, OER is the answer to all these questions along with some technological help. It's the onus of the institutions and educators to enhance and support awareness of such content as well as bring them into practice.

As RTE has come into play, a right to access free content can be brought alongside in the constitution. The recommendations of the 2012 Paris OER declaration can be considered as guidelines by various human resource agencies of various countries and can thus be applied in the education sector. They are as follows

- Foster awareness and use of OER.
- Facilitate enabling environments for use of information and communications technologies (ICT).
- Reinforce the development of strategies and policies on OER
- Enhance and support the understanding and use of open licensing frameworks
- Support capacity building for the sustainable development of quality learning materials.
- Foster strategic alliances for OER.
- Encourage the development and adaptation of OER in a variety of languages and cultural contexts.
- Encourage research on OER.
- Facilitate finding, retrieving and sharing of OER.
- Encourage the open licensing of educational materials produced with public funds.

10.7 ACADEMIC ASSOCIATION, COLLABORATION AND FORUM FOR TEACHING AND LEARNING: AN EXEMPLAR

Learning Management System

From a technical standpoint, a learning management system (hereinafter referred to as an LMS) is a server-based software program that interfaces with a database containing information about users, courses and content. In that sense, it resembles other systems designed for e-commerce, human resources, payroll, and learner records. An LMS is unique in its instructional nature. An LMS provides a place for learning and teaching activities to occur within a seamless environment, which is not dependent upon time and space boundaries (Ullman & Rabinowitz, 2004).these systems allow educational institutions to manage a large number of fully online or blended (part online and part face-to-face) courses using a common interface and set of resources. Face to- face courses that use an LMS for required or supplemental activities are often referred to as web-enhanced courses (Schmidt, 2002).

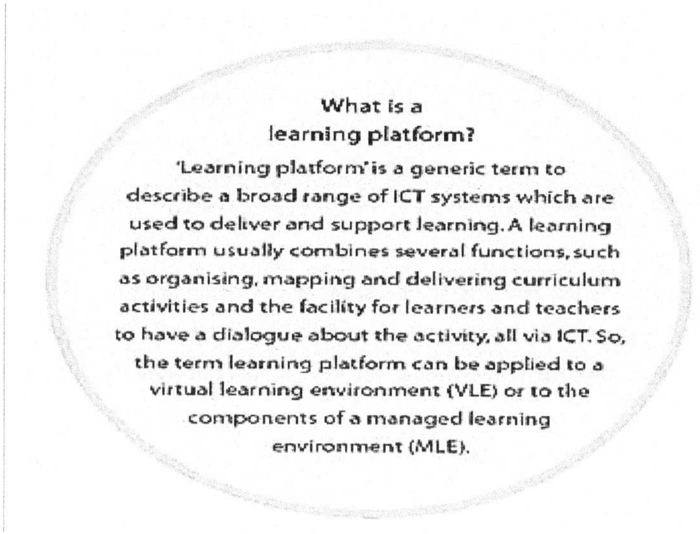
What is a learning platform?
'Learning platform' is a generic term to describe a broad range of ICT systems which are used to deliver and support learning. A learning platform usually combines several functions, such as organising, mapping and delivering curriculum activities and the facility for learners and teachers to have a dialogue about the activity, all via ICT. So, the term learning platform can be applied to a virtual learning environment (VLE) or to the components of a managed learning environment (MLE).

Significance of LMS

LMS has the potential to free us from constraints that currently prevent the full integration of technology in the classroom. The provision of a simpler, user friendly, group friendly system may help us to overcome the barriers we face now.

The change from command based computers to the GUI interface meant many more people were more comfortable using computers. The simplicity and ease of using a LMS has the potential to free learners and facilitators from poorly designed software and inhospitable organisational structures that currently constrain their use for learning and teaching.

The learning management system used by Lrnlab has vastly simplified the process of accessing information, creating documents, organizing our work, handing in assignments, communicating with the other learners or lecturers. Facilitators do not want to have to learn complicated software programs. As the ease of use improves so too would the frequency of use.

Description

Learning management systems are known by several different names. These include course management systems, virtual learning environments and e-learning courseware (Gibbons, 2005). Some authors recognize distinctions between course management systems and learning management systems (Ceraulo, 2005; Watson & Watson, 2007), while others argue that the term 'course management system' should be abandoned, since the acronym CMS is also used for content management systems and may cause confusion (Piña, Green & Eggers, 2008). Notwithstanding these minor controversies, the vast majority of US based journals and other printed and digital media tend to use the terms 'learning management system' (LMS) and 'course management system' (CMS) interchangeably, while the designation 'virtual learning environment' (VLE) is most popular in Europe and Asia.

Therefore, LMS is a

- Single piece of software that provides a platform for online learning content and communication tools.

+ It is used to deliver a blend of traditional classroom instruction and online delivery.
+ It allows easy management of the learning materials and tracking of learner's learning.
+ Used by learners, facilitators and administrators.
+ It supports a collaborative learning community and multiple modes of learning

There is a difference between a 'learning management system' (LMS) and a 'learning content management system' (LCMS). An LCMS is used to facilitate the organization of content from authoring tools, and presentation of this content to learners via the LMS.

Exemplars of LMS

Moodle, Webct, Blackboard, Edutools, Lrnlab, Atutor, Dokeos, Dotlrn, Ilias, Ion-capa, Openuss, Sakai, Spaghettilearning , Canvas by Instructure, Chamilo , Claroline , Efront , Fedena , Olat , Totara LMS and Webwork

While most LMS are commercially developed, there are also several free and open-source (FOSS) systems. One free LMS is Moodle. According to the Moodle website, this software package is a 'course management system', based on social constructionist pedagogical principles, which is designed to help educators create effective online learning communities. Moodle can be used by facilitators to create web-based courses. Such courses generally consist of several sessions, with each lesson including reading materials, activities (including tests and projects) and interactive elements to encourage learners to engage in group work.

One of the most important aspects of WebCT, and the reason why it is popular and versatile is its capacity to facilitate the creation of sophisticated World Wide Web based educational environment by non-technical users. Unique features of Prometheus include: equation editor, which allows learners/instructors to create maths/science equations online.

Structure of LMS

The composition of the LMS is composed of five parts: course management is divided into three groups of users levels that of learner, facilitator, and administrators. Learner can log on from anywhere at any time through the internet. The user and the system can support an unlimited number of lessons. It depends on hardware / software used and the system can support the full format. Content management system consists of tools to help create the content. The system can work well if the lessons are the text - based and lessons are in media streams. Test and evaluation system has a set of questions by a random test. It is a timed test. It has test automation solution with statistics, scores and statistics of attendance of learners. The communication between the facilitators and learners include a web board and course tools. The history of the chat room can keep them linked and connected for learning. Data management system includes a file management system. The facilitators have set the lessons in their own storage space. The area is set by the administrator.

Features LMS usually include

- Differential access for learners, facilitators and administrators. This includes login names and passwords
- Personalised working spaces,
- Individualised folders for participants home pages and work.
- Easy navigation, help pages, quick links, pervasive references (links for everyone)
- Easy-to-use content creation tools. Easy authoring tools for text, hyperlinks and graphics. Web page editing with templates for content pages.
- Information distribution including administrative information, calendar, news & course announcements.
- Communication and collaboration functions such as email, asynchronous collaborative learning (discussion forums for group learning, threaded discussions) synchronous collaborative learning (chats for live instruction in classroom settings).

Features that tutor interfaces have

- Access control
- Daily management tools
- Flexible course design and delivery.
- Support of reusable learning objects.
- Syllabus of teaching material.
- Ability to track learner progress.
- Assessment tools.
- Learner assignment management,
- Administrative applications.

Features that learner interfaces provide

- Access to learning resources with personalised study units, course materials, syllabus, basic teaching material for self-paced coursework.
- Learning management tools. Study toolkit.
- Collaborative tools- discussion forums, chat rooms
- Online support
- Other learning materials- glossary, Faqs, useful links
- Self-assessment such as online quizzes and exercises such as multiple-choice, true/false and one-word-answer (formative assessment)
- Assignment boxes or areas for submission of learner work (summative assessment).

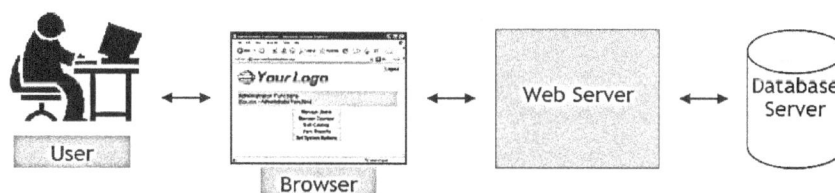

(LMS system architecture)

Some features of LMS

- Support for blended learning: People learn in different ways. An LMS should provide a curriculum that mixes classroom and virtual courses easily. Combined features enable prescriptive and personalized training.
- Administration tools: The LMS must enable administrators to manage user registrations and profiles, define roles, set curricula, chart certification paths, assign tutors, author courses, manage content, and administer internal budgets, user payments, and chargebacks. Administrators need complete access to the training database, enabling them to create standard and customized reports on individual and group performance. Reports should be scalable to include the entire workforce. The system should also be able to build schedules for learners, instructors, and classrooms. Most important, all features should be manageable using automated user-friendly interfaces.
- Content integration: It's important for an LMS to provide native support to a wide range of third-party courseware. When shopping for an LMS, keep in mind that some LMSs are compatible only with the supplier's own courseware, and others do little more than pay lip-service to learning content standards. An LMS supplier should be able to certify that third-party content would work within their system, and accessing courses should be as easy as using a drop-down menu.
- Adherence to standards: An LMS should attempt to support standards, such as Scorm and Aicc. Support for standards means that the LMS can import and manage content and courseware that complies with standards regardless of the authoring system that produced it.
- Assessment capabilities: Evaluation, testing and assessment engines help developers build a program that becomes more valuable over time. It's a good idea to have an assessment feature that enables authoring within the product and includes assessments as part of each course.
- Skill management: A skill management component enables organizations to measure training needs and identify improvement areas based on workers' collective competence in specified areas. Skill assessment can be culled from multiple sources, including peer reviews and 360-feedback tools. Managers determine whether results are weighed, averaged or compared to determine a skill gap.

Advantages
Enables leaders to

- Save time on administrative tasks
- Simplify organisation
- Easily and quickly communicate with parents

Enables parents to

- Help children with homework
- To know about that is going on in the school
- To get involved with the school

Enables administrators to

- Assist learners
- Communicate on a one-to-one or one-to-many basis
- Contribute to learning resources

Enables the facilitator to

+ Access resources and tools to support planning, information sharing within the school and outside the school.
+ Share the burden of creating resources with colleagues.
+ Import material from other sources.
+ Tailor the curriculum to individual learners' needs by supporting personalised learning.
+ Extend learning beyond the classroom and traditional timetables.
+ Submit and track activities, including evidence for assessment

Enables the learner to

+ Personalise home pages with learning tools such as tasks, diaries and files.
+ Gives every learner access to a personal online web-space where they can store course work and their achievements.
+ Store all their work.
+ Display their work to peers and facilitators.

Some More Advantages

Apart from using an LMS to deliver e-learning courses, schools and training institutions also use an LMS to assist with learner registration and sometimes to help with competency management, skills-gap analysis, certification, virtual classes and resource allocation (textbooks, instructors, etc.).

An LMS can be used on any computer and can be used to assist just one facilitator to manage one course or can be used to manage the e-learning content and delivery for several facilitators and thousands of learners

Limitations

There are limitations, however, as to how useful an LMS can be, and they are not a universal remedy for managing everything related to e-learning.

While an LMS is generally agreed to be a very useful administrative tool, some argue that an LMS provides so many tools and options; therefore it can be very confusing for learners to use. These critics of LMS argue that more efforts are needed to be put into designing the interface so that the users (learners) can utilize the tool to enhance their learning more easily. These critics recommend that an LMS should be designed with the facilitators' and learners' needs in mind.

Others argue that while an LMS is useful in delivering content to learners, it is not always an effective tool for encouraging interaction between learners. Therefore, for some aspects of course delivery, it may be better to use web-based 'social software' such as wikis, blogs and Skype, rather than an LMS, particularly if the type of subject being taught involves exploratory, constructivist thinking and learning.

In addition, some critics argue that an LMS is not suitable for all learning styles. These critics argue that LMS do not cater to the diversity of types of intelligence and the diversity of learning styles that exist. These critics also argue that most LMS provide knowledge in a sequenced, linear, one-way, managed way, which restricts the ability of learners to learn in the ways that best suit their needs.

Many educators believe that while an LMS can be very useful for administrative tasks and for certain learning functions, this one tool cannot address all aspects of learning. Facilitators and educators therefore need to have an array of tools and choose the relevant tool for the required task.

Wikispaces as an LMS

Wikispaces is a free web hosting service (sometimes called a wiki farm) based in San Francisco, California, launched in March 2005. Wikispaces is owned by Tangient llc and is among the largest wiki hosts, competing with Pbworks, Wetpaint, Wikia and Google sites.

Private Wikis with advanced features for businesses, non-profits and educators are available for an annual fee. As of march 2008, they had more than 920,000 registered members and hosted more than 390,000 wikis. By March 2009, that number had increased to over 2.2 million registered members and more than 900,000 wikis. Wikispaces has also given away more than 100,000 premium wikis to k-12 educators since 2010 wikispaces have cooperated with web 2.0 education platform Glogster edu. Glogster edu embeds glogs into wikispaces services.

A wiki

Wiki is a group of web pages that allows users to add content, similar to a discussion forum or blog, but also permits others (sometimes completely unrestrictedly) to edit the content (Arreguin, 2004). What distinguishes wikis from blogs, discussion fora, or other content management systems is that there is no inherent structure hard-coded: wiki pages can be interconnected and organized as required, and are not presented by default in a reverse-chronological, taxonomic-hierarchical or any other predetermined order. In essence, the wiki provides a vast simplification of the process of creating html page and thus is a very effective way to build and exchange information through collaborative effort.

Different user types on wikispaces

A guest: a guest is anyone who is visiting wikispaces.com but who has not signed in to a user account. Guests can view all public and protected spaces. They can also edit pages on public spaces but not create fresh and new pages. Guests can read, but not post on discussion pages.

A user account: anyone logged in to a user account on wikispaces.com can view all public and protected spaces on the site. They can edit and create pages in public spaces as well as post to the discussion pages in those spaces.

A member: when a user account is added to a space, they become a member of that space. They can then view and edit the space whether it is public, protected, or private. Members of a space are also able to upload images and files to that space. Any member of a space can be enhance and supported by the organizer to be a fellow organizer of that space.

An organizer: the organizer of a space has administrative access to that space. They can invite people to be members, enhance and support members to be organizers of the space, approve requests to join the space, delete pages, upgrade or delete the space, determine whether a space is public, protected, or private, change the look and feel of the space, and manage the subscription of that space. The creator of the space is an organizer with the ability to demote other organizers to the level of member.

A wikispaces look like

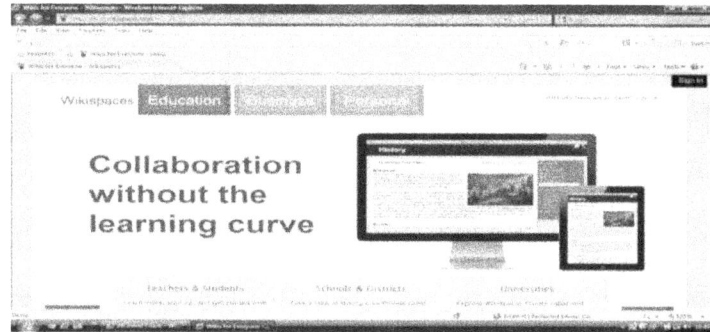

Characteristics of a wiki

The following are some typical characteristics of a wiki where a blog is (usually) the writings of one person to be read by many. The wiki is a website that allows a user to add content, but also allows that content to be edited by any other user; they involve the creation of documents (individual pages as well as the entire wiki) without a detailed technical knowledge of html; they tend towards expressing ideas as relationships between pages, thus creating a network of interrelated topics; they are a-temporal, that is, the nodes (or interlinking textual references) do not change according to time but by way of development within the evolving and edited text, they track the changes of individual pages over time; provides a space where knowledge becomes networked (situated, contextualized) but remains ephemeral: it changes, and can be changed and mediated by the community

Strategies for using wikis in teaching and learning

The following are some possible educational uses of a wiki: learners can use a wiki to develop research projects, with the wiki acting as on-going documentation of their work; a wiki can be used by learners to add summaries of their thoughts from the prescribed readings, building a collaborative annotated bibliography; in distance learning environments, the tutor can publish course resources like syllabus and hand-outs, and learners can edit and comment on these directly; wikis can be used as a knowledge base for facilitators, enabling them to share reflections and thoughts regarding teaching practices and allowing for versioning and documentation wikis can be used to map concepts: they are useful for brainstorming, and authoring a wiki on a given topic produces a linked network of resources; a wiki can be used to facilitate a presentation in place of conventional software like keynote and powerpoint; wikis are tools for group authoring of a document; wikis are being used for course evaluation. For a further exploration of some of these ideas, also see Pearce (2006), wikis in education and other tools for collaborative writing (2006), and exemplars Wikiuse (2006).

Features of wikispaces—how to sign in and create discussion topics

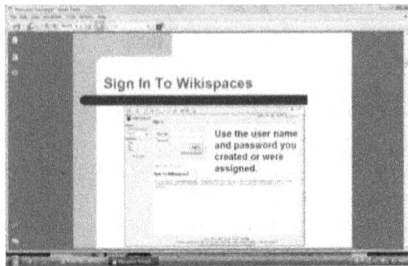

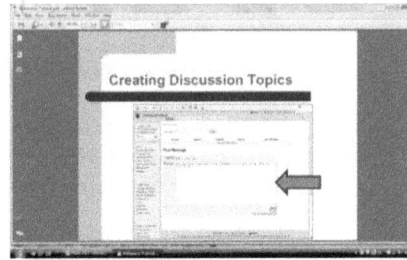

Educational advantages of wikis

In essence, wikis provide an online space for collaborative authorship and writing. They are available online for all web users or for members of specific communities and include version control tools that allow authors to track the history of specific pages and the history of their personal contributions. Using wikis, learners can easily create simple websites without prior knowledge or skill programming in html or current software used for website authoring, thus eliminating the time overhead necessary to develop these skills. Also, as more organisations adopt the wiki for internal and external collaboration and information, they work with wikis at the tertiary level to build crucial skills for the workplace.

A wiki also provides the ability to interact with an evolving document over time. It allows facilitators and learners to see the evolution of a written task, and to continually comment on it rather than providing comments only on the final draft. Considering learners' busy schedules, a wiki can also be very useful for tracking and streamlining group projects.

Wikispaces is great for any kind of group website. It's for families, classrooms, sports teams, community groups, book clubs, fan clubs, party organizers, wedding planners, and more.

Let us learn more about that wikispaces can do.

A) Keep a family scrapbook: a wikispaces is a great way to build a family website that the entire family can work on to put up family news, stories, and pictures. User's family members can then update, add and comment for family news. Wikispaces is so easy to use, everyone can participate

B) Energize user's classroom: need somewhere to work on essays together? A wikispaces for a class is a great place for learners to post their work so that facilitators and classmates can correct, improve and discuss their work.

C) Organize group activities: got a softball team, scout group or book club? A wikispaces lets users post schedules, plans and lists that the rest of user's group can update and edit any time they like. User's group members can also be notified of changes as they happen so that they never miss out on updates.

D) Share user's passion and learn:keep track of that users have learnt about user's latest passion on a wikispaces. By inviting others who share the same interest, user can build a better website than user ever could alone.

Permission settings provided by wikispaces

Wikispaces provides three types of space access: public, protected and private.

Public: a public space can be viewed by anyone and can also be edited by anyone.

Protected: a protected space can be viewed by anyone but can only be edited by members of the space.

Private: a private space can only be viewed or edited by members of the space.

Advantages of wikis in educational context

- ✦ The ability to easily control access at different levels through a simple 'manage space' interface (anyone can read and contribute; anyone can read but not contribute; only designated 'members' can read or contribute etc.)
- ✦ Few technical barriers for contribution to the site
- ✦ Few technical barriers for adding some quite sophisticated media to the site
- ✦ The ability to 'reverse' unintentionally destructive or unwanted editing through the simple 'history' function where user can restore to any earlier point, since every addition or editing is logged. There is a 'history' tab related to this option on every page, as user can see.
- ✦ The ability to monitor changes and additions to the site through the change record as well as e-mail forwarding of changes (which also enables a kind of tracking of contributions). There is a 'notify me' tab related to this option on every page too.
- ✦ The ability to incorporate discussion about page content through a bulletin board (like 'discussions' in UEL plus, but an 'unthreaded' list of messages). In the context of collaborative construction of pages, this facility is invaluable. But it also allows feedback from peers or the tutor on 'individually owned' pages. There is a 'discussions' tab on each page that lets user easily access the bulletin board.

Limitations

- ✦ Anyone can edit so this may be open for some applications, too, e.g. confidential documentation. However it is possible to regulate user access.
- ✦ Learners become easily distracted and use the computers for purposes other than course-related activities.
- ✦ Open to spam and vandalism if not managed properly. There are easy ways to restore a page however and on Wikieducator user must be logged in to edit pages so this reduces vandalism by automated spam bots.
- ✦ Requires internet connectivity to collaborate, but technologies to produce print versions of articles are improving.
- ✦ The flexibility of wiki's structure can mean that information can become disorganised. As wiki grows, the community plans and administers the structure collaboratively.
- ✦ Are users building a freely editable and public wiki, or do users need to be conscious of privacy and security? There can also be issues of legal liability and risk to reputation, particularly if user publishes to the web.

Options such as a moderated wiki format, user agreements and locking some pages from public view can provide protection.

Recapitulation

Just as there are strengths in collaborative, co-authored online spaces there are also some challenges. Some wikis have no page locking system, so if two people edit the page simultaneously, one set of changes would be silently deleted. Some wikis do not include a versioning system, making them inappropriate for the task. Also, there are the social issues that occasionally crop up, particularly on very large projects such as the Wikipedia. Some pages on Wikipedia, dealing with controversial topics such as abortion or religious perspectives, can exhibit a phenomenon known as an 'edit war' (Wikipedia, 2006). This is the continuous editing and re-visioning of content by a community member with a particular agenda. The easiest way to circumvent such disagreements is to place a block on the page edit functionality for a period of time.

Asking learners to develop fresh and new wiki pages can present considerations from an educational perspective which are comparable to teaching learners the processes of authorship in any other written task. Depending on the nature of the task at hand, wiki entries may be structurally and procedurally different from standard writing tasks that learners may be already used to – therefore, it is important that facilitators provide sufficient help and instruction to learners as they come to understand the requirements of the wiki writing genre.

The future of LMS while still a relatively fresh and new field, LMS continues to evolve and adapt to fresh and new learning challenges and technological capabilities, including

- ↠ Fresh and new uses for e-learning content ranging from the arts to marketing communications.
- ↠ Tighter integration into collaborative software platforms and messaging frameworks, such as GroupWise and Microsoft outlook.
- ↠ Migration of data storage to network-based methods, commonly known as 'the cloud.'
- ↠ Further integration with talent management software systems.

10.8 JOURNALS AND OTHER RESOURCES: AN EXEMPLAR

Directory of open access journals (DOAJ): Journal database

A Journal

A journal is a daily record of events, occurrences, experiences etc.; a daily newspaper; and a periodical or magazine published for a special group or a learned society (www.dictionary.com). Directory of open access journals defines a journal as a periodical or a magazine published for a special group connected by means of a common interest.

With the content explosion on the internet, people started sharing the soft copies of books, articles, journals, etc. That is when the journal assumed the bifurcation of the hard copy format and the soft copy format. With the rapid expansion of internet, content sharing became very easy unlike the case with the hard copies. Due to this content sharing, the publishers started losing the money that they would have earned by means of selling the content. So, the various laws around piracy emerged and laws came into action that would protect the content and the interest of the publisher so that piracy is controlled. While the

laws were not sufficient, several technologies emerged that started protecting the content so that sharing was made increasingly difficult. While this was happening at one end, the hacker community was also developing their expertise further to meet the toughest challenge. Technology continued evolving with time. And today, the security technologies have reached great heights with complex algorithms.

Also, since copying can impact one's business badly, original creators of content and technologies maintain the copyright and patents to the content, technology or the idea so that they get due credit for their innovation and put a value against their innovation, which becomes a very good means of earning for them.

However, there is a philosophy that is completely contrary to this thought of protection of content and ensuring appropriate credit to the creator/inventor. With monetary implications of such prevention of copying content, the pace of growth in technology and sharing of information is impacted negatively. Such an impact is not good for the further evolution of technology and content. So, the people who follow this philosophy believe in open access.

Open access: Content that people develop is shared with others without any monetary involvement. This content is shared freely across people without any barriers. Such a free access to content without any restriction is known as open access. Hence, open access journals are those which are available at no cost across the entire world and pose no restriction to their access. Such journals are more like a service to the entire community which provide a lot of information free of cost, which helps people of all strata enjoy the advantages of such information than the limited few who can afford the content.

Now, coming to 'directory of open access journals' (DOAJ), it can be defined as an online database of free or open access journals. It contains a list of various open access journals.

Significance

With a lot of content being created by people who wanted the content to proliferate freely, information sharing became a common activity and people could get access to any information that they felt necessary very easily. But, with continuous increase in content creation and an increase in the rate of content creation, the problem of finding the exact information required increased. Finding information that is accurate became a big concern. Finding information that is relevant became difficult due to the very enormity of information.

There were a huge number of free journals out there, which didn't require one to shell out big bucks, but was available for general consumption, which was

a valuable resource. But, there wasn't any way that one could search for the relevant journal or the relevant article. Also, there was this question that after the search ended, the journal may happen to be a costly one and after hours of effort, one may realize that the information they received was inaccurate. With all such problems emerging due to information explosion on the internet, it was increasingly becoming important for a kind of database that would index all the journals out there that are available free of cost and sort them according to the various areas of interest. So, this was the problem that Budapest Open Access Initiative (BOAI) decided to solve. They created DOAJ, which would collect information about all the different freely available journals and store them in a single database for public consumption.

This initiative led to the birth of DOAJ, which is a methodical arrangement of information that user would need before looking out for valuable information. Within a short span of time, people realized the significance of such a collection of information.

DOAJ

The aim of the directory of open access journals is to increase the visibility and ease of use of open access scientific and scholarly journals thereby promoting their increased usage and impact. The directory aims to be comprehensive and cover all open access scientific and scholarly journals that use a quality control system to guarantee the content. In short it is a one stop shop for users to open access journals.

Evolution and emergence of DOAJ

The proliferation of freely accessible online journals, the development of subject specific pre- and e-print archives and collections of learning objects provide a very valuable supplement of scientific knowledge to the existing types of published scientific information (books, journals, databases etc.). However these valuable collections are difficult to overview and integrate in the library and information services provided by libraries for their user constituency.

Available technologies make it possible to collect and organize these resources in a way that allow libraries worldwide to integrate these resources in

228

existing services thus providing added value both for the service providers of these resources and for the global research and education community.

Some of the terms defined by DOAJ

Open access journal: we define open access journals as journals that use a funding model and do not charge readers or their institutions for access. From the BOAI definition [http://www.earlham.edu/~peters/fos/boaifaq.htm#openaccess] of 'open access' we take the right of users to 'read, download, copy, distribute, print, search or link to the full texts of these articles' as mandatory for a journal to be included in the directory.

Quality control: the journal must exercise peer-review or editorial quality control to be included.

Research journal: journals that report primary results of research or overviews of research result to a scholarly community.

Periodical: a serial appearing or intended to appear indefinitely at regular intervals, generally more frequently than annually, each issue of which is numbered or dated consecutively and normally contains separate articles, stories or other writings.

Criteria for listing of journal by DOAJ

a. Coverage

    1.   Subject: all scientific and scholarly subjects are covered

    2.   Types of resource: scientific and scholarly periodicals that publish research or review papers in full text.

    3.   Acceptable sources: academic, government, commercial and non-profit private sources are all acceptable.

    4.   Level: the target group for included journals should be primarily researchers.

    5.   Content: a substantive part of the journal should consist of research papers. All content should be available in full text.

    6.   All languages

b. Access

    1.   All content freely available.

    2.   Registration: free user registration online is acceptable.

    3.   Open access without delay (e.g. No embargo period).

c. Quality

    For a journal to be included it should exercise quality control on submitted papers through an editor, editorial board and/or a peer-review system.

d. Periodical

    The journal should have an ISSN (international standard serial number, for information see http://www.issn.org).

e. Metadata information

Resources would be catalogued on journal title level. To make article level content searchable in the system, journal owners are encouraged to supply us with article metadata when a journal has been added into the directory.

Advantages

Following are some of the boons that DOAJ has given to the community.

1. Due to the exhaustive rules and the process followed by DOAJ, like the peer review and the editorial review, the quality of the journals and accuracy of content is high.
2. DOAJ has broad subject coverage and thus caters to a wider group of people.
3. The access to the journals in over 100 countries is quite indicative of the geographic coverage that DOAJ has and it makes it easy for people to access the journals created in different parts of world without any trouble.
4. The site itself is well designed and is structured for quick search and browsing so that the user can arrive at the required content quickly and would get more relevant content.

Limitations

There are some limitations that DOAJ has. Some of the key limitations are as follows.

1. One of the requirements of the journal being its periodicity restricts the list to journals that are more frequently published. Some annual publications cannot make the cut due to such restrictions.
2. The high quality journals that have a cost associated with it, cannot figure in this list. Although there are other databases that cater to that need and do not distinguish between the free journals and the paid journals, DOAJ can have a separate section where low cost journals are also showcased. However, it may go against the philosophy with which DOAJ came into existence.
3. The strictness of DOAJ may leave out a lot of other articles which do not fit the hard requirements that DOAJ has laid down. Although this maintains a high quality of the content of the material hosted, it may leave out some branches and fields where content is too advanced to meet the requirements.

Chief points

Some of the chief points about DOAJ are as follows.

1. It provides an extensive database of free and open access journals across the globe.
2. The rules make the content authentic and genuine.
3. The reputation gained by DOAJ over the time is enormous due to the adherence to the quality.
4. They have created a common platform which makes life easy for people in search of the information.
5. The structure of the website is such that it is optimized for search and makes the browsing experience a smooth one.

Recapitulation

DOAJ has created a platform for people to come and search for information in a very structured manner. The collection of very authentic and genuine journals through a strict means of review process makes it convenient for people looking for free but authentic information.

DOAJ has established itself as a pioneer in the open access journal collections and has led the path from the front. Their definition of open access is something that allows copying and saving, even if it requires registration etc. makes it possible for them to include a lot of content.

Their effort would be very useful to people who look for information and search for content on multiple places. Now they would have a single point where they can access all the content. The service that DOAJ has done to the community is really great and it deserves applause for the work.

10.9 STATISTICAL TOOLS: EXEMPLARS

SOFA - Statistics Open For All

SOFA is a user-friendly statistics, analysis and reporting program with an emphasis on ease of use, learn, and beautiful output. SOFA lets user display results in an attractive format ready to share and it would help user learn as user want.

SOFA Statistics is useful to

- ✦ Make charts
- ✦ Produce attractive report tables
- ✦ Perform a range of basic statistical tests

SOFA can help a

- ✦ Researcher
- ✦ Learner
- ✦ Business Analyst
- ✦ Or anyone who wants to understand their data

SOFA Statistics is a fresh and new project and features are being added on an ongoing basis. Priority areas are being completed first.

Beauty - Attractive Output

Beautiful output is a feature, even in a statistics/analysis program! It means that SOFA output can be used for presentations or automated reporting without manual formatting or reworking. Many statistical programs do not place much emphasis on aesthetics.

Database Friendly

Many statistics programs make user import data from a database before user can use it. But in SOFA one can connect directly to user's database and all its tables with login details. We can even edit data from within SOFA or apply a simple data filter to focus on the subset of a table user are interested in. SOFA currently supports MySQL, Microsoft Access, SQLite, PostgreSQL, Microsoft SQL Server and CUBRID. SOFA lets user work with any tables wherever they may be and whichever (supported) database type they are stored in.

Spreadsheet Friendly

a. Output

SOFA tabular output is already in a form that can be directly opened in MS Excel or pasted into Open Office Calc.

b. Importing

SOFA can import data from Excel spread sheets into its built-in SQLite database. ODS spread sheets can be imported from both Open Office Calc and Gnumeric. Data in CSV format can be imported into SOFA Statistics.

Data can be imported from on-line Google Docs Spread sheets.

All imported data can be viewed and edited within SOFA.

c. Exporting

SOFA can export data into an Excel spread sheet format (readable by open source spread sheets as well).

Data Entry Friendly

We can now add data directly to SOFA Statistics by configuring fresh and new tables in the built-in SQLite database and adding data directly to them. It is also possible to redesign and delete tables.

Easy Data Recoding

It is easy to recode the data using a simple form - e.g. if the data contains age but we need to analyse by age group user can recode MIN TO 19 as 1 with a label of 'Under 20', 20 TO 39 as 2 with a label of '20-39' etc.

Output User Can Share Easily

Tabular output is in HTML, which means we can put it directly on user's intranet or website or put it in a spread sheet.

SOFA has a wide range of attractive, high quality charts including simple bar charts (frequency or means), clustered bar charts (frequency or means), pie-charts, single and multiple line charts (frequency or means), area charts (frequency or means), histograms, scatterplots and box and whisker plots, etc.

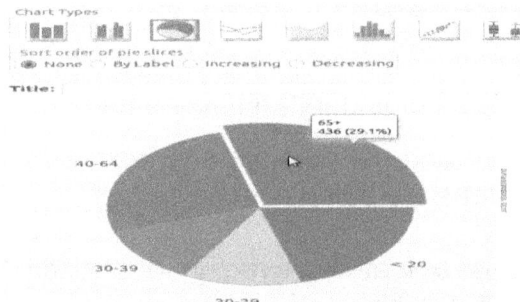

It is also possible to create chart series. There is even some eye candy.

Main Tests and Measures Made Easy

Most analysis uses a small subset of all available statistical options. The goal of SOFA Statistics is to make this subset as easy to use as possible.

SOFA would make it easy to conduct and report on the use of:

Row and column percentages, with the ability to nest variables e.g. look at Ethnicity and Gender vs. Age, Mean, Median, Lower Quartile, Upper Quartile, Standard Deviation, Sum of N items, Min, Max, Range, Pearson's Chi-Square with Contingency Tables, Independent samples t-test, Paired samples t-test, One-way ANOVA, Mann Whitney U, Wilcoxon Signed Ranks, Kruskal Wallis H, Pearson's Correlation and Spearman's Correlation

Learn As User Go

A central goal of SOFA Statistics is to make Statistics Open for All. Secondary school learners, e.g., should be able to use SOFA to learn more about statistics and other users would also be benefitted from the educational orientation of the program.

SOFA helps users make the correct choice of test in a graphical and interactive way.

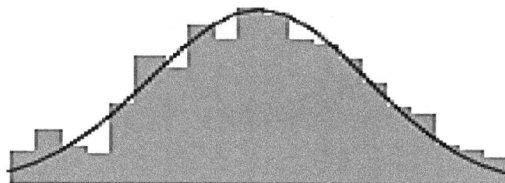

SOFA would supply visual and numerical tests which let the user know if a test is suitable for the data they are working with. Users can now view graphs showing the distribution of a selected variable against a normal distribution curve; histograms for independent t-tests and ANOVA; and scatterplots for Pearson's and Spearman's correlation analyses.

When making tables, SOFA lets users see the impact of configuration changes in a demonstration table before running the actual analysis.

Automated Reporting

SOFA lets users export Python scripts for use in their own simple (or complex) reporting programs. Imagine running a detailed monthly report for management with a single script. Python was originally designed with beginner programmers in mind and has a gentle learning curve. Novices can become productive very soon. Python is included in the installation process and is free and open source.

Speaking user's language

SOFA now has support for a variety of languages including English, Croatian, Spanish, Russian, Galician and Breton. It can help with translation if user likes with the help of SOFA Statistics Translations.

Some screenshots

Start Menu

Everything can be done from the same start screen.

Making Attractive Charts

SOFA Statistics generates attractive and dynamic charts that user can share with others easily. The output is HTML and JavaScript so it is web-friendly from the start.

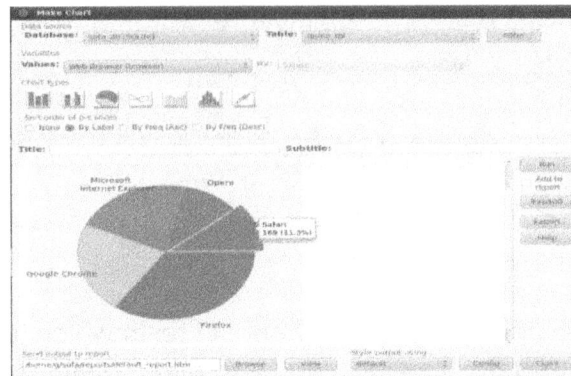

Selecting a Statistical Test
SOFA Statistics helps user choose the correct test but also makes it easy for user to work quickly if user already know which one user need.

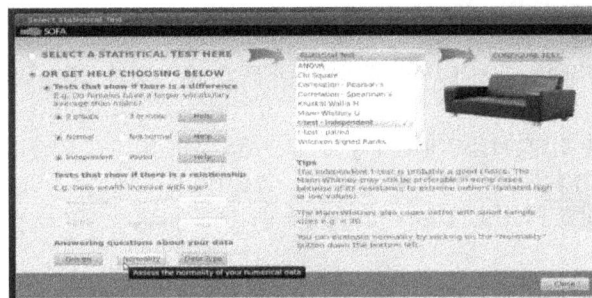

Project configuration
Projects are entirely optional but they make it easy to keep all user's settings (labels, data sources etc.) together. And user can easily switch from one project to another.

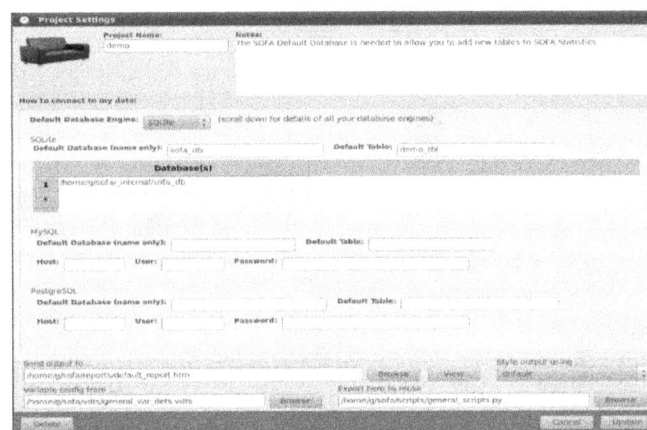

Data Editing
Data can be viewed or edited and fresh and new records can be added - irrespective of which database the data is stored in e.g. MySQL, SQLite, and MS Access etc. Very large datasets can be displayed.

Making a Table

All users' tables can be made from the same dialog. User can easily change user's mind or experiment until user get the exact table user want.

While interacting with the data user can see a demonstration table changing in sync with user's changes. This makes it easier to design the table before running it.

Some important tutorials for SOFA

How to use SOFA for *Mann-Whitney U-test*

    Video can be referred at http://www.youtube.com/watch?v=Zvg1Bl852EQ

How to use SOFA for a *paired t-test*

    Video can be referred at http://www.youtube.com/watch?v=DiAYu0aM9Zw

How to use SOFA for a *chi-square test*

    Video can be referred at http://www.youtube.com/watch?v=tr1u-OuT0Ow

How to use SOFA for an *independent t-test*

    Video can be referred at http://www.youtube.com/watch?v=-mc_pLdd6Jg

How to use SOFA for *filtering the data*

    Video can be referred at http://www.youtube.com/watch?v=_rcgNW-Zcxo&feature=relmfu

How to use SOFA for *making report tables*

    Video can be referred at http://www.youtube.com/watch?v=rlkeG8lGoN0

R-project: Statistical research tool

    R-project is an environment for statistical computing and graphics. R can be considered as a different implementation of s. There are some important differences, but much code written for s runs unaltered under R.

One of R's strengths is the ease with which well-designed publication-quality plots can be produced including mathematical symbols and formulae where needed. Great care has been taken over the defaults for the minor design choices in graphics but the user retains full control.

R is available as free software under the terms of the free software foundation's gnu general public license in source code form. It compiles and runs on a wide variety of UNIX platforms and similar systems (including FreeBSD and Linux), windows and mac.

Significance

R is an integrated suite of software facilities for data manipulation, calculation and graphical display. It includes:
↳   An effective data handling and storage facility,
↳   A suite of operators for calculations on arrays in particular matrices,
↳   A large, coherent and integrated collection of intermediate tools for data analysis,
↳   Graphical facilities for data analysis and display either on-screen or on hardcopy, and
↳   A well-developed, simple and effective programming language which includes conditionals, loops, user-defined recursive functions and input and output facilities.

R is an environment within which statistical techniques are implemented. R can be extended (easily) via *packages*. R has its own latex-like documentation format, which is used to supply comprehensive documentation, both on-line in a number of formats and in hardcopy.

Advantages

R has several major advantages for learner or collaborator:

↳ It is completely free and would always be so, since it is issued under the gnu public license;
↳ It is freely-available over the internet via a large network of mirror servers; see appendix a for how to obtain R;
↳ It runs on many operating systems: UNIX© and derivatives including Darwin, mac OS, Linux, FreeBSD, and Solaris; most flavours of Microsoft windows; apple Macintosh OS; and even some mainframe OS.
↳ It is the product of international collaboration between top computational statisticians and computer language designers;
↳ It allows statistical analysis and visualisation of unlimited sophistication; user are not restricted to a small set of procedures or options and because of the contributed packages, user are not limited to one method of accomplishing a given computation or graphical presentation;
↳ It can work on objects of unlimited size and complexity with a consistent and logical expression language;
↳ It is supported by comprehensive technical documentation and user contributed tutorials. There are also several good textbooks on statistical methods that use (or s) for illustration.
↳ Every computational step is recorded and this history can be saved for later use or documentation.

- It stimulates critical thinking about problem-solving rather than a 'push the button' mentality.
- It is fully programmable, with its own sophisticated computer language. Repetitive procedures can easily be automated by user-written scripts. It is easy to write user's own functions, and not too difficult to write whole packages if user invent some fresh and new analysis;
- All source code is published, so user can see the exact algorithms being used; also, expert statisticians can make sure the code is correct;
- It can exchange data in MS-excel, text, fixed and delineated formats (e.g. Csv), so that existing datasets are easily imported, and results computed in rare easily exported.
- Most programs written for the commercial S-plus program would run unchanged, or with minor changes in R.

Limitations

- The default windows and mac OS x graphical user interface (GUI) is limited to simple system interaction and does not include statistical procedures. The user must type commands to enter data, do analyses and plot graphs.
- The user must decide on the analysis sequence and execute it step by-step.
- The user must learn a fresh and new way of thinking about data, as data frames and objects each with its class, which in turn supports a set of methods. This has the advantage common to object-oriented languages that user can only operate on object according to methods that make sense and methods can adapt to the type of object.
- The user must learn the S language, both for commands and the notation used to specify statistical models. The S statistical modelling language is a lingua franca among statisticians and provides a compact way to express models.

Screen shots
Different types of graphs and diagrams

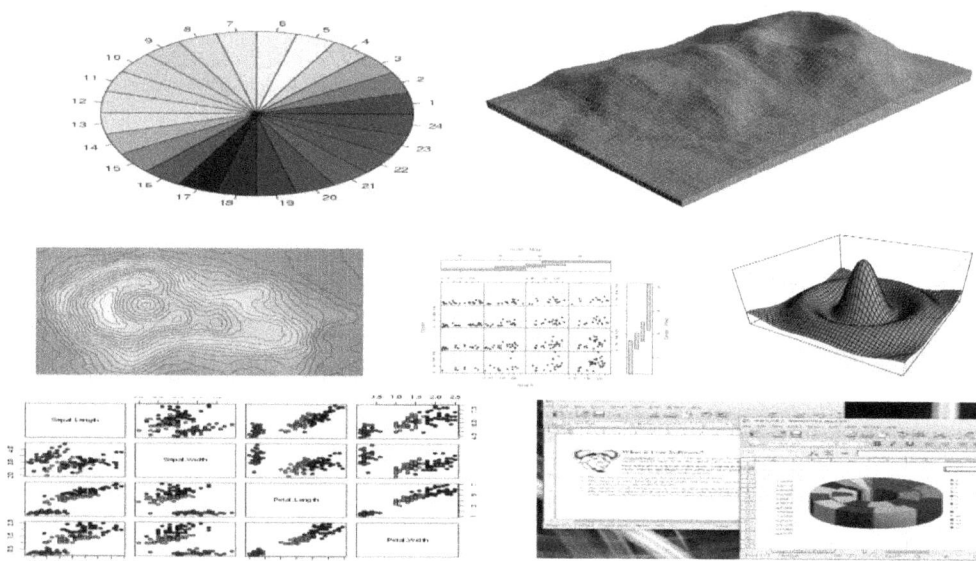

Recapitulation

R is a language and environment for statistical computing and graphics. R provides a wide variety of statistical (linear and nonlinear modelling, classical statistical tests, time-series analysis, classification and clustering,) and graphical techniques and is highly extensible. The S language is often the vehicle of choice for research in statistical methodology, and R provides an open source route to participation in that activity.

10.10 WEB CONFERENCING: AN EXEMPLAR

Big blue buttons: web conferencing platform

The BigBlueButton name comes from the initial concept that starting a web conference should be as simple as pressing a metaphorical big blue button. It is an open source web conferencing system developed primarily for distance education which enables universities and colleges to deliver a high-quality learning experience to remote learners. The main aim of the website is to enhance learner's learning experience.

'Big blue button' is essentially an open source web conferencing system which supports multiple audio and video sharing, presentations with extended whiteboard capabilities - such as a pointer, zooming and drawing - public and private chat, desktop sharing and support for presentation of PDF documents and Microsoft Office documents

Open-source software is software whose source code is published and made available to the public, enabling anyone to copy, modify and redistribute the source code without paying royalties or fees. Open-source code can evolve through community cooperation.

While developing this software, the developers wanted the web conferencing as easy as literally pressing the big blue button, hence the name Big Blue Button. The sole aim for this web conferencing system is to improve the distance learning experience and reach remote people.

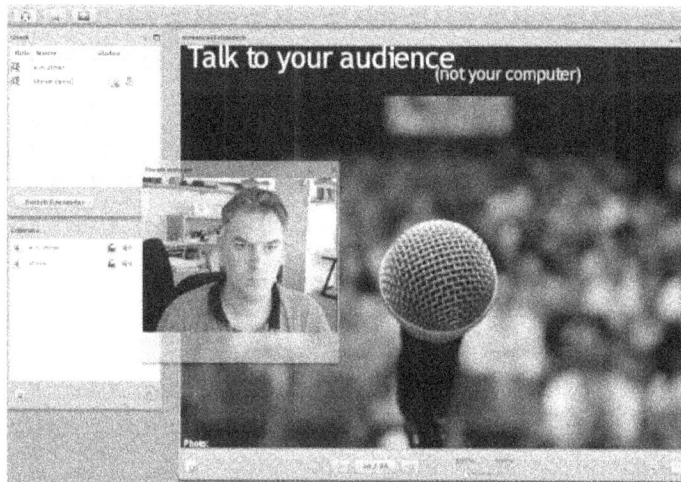

Features

BigBlueButton supports multiple audio and video sharing, presentations with extended whiteboard capabilities – such as a pointer, zooming and drawing, public and private chat, desktop sharing integrated VoIP using free switch, and support for presentation of pdf documents and Microsoft office documents. Users may enter the conference in one of two roles:-

✦ As a viewer, a user may join the voice conference share their webcam, raise their hand and chat with other.

✦ As a moderator, a user may mute/unmute others, eject any user form the session and make any user the current presenter (the presenter may upload slides and control the presentation).

(The above picture shows moderator and viewers on going video conference)

Idea behind the BigBlueButton

The idea behind the big blue button is to build software to make web conferencing easier so that the sharing of knowledge is the maximum. Interaction is a major focal point in big blue button. It allows user to not just talk to user computer screen but to viewers whom he can see. This enables him to convey his ideas in the best possible manner and for learners to learn.

Features such as whiteboard capabilities and desktop sharing enables user to focus on important points during a presentation thus increasing his freedom how he wants to explain.

Moreover, users may enter the conference in one of two Roles- viewer or moderator.

Installing BigBlueButton:

1. Go to www.BigBlueButton.org
2. Click on download button.

       A fresh and new window would open. In install notes read 'before installing' so as to know if user system meets the minimum requirement
3. Click on Installation of BigBlueButton 0.80

Using Big Blue button
       Using big blue button is very easy. A person can either enter conference as a participant or a moderator.

Language can be set from the drop down box on the top most corner
   a. The BigBlueButton is highly error prone. This is mainly due to its open-source structure.

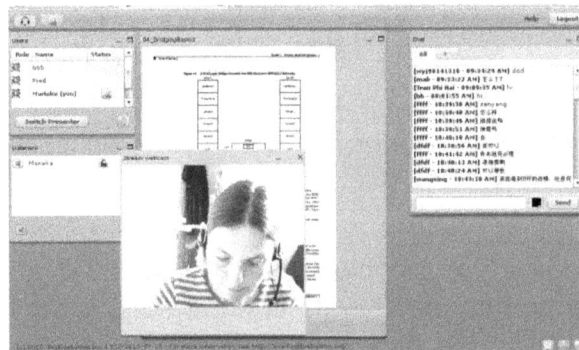

   b. While sharing Desktop there is a large amount of lag of at least 2-3 seconds.

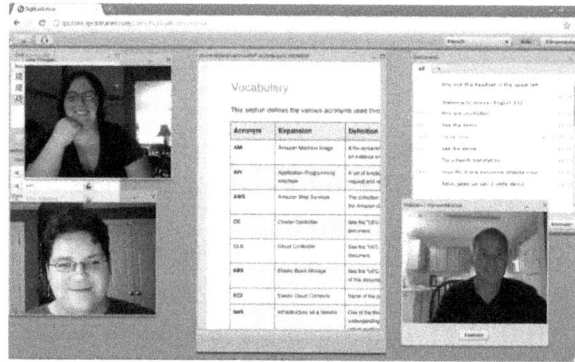

c. The installation procedure is hard and even if all mentioned steps are followed correctly there is still a probability of occurrence of an error or more.

Advantages

↣ User friendly Interface, It is very easy to join a conference and provides a satisfying learning experience.

↣ With help of 'whiteboard capabilities' user can easily highlight a particular part of slide.

↣ Provides Record and Playback option.

↣ It has integrated VOIP (Voice over IP), so people need headphones and microphones to make it an interactive session as the speaker can see his learners and they can ask doubts by raising hands as it would be visible to the facilitator.

↣ Smooth conference running capabilities are provided in form of a moderator who can mute, unmute and kick people out of conference as needed.

↣ There is no limit on how many people can be simultaneously active.

↣ Open-source, therefore easy to improve upon if needed.

Delimitations

↣ The software is only for Ubuntu, making it a little harder for windows and mac user to set up a conference.

↣ It is based on flash based plugin.

↣ As simultaneous sharing is there during conference with many people, high speed connection is prime requirement.

EXEMPLARY QUESTIONS

1. What do you understand by professional development of teachers and teacher-educators?
2. Describe two technology tools which can be helpful for instruction and learning.
3. What can be the possible advantages and limitations of using an OER in instruction and learning?
4. What is DOAJ and how it is helpful in professional development of teachers and teacher-educators?

Bibliography

Balki, R. S. (2010). Learning management system. USA: Lambert academic publishing.

Baylen, D. M., Hancock, M., Mullen, C. M. & Coleman, M. A. (2010). Development of a web-based system for diagnosing learner learning problems on English.

Beckmann, C. E., Thompson, D. R. & Rubenstein, R. N. (2010). *Teaching and Learning High School School subjects,* New Jersey: John Wiley and Sons Inc.

Behari, A. (2008). 'Trends in Teacher Education'. In Saxena, V. (ed.) *Nurturing the Expert Within*, Delhi: University of Delhi.

British Educational Communications and Technology Agency (BECTA) (2003-2004). An introduction to learning platforms.

Clements, M. A. & Ellerton, N. F. (1996). *School subjects Education Research: Past, Present and Future*, Bangkok: UNESCO Principal Regional Office for Asia and the Pacific.

Corbitt, B., Holt, D. & Segrave, S. (2006). Education: Concepts, methodologies, tools and applications (pp. 1825-1843). *International journal of web-based learning.* California: Corwin Press.

Crisan, C., Lerman, S. & Winbourne, P. (2007). 'School subjects and ICT: A Framework for Conceptualising Secondary School Teachers' Classroom Practices', *Technology, Pedagogy and Education.* 16 (1).

Cunningham, W. & Leuf, B. (2001). The wiki way: Quick collaboration on the web. Addison-Wesley.

Daskalakis, S. & Tselios, N. (2011). Design for web-based teaching and learning: Making corporate technology systems work for the learning organization. *Teaching Technologies. pp. 15-35.*

Exemplarswikiuse. (2006) [online], http://www.malts.ed.ac.uk/idel/assignment/wiki/000022.html

Freedman (2006). Learning platforms.

Gillmor, D. (2007). We the media - 2. The read-write web. [online],

Graf & Beate (2005). An evaluation of open source e-learning platforms stressing adaptation issues. Women's Postgraduate College of Internet Technologies, Vienna University of Technology@wit.tuwien.ac.at.

Hall, J. L. (2003). Assessing learning management systems. Oracle University.

Helsing, D., Howell, A., Kegan, R. & Lahey, L. (2008). 'Putting the Development in Professional Development: Understanding and Over tuning Educational Leaders' Immunities to Change', *Harvard Educational Review.* 78 (3).

http://cnx.org/

http://col-oer.weebly.com/module-5:using-oer.html

http://col-oer.weebly.com/module-6:the-oer-life-cycle.html

http://deoracle.org/online-pedagogy/emerging-technologies/open-educational-resources.html

http://educationaltechnology20.wikispaces.com/wikis

http://en.wikipedia.org/wiki/doaj

http://en.wikipedia.org/wiki/Open_educational_resources

http://en.wikipedia.org/wiki/wikipedia:edit_war.

http://en.wikiversity.org/wiki/Open_educational_resources

http://facultyfiles.deanza.edu/gems/deansusan/CMC32008Conf.ppt

http://icommons.org/2007/03/01/virtual-learning-10-open-education-resources/#more-491

http://oalibrarian.blogspot.in/2007/08/doaj-review-for-charleston-advisor.html

http://poeticeconomics.blogspot.in/2008/01/directory-of-open-access-journals-doaj.html

http://tep.uoregon.edu/shared/blogswikispodcasts/wikisbiblio.pdf

http://wikieducator.org/oerf—home

http://wikieducator.org/open_content_licensing_for_educators/home

http://wikieducator.org/Open_Educational_Content/olcos/CHOOSE_a_licensehttp

http://wikieducator.org/Open_Educational_Content/olcos/PRODUCE_%26_REMIX

http://wikieducator.org/Open_Educational_Content/olcos/SEARCH

http://www.bepress.com/

http://www.collegeopentextbooks.org

http://www.creativecommons.org./licenses/

http://www.curriki.org/xwiki/bin/view/Main/WebHome

http://www.DOAJ.org/

http://www.doaj.org/doaj?func=loadtempl&templ=about&uilanguage=en

http://www.educause.edu/content.asp?page_id=7495&bhcp=1

http://www.gale.cengage.com/reference/peter/200912/doaj.html

http://www.geogebra.org/

http://www.intellogist.com/wiki/doaj

http://www.knowledgeboard.com/cgibin/item.cgi?id=96934&d=744&h=746&f=745

http://www.knownet.com/writing/weblogs/Graham_Attwell/entries/beijing_paper/7106458966/attach/OpenContentBeijing.rtf

http://www.merlot.org/merlot/index.htm

http://www.moodle.org/

http://www.oercommons.org/

http://www.oerderves.org/wp-content/uploads/2007/03/a-review-of-the-open-educational-resources-oer-movement_final.pdf

http://www.opensourcescripts.com/help.html

http://www.oreilly.com/catalog/wemedia/book/ch02.pdf

http://www.scienceofspectroscopy.info/edit/index.php?title=using_wiki_in_education.

http://www.sitejabber.com/reviews/www.doaj.org

http://www.teacherswithoutborders.org/about

http://www.un.org/esa/socdev/enable/disacc00.htm

http://www.vanderwal.net/random/entrysel.php?blog=1781wikipedia. (2006) The Edit War. [online],

http://www.w3.org/WAI/WCAG20/quickref/

https://openeducationalresources.pbworks.com/w/page/24838012/stakeholders%20and%20benefits

https://openstaxcollege.org/books

Hwang, G., Cheng, H., Chu, C. H. C. & Tseng, J. C. R. (2010). Home instructionaldesign.com.au

Managal, S. K. (2009). Essentials of educational technology. New Delhi: Phi Learning.

Management system technologies and software solutions for online teaching: Tools and applications. Moodle.com

NCERT (2005). *National Curriculum Framework-2005*, New Delhi: NCERT.

NCERT (2006). *Position Paper National Focus Group on Teaching of School subjects*, New Delhi: NCERT.

NCERT (2012). *Textbook on Pedagogy of Mathematics*, New Delhi: NCERT.

NCTE (2009). *National Curriculum Framework for Teacher Education,* New Delhi: National Council for Teacher Education.

Nunes, T & Bryant, P. (eds) (1997). *Learning and Teaching School subjects: An International Perspective,* UK: Psychology Press Ltd Publishers.

Oblinger, D. (2003). Boomers, Gen-xers, and Millennials: Understanding the 'new learners'. Educause Review.

Oregon. [online],

Organization Science, vol. 3, no. 3, focused issue: Management of Technology. (Aug., 1992), pp. 398-427.

Orlikowski, W. J. (1992). The duality of technology: Rethinking the concept of technology in organizations.

Paquet, S. (2003). Personal knowledge publishing and its uses in research. Knowledge Board [online].

Pearce, J. (2006). Using wiki in education. The science of spectroscopy. [online]

Prensky, M. (2004). Digital game based learning. New York: McGraw-Hill.

Preparing faculty for a learning management system transition

Ramadas, V. (2010). 'Training of Teacher Trainers: Developing Training Competence Through Teleconferencing', *Staff and Educational Development International.* 14 (1).

Richardson, W. (2006). Blogs, wikis, podcasts, and other powerful web tools for classrooms. Thousand Oaks.

Robbins, S. R. (2002). The evolution of the learning content management system.

Roblyer, M. D. (2008). *Integrating Educational Technology into Teaching,* New Delhi: Pearson Education.

Siddiqui, M. H. (2008). Educational technology. Delhi. Balaji Offset.

Simmons, C & Hawkins, C. (2010). *Teaching ICT: Developing as a Reflective Secondary Teacher,* New Delhi: SAGE.

Tanner, H. & Jones, S. (2000). *Becoming a Successful Teacher of School subjects,* London: Routledge Falmer.

Towards a pattern language for learning management systems: Paris Avgeriou , Andreas Papasalouros Symeon Retalis , Manolisskordalakis 1999

Utilizing web tools for computer-mediated communication to enhance team-based learning *Web-based learning and teaching technologies, pp. 21-37.*

Wikis in education and other tools for collaborative writing. (2006). Teaching effectiveness program.

www.irma-international.org/article/evaluating-learning-initiatives/55555/

www.irma-international.org/article/strategic-design-web-based-teaching/2972/

www.irma-international.org/article/utilizing-web-tools-computer-mediated/2981/

www.irma-international.org/chapter/development-web-based-system-diagnosing/41447/

www.irma-international.org/chapter/preparing-faculty-learning-management-system/43449/

www.UNESCO.org/new/fileas\dmin/multimedia/hq/ci/ci/pdf/events/english_paris_oer_declaration.pdf

A Comprehension on Educational Technology and ICT for Education

Vinod Kumar Kanvaria is currently associated with Department of Education, University of Delhi (India), which is popularly known as Central Institute of Education. He has a teaching and research experience of more than twelve years from Secondary School level to University level, including Govt of NCT of Delhi, NCERT and University of Delhi. His research interest areas are educational technology, mathematics, pedagogy of mathematics, experimental education, measurement and evaluation and ICT and its use in education. He is holding JRF award of UGC in Education and Population Studies and holds CSIR-NET in Mathematical Sciences. He has presented a number of research papers in national seminars and conferences. His numbers of research papers have been published in the national and international journals. He had been associated with developing the semesterised curriculum of the four year integrated B.Sc. B.Ed. of Barkatullah University, Bhopal and the draft curriculum of the two year B.Ed. programme of University of Delhi. He has been associated as a resource person with a number of programmes especially of Distance Education Programme – Sarva Shiksha Abhiyaan (IGNOU and MHRD, Govt. of India), NCERT, New Delhi, RIE, Bhubaneswar (Odisha) and SCERT, Delhi. His single authored book 'Developing a Standardized Achievement Test: VTAT' and co-authored book 'Evaluating a Textbook: A Case of Class IX Mathematics' have been published by LAP, Germany and VDM, Germany, respectively. He is the member, author team of 'Package on ICT-Pedagogy Integration for Teacher-Educators' and 'Package on Open Education Resources for Teacher-Educators' published by RIE (NCERT) Bhubaneswar and the member, author group of 'CCE Manual for Class VIII Students' published by SCERT, DELHI, and 'Textbook on Pedagogy of Mathematics' for two year B.Ed. course of NCERT, New Delhi. He has been a member of review team for the Hindi version of the book, 'Exemplar Problems in Mathematics' for Class X of NCERT, New Delhi and 'Package on ICT-Pedagogy Integration for Teachers' of RIE (NCERT), Bhubaneswar. He is member, editorial board of Turkish Online Journal of Educational Technology and member, reviewer panel in a number of international journals. He is member of several academic associations including IATE, AIATE, AIAER, ISOC, AMTI and AITEA. He is also member, advisory board, international educational technology conference, Turkey. Moreover the author has a privilege for acting as a resource person in several national seminars, conferences and workshops across the India.

www.ingramcontent.com/pod-product-compliance
Lightning Source LLC
Chambersburg PA
CBHW080934040426
42443CB00015B/3405